George Washington Sprott

The Worship and Offices of the Church of Scotland

being lectures delivered at the Universities of Aberdeen, Glasgow, St. Andrews, and Edinburgh

George Washington Sprott

The Worship and Offices of the Church of Scotland
being lectures delivered at the Universities of Aberdeen, Glasgow, St. Andrews, and Edinburgh

ISBN/EAN: 9783337285593

Printed in Europe, USA, Canada, Australia, Japan

Cover: Foto ©Lupo / pixelio.de

More available books at **www.hansebooks.com**

THE WORSHIP AND OFFICES

OF THE

CHURCH OF SCOTLAND

THE
WORSHIP AND OFFICES

OF THE

CHURCH OF SCOTLAND

OR

THE CELEBRATION OF PUBLIC WORSHIP,
THE ADMINISTRATION OF THE SACRAMENTS, AND OTHER
DIVINE OFFICES, ACCORDING TO THE ORDER
OF THE CHURCH OF SCOTLAND

BEING

Lectures

DELIVERED AT THE UNIVERSITIES OF ABERDEEN,
GLASGOW, ST ANDREWS, AND EDINBURGH

BY

GEORGE W. SPROTT, D.D.

MINISTER OF NORTH BERWICK

ONE OF THE LECTURERS ON PASTORAL THEOLOGY APPOINTED BY THE
GENERAL ASSEMBLY OF THE CHURCH OF SCOTLAND

WILLIAM BLACKWOOD AND SONS
EDINBURGH AND LONDON
MDCCCLXXXII

TO THE

REV. WILLIAM MILLIGAN, D.D.

PROFESSOR OF DIVINITY AND BIBLICAL CRITICISM IN THE UNIVERSITY
OF ABERDEEN, CONVENER OF THE COMMITTEE OF THE
CHURCH OF SCOTLAND ON PASTORAL THEOLOGY,
AND MODERATOR DESIGNATE OF THE
GENERAL ASSEMBLY

WHO, IN A TIME OF UNBELIEF, SCHISM, AND CONFUSION,

HAS WITNESSED FOR CATHOLIC TRUTH,

UNITY, AND WORSHIP,

This Volume

IS INSCRIBED BY HIS OBLIGED FRIEND

THE AUTHOR.

PREFACE.

THE following Lectures are based on the Westminster Directories for Public Worship, Ordination, and Church Discipline; and they treat of the public devotional services which have to be conducted by the clergy of the Scottish Church. Owing to the circumstances in which they were delivered, I thought it advisable not only to avoid disputed questions, such as the use of a Liturgy, the observance of the Christian Year, and the degree in which beauty and splendour are admissible or obligatory in Divine Service, but to abstain even from enlarging on the fundamental principles of Christian worship, and to restrict myself to historical details and practical suggestions. They are published at the request of many who heard them, and of the Church Service Society; and I hope they may be of some use, as there has hitherto been no book on the same plan, and mistaken notions on many of the points discussed are prevalent. If the Scottish people, as a rule, have little respect for the authority of the Church from the days of the Apostles till the time of John Knox, they at least pay great deference to the opinions of the Reformers, and of the Westminster Divines; and it is important that they should be able to distinguish betwixt them and the "sectarian conceits" which were imported from England, and which infected the party that was responsible for the Disruption of 1651.

Apart from original sources, the work to which I have been chiefly indebted is the Directory of Worship, as edited, with Introduction and Notes, by my friend and fellow-labourer in these studies, —the Rev. T. Leishman, D.D., minister of Linton. For permission to make free use of the results of his researches, of which I have largely availed myself, and for many valuable suggestions while this volume has been going through the press, I owe him my warmest thanks.

G. W. S.

THE MANSE, NORTH BERWICK,
April 1882.

CONTENTS.

LECT.   PAGE

I. MORNING OR EVENING PRAYER, . . . 1

    Introduction—Law of the Church as to worship—Order of service: 1. Scriptural order—2. Order of the Primitive Church—3. Order of the Church of Scotland—Preliminaries to public worship: 1. Private prayer on entering Church—2. Introductory psalm—3. Prefacing—The service: 1. Prayer—2. The psalter and lessons—3. Psalms and hymns—Reading the line—Chanting—4. Second prayer—Lord's Prayer—5. Third prayer—6. Praise—7. Benediction—Suggestions—Books of reference.

II. BAPTISM AND THE ADMISSION OF CATECHUMENS, ... 54

    Baptism of infants—Not to be delayed—To be celebrated in Church—The sponsors—The service: The address—Questions to Sponsors: 1. The Creed—2. The baptismal engagement—3. Promises—Prayer—The rite—The blessing—The declaration — Naming the child — Concluding prayer—Baptism of adults—The address—Vows—The blessing—The exhortation—The declaration.

Admission of catechumens—History of the service—Preparation for—The renewal of baptismal vows—The blessing—Prayer—Exhortation—Importance of the service.

III. THE HOLY COMMUNION, ... 98

Frequency of Communion—Preparatory services—Fast Days—The Lord's Supper the normal service of the Lord's Day—Exhortation before Communion—1. Words of institution—Explanation of—2. Taking the elements—3. Consecration prayer—Lord's Prayer—4. Declaration that the consecrated bread and wine are sacramentally the Body and Blood of Christ—5. Commemoration and communion—The fraction—The minister to partake first—The distribution—Private devotion—Table addresses—Simultaneous communion—Singing during the service—6. Call to Thanksgiving—7. Post-communion prayer—8. Concluding hymn—Alms—Thanksgiving service—Scottish Communion seasons.

IV. THE SOLEMNISATION OF MATRIMONY — THE BURIAL OF THE DEAD — PUBLIC SOLEMN FASTING — DAYS OF PUBLIC THANKSGIVING, ... 143

Marriage—Proclamation of banns—Marriage to be celebrated in Church—Formerly on Sundays, during public worship—The service : 1. Exhortation—2. Prayer—3. Vows—Use of the ring—Declaration—Marriage blessing—Words of counsel—4. Prayer—5. Psalm cxxviii.—Greatest care should be taken with the service.

Visitation of the Sick.

Burial of the Dead — Scottish funeral-rites since the Reformation—The service in the House or in the Church—At the grave—Funeral prayers.

Public Fasts—Practice of the early Church—Lent—Fasting on Sunday—Scottish usages—Fast-day services.

Thanksgiving Days—The service in Church—How to spend the rest of the day—Absence of religious festivals in Scotland.

V. ORDINATION—LICENSING OF PROBATIONERS—ADMISSION OF ELDERS—CHURCH DISCIPLINE, ... 184

Power of ordination belongs to Presbyters—The successors of the Apostles—Two orders of the ministry of divine right—viz., bishop or presbyter, and deacon—Lawfulness of superintendents—Episcopacy a phase of Presbytery—Opinions of the Pre-Reformation Church—Of the English Reformers—The English ordinal—Many of the English clergy formerly in Presbyterian orders—Scottish superintendents—Old Celtic Church—Westminster divines on the necessity of a lineal succession from the Apostles—The succession in Scotland—Scottish clergy bishops in the ecclesiastical sense — Scottish Episcopal ministers in Presbyterian orders— Importance of subject—Scottish forms of ordination—A fast to be kept—The service—Induction—Old usages.

Licensing probationers — The diaconate — Admission of elders — Formerly elected annually — Elders continued under Episcopacy — Westminster Assembly rejected presbyter theory of the office—Representatives of the laity—Deacons.

Church discipline : 1. Admonition—2. Suspension from the Communion—Oath of purgation —3. Excommunication—Absolution.

VI. CHURCH ARCHITECTURE — INTERNAL ARRANGEMENTS OF CHURCHES, FITTINGS, AND OTHER REQUISITES FOR DIVINE SERVICE —LAYING OF A FOUNDATION-STONE, AND DEDICATION OF A CHURCH—CONCLUDING OBSERVATIONS, ... 227

Deplorable condition of Scottish Churches—Causes of this — Revival of a better spirit — Different styles of Architecture—Pews—Postures in worship—Arrangements for the administration of the Sacraments—Church plate—Communion elements —Clerical robes—Hoods—Degrees in divinity—Service for the laying of a foundation-stone—Naming of Churches—Celtic Saints—Relative holiness of Churches—Desecration of—Service for the dedication of a Church—Concluding remarks —Degradation of worship—Revival in England ; in Scotland—The Church Service Society—Necessity of the clergy devoting much attention to the subject.

THE WORSHIP AND OFFICES

OF THE

CHURCH OF SCOTLAND.

LECTURE I.

MORNING OR EVENING PRAYER.

As you have already been informed, I am about to address you on "The Celebration of Public Worship, the Administration of the Sacraments, and other Divine Offices, according to the Order of the Church of Scotland." While desirous of imparting as much historical information on these subjects as possible, my chief aim will be to be helpful to you in your preparation for a department of ministerial duty, which is happily attracting much more attention now than it did for a long period.

Scripture everywhere shows us the supreme importance of Worship in the sight of God. Under the Old Testament Dispensation it was regulated from Heaven down to the minutest details; and though in Christian times great liberty is allowed in the manner of conducting Divine Service, the subject is invested with peculiar sacredness because of our membership in Christ, and from the fact that the Holy Ghost has now made the Church His dwelling-place. The glorifying of God in its public acts of homage and devotion is the highest function of the Church, and adequate provision for this service is one of its most essential requirements.

In Communions like our own, which have thought fit to prescribe only general directions for the Offices of Worship, those on whom the great responsibility rests of guiding the devotions of the people, and of bringing their sacrifices of praise and prayer into the sacred presence of God, ought at the least to be specially trained for these holy duties, and they should spare no pains to qualify themselves for discharging them in a manner acceptable to Him, who has repeatedly declared that in this matter He is jealous for His own glory.

I purpose taking up the Public Services of the

Church in order, and the subject of Lecture today will be the Ordinary Worship of the House of God. Before entering upon this, however, it is necessary that I should state shortly

THE LAW OF THE CHURCH AS TO WORSHIP.

In 1557 the Scottish Protestant Lords in Council resolved that "the Common Prayers be read weekly on Sunday and other festival days publicly in the parish kirks, with the lessons of the Old and New Testaments, conform to the Order of the Book of Common Prayers." The Liturgy thus authorised was the version of the English Prayer-Book, known as the Second Book of King Edward VI. In 1559 the Book of Geneva began to be used; and after it had been modified and added to by the Reformers, the General Assembly in 1564 "ordained that every Minister, Exhorter, and Reader shall . . . use the Order contained therein in Prayers, Marriage, and ministration of the Sacraments." From that time till 1645 this Liturgy, or Book of Common Order, was of public authority in the Church, was used on Sundays by the Readers, and partially by the Clergy, and was read daily at Morning and Evening Prayer in all the towns and in many of the villages of the country. In 1645 the Directory of Worship was adopted as part of the uniformity with England, and was sanctioned both by Church and State. It had been drawn up by the English Divines at Westminster with the assistance of Commissioners from the Church of Scotland, some of whom regarded it as a minimum in the way of formal service, to which they gave a somewhat reluctant consent. Principal Baillie, whose graphic letters shed so much light on the proceedings of the Assembly, tells us that he was anxious to retain all the Scottish usages, and that Henderson was not far from his mind, but that they were overruled by others.[1] The Directory was accepted in Scotland with some qualifications as to the Communion Service, which will afterwards be referred to, and also with the proviso, that the old laws and regulations as to worship were to remain in force, except in so far as altered by it.

After the restoration of Episcopacy in 1661, the Scottish Parliament, by the Act Rescissory, declared the whole Covenanting Legislation from 1640 null and void, and the Directory thus lost its civil sanction. During the "Second Episcopacy"—from 1661 to 1690—there was no attempt to revive Laud's Liturgy, the introduction

[1] Letters, vol. ii. p. 258.

of which had been the occasion, if not the main cause, of the outbreak in 1637. The new Bishops, as was said, had no wish to ride the ford where their predecessors were drowned, but contented themselves with falling back on the Book of Common Order, and this was now used merely as a Directory. The reading of prayers by the Clergy had fallen into disrepute; and those Bishops who touched the thorny subject of worship, went no further than to recommend reverence in God's House, the reading of large portions of Scripture, the use of the Lord's Prayer, Doxology, and Creed; and daily common prayer in the churches, with reading of Scripture when convenient,[1]—all which had been usual in the Church since the Reformation.

[1] See Leighton's Recommendations to the Synod of Dunblane in 1662; Synod Register, pp. 2, 3. There is no rule, however, without an exception; and in the Parish of Salton, near Haddington, the English Liturgy was read from 1665 to 1669, when Gilbert Burnet, afterwards Bishop of Salisbury, was Minister.

Anderson, Minister of Dumbarton, writes thus in 1714: "In the late times, before the Revolution, the Episcopal Clergy did not so much as essay to bring in a Liturgy. For many years after the Revolution none of them publicly used any either in their churches or meeting-houses; and to this day some of the best of them, to my certain knowledge, are against the English Liturgy."—Defence of the Church Government, &c., of the Presbyterians, p. 10. For long after that time the use of the English Liturgy among the Scottish Episco-

In 1690, when Episcopacy was again abolished, the Scottish Parliament passed an Act ratifying the Westminster Confession of Faith, and restoring the Presbyterian Government of the Church as it had been settled in 1592; but the Act Rescissory was not repealed, the Covenanting Legislation remained under the ban, and the Church was left for the time without a legal order of worship. The Confession of Faith lays down the general principle that God is not to be worshipped in any way not prescribed in the Holy Scripture;[1] but this is qualified by another statement, "that there are some circumstances concerning the worship of God . . . which are to be ordered by the light of nature and Christian prudence, according to the general rules of the Word,"[2] and there have always been differences of opinion as to what is prescribed and what left free. A further Act of Parliament was passed in 1693, in which it was ordained "that uniformity of worship, and of the administration of all public ordinances within this Church, be observed by all the ministers and preachers, as the same are at present performed and allowed therein, or shall be

---

palians was discretionary, and the clergy were in the habit of interpolating long prayers of their own.

[1] Ch. xxi. sec. 1.   [2] Ch. i. sec. 6.

hereafter declared by the authority of the same." This Statute contemplated the fact that the provision for worship was incomplete, and acknowledged the right of the Church to legislate further on the subject. Accordingly, in 1705, the Assembly "seriously recommended to all ministers and others within this National Church, the due observation of the Directory for the Public Worship of God, approven by the General Assembly, held in the year 1645, Sess. 10."[1] At this period the greatest alarm was felt lest the proposed Union with England should prove destructive of those ecclesiastical principles with which Scottish Nationality was felt to be more than ever identified, and every precaution was taken, both by Church and State, to guard against this danger. In January 1707, Parliament passed an Act establishing and confirming not only the Discipline and Government, but the Worship, of the Church, "to continue, without any alteration to the people of this land, in all succeeding generations;" and in April of the same year, the Assembly made the law against "Innovations in the Worship of God," to which all the ministers of the Church have still at their ordination to promise obedience.

That there were departures from the Directory

[1] Sess. 12, Act X.

at that time is certain; but as the Assembly had so recently recommended its observance, it is reasonable to regard the Act of Parliament of 1707, which is embodied in the Treaty of Union, as referring to it. Some hold that it refers to the actual worship then in use; but if this were so, and the law enforced, I suspect that even the advocates of this opinion would think the absence of Hymns, of Scripture-reading, and of the Lord's Prayer, inadequately compensated for by the reading of the line by the precentor, and the minister's address to the penitents clad in sackcloth on the stool of repentance. Whether the liberty allowed to the Church, by the Act of 1693, to modify the worship without further sanction of the Legislature is affected by the Treaty of Union, may be questioned; but it is evident that the Assembly did not consider itself precluded from making further changes, for in 1707 it appointed a Committee to revise the Scriptural Songs, with the view of having them sung in Divine Service, and it sanctioned the Form of Process which provides complete rules for the exercise of discipline, and the devotional acts connected therewith.

The Westminster Directory, as enjoined in 1705, with whatever it did not abrogate of the earlier regulations of the Church, and all special

Acts on the subject passed since 1690, may thus be regarded as embodying the law of the Church as to Public Worship. I purpose, accordingly, making the Directory, so far as it goes, the basis of these Lectures.

Morning or Evening Prayer.

I now proceed to take up the ordinary service for Morning or Evening Prayer, and shall notice first, the Order, and then the different parts successively.

THE ORDER OF SERVICE.

There must be some order in conducting public worship, and it is a matter of great moment that each part of the service should have its due place and proportion, that nothing should be neglected, and that "none of the permanent wants of the soul, and none of the classes for whom the Church ought to pray," should be neglected. The same order should be followed on all ordinary occasions; and when it is necessary to shorten the service, this is best done, not by omitting any part, but by shortening all, so as not to destroy its completeness. A fixed order is advantageous to minister and people alike; it simplifies the duties and aids the memory of the one, and it enables the other to join in the service without distraction.

1. *The Scriptural Order.*—No order is definitely prescribed in the New Testament, though it may indeed be held that the example of our Lord is an express rule for the administration of the Holy Communion, which is the normal service of the Church, and the only one appointed by Him. There are those who hold that the order did not need to be prescribed, inasmuch as it was already foreshadowed for all time in the service of the Tabernacle and the Temple. According to this view, every feature in the Morning and Evening Service of the Jewish ritual should have its corresponding reality in that worship, in spirit and in truth, which we are required to offer in Christian times. The brazen altar and the laver at the door of the Tabernacle show us that "atonement is the ground of all acceptable service," and that confession of sin and absolution have their proper place at the threshold of every act of worship; the consuming of the lamb on the brazen altar symbolises the dedicating of ourselves to God when pardoned and reconciled to Him; and so on with the other symbols which are held to foreshadow our meditations on His

Word, our singing His praises with gratitude and joy, our supplications, intercessions, and thanksgivings.[1] Whatever truth there may be in this view, the order thus indicated agrees substantially with that of our own and other branches of the Reformed Church. Indeed, the most important feature of it—beginning with confession and prayer for pardon—was first introduced by Calvin in his Strasburg Liturgy, and the English Reformers borrowed it from the Service Books used by Reformed immigrants in England. No ancient Liturgy began with confession, but Calvin substituted this for the private confession and absolution previously in use.

2. *The Order of the Primitive Church.*—In the Primitive Church, the order of Daily Morning and Evening Prayer varied considerably in different places. In the Sunday service there was substantial agreement, but not without minor variations also. Justin Martyr, about 150, describes the order thus: " First the memoirs of the Apostles and writings of the Prophets are read ; " then " the president verbally instructs, and exhorts to the imitation of these good things; then all

[1] See 'Readings upon the Liturgy,' and 'Worship in Spirit and in Truth.' Bosworth : London.

rise together and pray, and when our prayer is ended, bread and wine and water are brought;"[1] and then follows an account of the Communion service. The order is thus referred to in the Apostolic Constitutions: "When you go to prayer after the lessons, and the psalmody, and the instruction out of the Scriptures."[2] Tertullian also says: "In our Public Assemblies, the Scriptures are read, psalms sung, sermons preached, and prayers offered." In some churches, however, psalms were sung before the lessons, and in others intermixed with them.[3] A collect for Divine assistance was also sometimes offered before the sermon; but prayer in the early part of the service was so informal and exceptional as to be seldom noticed in the accounts of primitive worship that have been handed down. After the sermon, which was always concluded with a doxology to the Holy Trinity, the common prayers, popularly so called, began. In some of them the catechumens, energumens, candidates for baptism, and penitents, were permitted to join, but they were all dismissed at or before the close of what was called "the service of the catechumens," and then the Communion service was celebrated by

---

[1] 1st Apol., ch. vi.   [2] Book II. sec. 54.
[3] Bingham's Antiq., Book XIV. ch. i.

the faithful. It was usual to preface each part of the service—lessons, sermon, and prayers—with the salutation, "Peace be with you," to which the people responded, "And with thy spirit;" and the practice was believed to be apostolical.[1] This service may have been partly modelled on that of the synagogue, but it was specially adapted to those times, when the congregations were so mixed, and only the baptized who were in full communion were allowed to remain to the close.

3. *The Order of the Church of Scotland.*—The order of worship followed in our Church before 1661, while the Directory had both civil and ecclesiastical sanction, as we learn from Ray, the English Naturalist, who paid a visit to Scotland at that time, and from other authorities, was usually as follows: After an introductory Psalm, which was often sung before the Minister came in,— 1. Prayer; 2. Reading the Scriptures; 3. Praise; 4. Prayer; 5. Sermon; 6. Prayer of Intercession; 7. Praise; 8. the Benediction. This closely resembled the order followed when Knox's Liturgy was used, although then the first part of the service was commonly conducted by the

---

[1] Apost. Con., Book VIII. ch. 5. In some cases the Apostolic Benediction was used instead of "Peace be with you."

Reader.[1] Indeed, in many parishes this practice was continued after 1645. The Directory had not had time fully to take root before the country was thrown into anarchy by Cromwell's invasion, and the Church divided into two hostile camps—those of the Resolutioners and the Protesters. The Readers' service was further revived during the Second Episcopacy, and in a mutilated form lingered on till our own day. Within the memory of many still living, both in the South and North, precentors and schoolmasters were in the habit of reading psalms and chapters from the Lectern while the people were assembling, and a few generations earlier, they read also the Belief, Lord's Prayer, and Ten Commandments.[2] The order prevalent from 1645 to 1661 is that now generally followed, except that it has become common to sing after the sermon, and also in

[1] Probably in the post-Apostolic Church the Scriptures were read by the Deacons, but in the third century the order of Readers was instituted.

[2] In 1697 the Session of Whitekirk "appoints the Precentor to read every Lord's Day the Belief, Lord's Prayer, and 10 Commandments."—Rec. The author of the 'Lamp of Lothian,' published in 1844, states that the practice of reading Scripture in Church before the Minister entered still continued in the South Country, and that he had heard it done by the schoolmaster in the Church of Hawick—p. 436. M'Gillivray, in his 'Life of Chrysostom,' says that the practice was kept up in the Highlands till the beginning of this century.

many churches between the lessons, according to a custom of the Primitive Church.[1]

Some of the clergy have recently adopted the practice of introducing the Prayer of Intercession before the sermon. The Directory favours this use, while leaving it an open question; but the Book of Common Order, like all the Reformed Liturgies, and those of the Primitive Church, placed the intercessions after the sermon, and this rule has always been generally followed in Scotland. Besides the weight of authority in its favour, there is something in the view that the sermon most naturally follows soon after the reading of the lessons of one of which it was often at first an exposition, and that the order of service should be cumulative, rising in devotion towards the close. Further, the introduction of the intercessions after the sermon keeps the ordinary service in harmony with that of a Communion Sunday, and is a testimony, as Calvin meant it to be, for the Lord's Supper as part of the complete service of the House of God. In the English Church there is no fixed rule as to the time when the sermon is to be preached at Morning or Evening Prayer. It is most commonly done near the close of the service, but not unfrequently

[1] Apost. Con., Book II. ch. 57.

before the intercessions and thanksgiving. Indeed, in Cathedrals, where the ideal service is to be looked for, the order of worship is often almost the same as that now common in Scotland.

For the greater part of two centuries, the service of our Church consisted only of praise, prayer, [praise] sermon, prayer, praise, and benediction. This mutilated order began during the years of anarchy, and was simply the old service minus the Reader's part of it. In our own day the Church has enjoined the restoration of the reading of Holy Scripture, and in its own Book of Prayer provided for those without a ministry, it has deviated from the order long in use, with the avowed object of bringing the services into closer agreement with the recommendations of the Directory. The order given in the Assembly's 'Prayers for Social and Family Worship; or Aids to Devotion,' is as follows: (after an introductory Psalm) 1. Prayer; 2. Reading of portion of Psalter and Lessons from the Old and New Testaments; 3. Praise; 4. Prayer and Lord's Prayer; 5. Sermon; 6. Prayer of Intercession; 7. Praise; 8. Benediction.

As this order has thus been virtually sanctioned by the Church, no part of it should be omitted, and if more Psalmody is desired, this may be introduced between the Lessons, as in the first edition of Aids to Devotion, and again, after the Sermon, in accordance with usual practice.

With these additions the order would stand as follows:—

[Introductory Psalm.]
1. Prayer.
2. Psalter, and Lesson from Old Testament.
3. Praise.
4. Lesson from New Testament.
5. Praise.
6. Prayer and Lord's Prayer.
7. Sermon.
8. Praise.
9. Prayer of Intercession.
10. Praise.
11. Benediction.

PRELIMINARIES TO PUBLIC WORSHIP.

Before entering upon the separate parts of Public Worship, there are some *preliminaries*, properly so called, which deserve notice.

1. *Private Prayer on entering Church.* — The Directory is silent on this subject so far as the Minister is concerned; but while forbidding "adoration,"—that is bowing towards the Communion Table, which had been common in England,—it favours the practice on the part of the

people by ordering that, "If any, through necessity, be hindered from being present at the beginning, they ought not when they come into the congregation, to betake themselves to their private devotions, but reverently to compose themselves to join with the assembly in that ordinance of God which is then in hand." This is obviously a case where the exception confirms the rule. George Gillespie, one of the Scottish Commissioners at Westminster, tells us in his Notes on the Assembly, that this regulation was made at the instance of the English Clergy, who said, "This is very necessary for this Church; for though the Minister be praying, many ignorant people will not join in it till they have said over the Lord's Prayer."[1] With regard to the Ministers engaging in private prayer, Baillie writes: "Besides the vehemency of the Independents against it, there is no such custom used here"— *i.e.*, in England—" by any;" but he adds, "we intend in due time to do the best for it we may."[2] Up till that period the custom had been general in Scotland. There had already, however, been some keen controversy on the subject. After 1638, a party arose in the Scottish Church, which sympathised with many of the notions of the

[1] Notes, p. 102.   [2] Baillie, ii. p. 123.

fanatical sects which then began to flourish in England. This party, which was destined to have a great and disastrous influence, commenced with "scrupling the three nocent ceremonies," as they were called—viz., the Ministers bowing for private devotion, the singing of the Doxology at the end of the Psalms, and the use of the Lord's Prayer. The leading Clergy, such as Henderson, Baillie, and others, "expressed themselves passionately against these conceits;" and the Church, as a whole, had such an aversion to them, that the Commission of the Covenanting Assembly of 1642 of which the famous Robert Douglas was Moderator, threatened with deposition some Ministers in the South and West, who had given up these laudable customs—gave orders that none should forbear ordinarily to practise them—and issued injunctions to Presbyteries, "to take heed that every one received into the ministry should be free both in their judgment and practice from the foresaid novations." Even before this order was given Presbyteries had begun to "pose" entrants to the Ministry as to these points, and to require them to own the lawfulness of read prayers,[1] which was denied by those

[1] Thus in 1640, Mr Andro Donaldson "was posed before the Presbytery (of Perth) whether it was lawful to read prayers;

"in the sectarian way." So rapid had been the change of sentiment, that within three years the same men who had contended for liberty to use free prayer, had to defend the right of using forms of prayer. Instead of the English being induced to adopt the Scottish practice of the Ministers "bowing in the pulpit," as Baillie had hoped, our Assembly, in 1645, recommended that "though a lawful custom in this Kirk," it "be hereafter laid aside for satisfaction of the desire of the reverend divines in the Synod of England, and for uniformity with that Kirk so much endeared to us." When the Ministers gave up the practice the people followed their example. In our own day the "lawful custom" has been revived; but it was at first such a startling novelty, that a beadle, seeing the Minister bow, has been known to rush to the pulpit with a glass of water, under the impression that he had been taken suddenly ill.

2. I pass on to the second *preliminary*—viz., the *Introductory Psalm.*—The daily service of the Primitive Church, and in some cases the Sunday service, as has already been stated, began with Psalmody. As the Jews sung invitatory Psalms

---

because there went a report of him that he disdained reading of prayers altogether."—Pastoral Work in Covenanting Times (Ross), p. 79.

in ascending the steps of the Temple, the practice was continued by the early Christians as they entered their Assemblies: and it has been partially followed by the Reformed Churches. It is not mentioned in Knox's Liturgy, the Directory, or the English Prayer-Book, though it is not uncommon to sing before the Service in the English Church. Among the Reformed this first singing has usually been regarded, not as a part of Public Worship, but as a fitting prelude to it. You have a trace of this in the phrase still used by some of the Clergy: " Let us compose our minds for the worship of God by singing the —— Psalm." This should be kept in view, and Psalms selected such as the 95th, 100th, and 122d, which do not directly address the Most High, but in which we call upon one another to worship Him, or express our joy at entering His Courts.

3. There is still another preliminary, which is thus referred to in the Directory: "The congregation being assembled, the Minister, *after solemn calling on them to the worshipping of the great Name of God,* is to begin with prayer." This solemn call to worship was formerly called *Prefacing.* You have traces of this in all Liturgies. Thus, the Book of Common Order directs that, when the people are assembled, the Minister

is to exhort them diligently to examine themselves, and to follow in their hearts the tenor of his words; and in one of the proposed emendations of that Book, you find the following form: "The Minister or Reader shall say—

"Come, let us worship and fall down before the Lord our Maker; let us try our ways, confess and forsake our sins, and lift up our hearts and hands to God in the heavens, saying:"

The French and Genevan Liturgies begin with the reading of Chapters and the Decalogue, by a Reader or Proponent. The Pastor then says: "Our help is in the name of the Lord who hath made heaven and earth. 'Amen.' Brethren, let each of you present himself before the Lord, with confession of his sins and offences, following in heart my words." The text quoted is one of those with which the Roman Office commences. It was from the Reformed Service on the Continent that the English practice was borrowed of reciting passages of Scripture, and founding the call upon them. In Scotland, where, since the middle of the Seventeenth Century, instruction has been amplified at the expense of devotion, an exposition of the opening Psalm came to be substituted for prefacing. This was long highly popular, but too much of anything is sure to be followed by too little, and the solemn call of the Directory is now represented by the short and abrupt phrase —"Let us pray." There are signs of a return to the older practice, but such transitions must always be gradual.

THE SERVICE.

1. *First Prayer.*—We come now to the proper commencement of Divine Service—viz., the first prayer, which, according to the usage of our Church, should consist of invocation, confession, petitions for pardon and peace, and supplications for grace. That given in the Directory is little more than an invocation, but it has been the general practice to introduce after this the other topics I have mentioned. There is the same reason for order and proportion in the several parts of each prayer as in the whole service.

The *invocation* should be short as in the Directory, and should close with a petition for assistance and acceptance in the whole service. It had been a complaint of the English Puritans, that there was nothing of this in the Book of Common Prayer, and this defect was remedied in the Directory.

The next topic is *the confession of sin.* As all

our acts of worship are offered in the communion of the Universal Church, it is proper to confess the sins of the whole family, and this gives a prominent place to Church sins, and the part we have in them. It is an obvious and usual arrangement to confess our sins against God, our neighbour, and ourselves; but this is not the time or place for noticing merely individual or personal transgressions. It is further fitting to acknowledge that our sins deserve death, as was done of old by the worshippers bringing their sacrifices to the altar; and as they put their hands on the head of the victim, so should we follow our confessions by laying hold upon Christ, as our surety and substitute, and by earnest prayers that, for the sake of His sufferings and merits, our sins may be blotted out.

And we should pray not only for pardon, but for *peace*, or the assurance of forgiveness. Calvin held that something of the nature of a general absolution should follow the public confession of sin. "There is none of us," he says, "but must acknowledge it to be very useful, that after the general confession, some striking promise of Scripture should follow, whereby sinners might be raised to the hopes of pardon and reconciliation."[1]

[1] See Eutaxia, p. 21.

In several of the Reformed Liturgies this suggestion was carried out, and from this source came the "comfortable words" of the English Communion Office. Absolution, in this sense, is God's answer to our confession. It is quite easy to introduce such verses without breaking the continuity of the prayer, or indeed to introduce those precative forms of absolution which were alone used for many centuries.[1] As all true penitents are then in reality forgiven, there should ordinarily be no renewal of confession during the remainder of the service, unless at the close, when pardon may be asked for its imperfections; but we should go on to worship God in joy and peace, as His reconciled children.

As such, it is appropriate for us to consecrate ourselves anew as a living sacrifice to God, and the

[1] *E.g.*, "Almighty God, who hath given His Son Jesus Christ to be the Sacrifice and Propitiation for the sins of the whole world, grant unto you for His sake full remission and forgiveness; absolve you from all your sins; and vouchsafe to you His Holy Spirit."—Lit. of the Cath. and Apost. Church.

In "The practice of the Lord's Supper, as used in Berwick by John Knox," after the confession, we have the following direction: "Some notable place of the Evangel, wherein God's mercy is most evidently declared, should then be read, plainly to assure the penitent of full remission of all offences; and thereafter ought the minister openly to pronounce to such as unfeignedly repent and believe in Jesus Christ, to be absolved from all damnation, and to stand in the favour of God."—Knox and the Church of England (Lorimer), p. 291.

rest of the prayer should consist of supplication for grace, that we may be enabled hereafter to serve Him in newness of life. In prayer for the assistance of the Holy Ghost, we should avoid expressions which ignore the great fact of Pentecost, when He was sent to earth by our ascended Lord to establish the Church, and to abide with it for ever. The gift of the Comforter "is to be regarded as a perennial fountain, ever sending forth its living waters, or as one continual river, ever flowing from the throne of God;" but we might as well pray for the Creation of the Universe, or the Incarnation of Christ, as for the Descent of the Holy Spirit in any sense that overlooks His indwelling in the Church and all the true members thereof.

Having offered our petitions in the name of Christ, it is proper to conclude with an ascription of praise to the Ever-blessed Trinity—thus: To Whom, with Thee the Father and the Holy Ghost, be Glory, &c.; or, And to Thee we ascribe the Glory, to the Father, to the Son, and to the Holy Ghost, as it was, &c. I have sometimes heard it done in the form in which it is sung: Glory be to the Father, &c.—but this is for praise, not for prayer, and should be avoided.

2. *Reading of Psalms and Scripture Lessons.—*

The next feature of the service is the reading of Holy Scripture. The amount to be read as required by the Directory is, besides a portion of the Psalter, at least one chapter from each Testament. "It is convenient," says the Rubric, "that ordinarily one chapter of each Testament be read at every meeting, and sometimes more, where the chapters be short, or the coherence of matter requireth it." It is added, "We commend also the more frequent reading of such Scriptures, as he that readeth shall think best for edification of his hearers, as the Book of Psalms and such like." Gillespie, in his Notes, says: "The Assembly added a direction to read a portion of the Psalms before the chapters,"[1] and in the Directory turned into a Liturgy, and published by authority in 1645 for the use of the laity in the absence of a Clergyman—a copy of which almost unknown work is extant in the British Museum,—it is ordered that "some Psalms and chapters out of both Testaments shall be read." These notices not only make the meaning of the Directory plain, but they show the order that should be followed,—psalms first, and then the chapters. This had been the previous Scottish custom. We find Archbishop Leighton, who tried hard to revive the old wor-

[1] P. 102.

ship of the Church in the face of the fanaticism which affected many of those even who submitted to Episcopacy in 1661, earnestly urging the clergy of Dunblane to read both Psalms and two chapters at each service.[1]

The Psalter may either be read continuously on Sundays in such portions as to overtake it in a year, or by taking the Psalms for the day, according to the common monthly division.[2]

As to the selection of lessons, the Directory requires—1. "That all the Canonical Books be read over in order, that the people may be better acquainted with the whole body of the Scriptures;" and 2. "That ordinarily, where the reading in either Testament endeth on one Lord's Day, it is to begin the next." A similar recommendation had been given in the First Book of Discipline, which, though never law—civil or ecclesiastical—had always largely influenced the practice of the Church. "We think it most expedient," say the Authors of that Book, "that the Scriptures be read in order—that is, that some one Book of the Old or New Testament be begun and orderly read to the end; and this same we

---

[1] Synod Register of Dunblane, p. 2.

[2] Knox was in the habit of reading through the Psalms monthly, with chapters of the Old and New Testaments daily.—Calderwood, Hist., vol. iii. p. 232.

judge of preaching, where the Minister for the most part remains in one place; for this skipping and divagation from place to place of Scripture, be it in reading or be it in preaching, we judge not so profitable to edify the Kirk as the continual following of one text."

The practice of selecting chapters at random, or to suit the sermon, is contrary to the regulations of our own and of all other Churches. It is apt to result in the reading and re-reading of a few favourite chapters, and tends to make ill-informed and ill-balanced Christians. We should read on some plan which contemplates the going through the Books and principal chapters of Scripture in order. This is the aim of all Tables of Lessons. It is best to read at the Morning Service the Historical Books and the Gospels, and in the Evening the Prophetical Books and the Epistles, all in the order of the Canon, but omitting such chapters as are less suitable. In Aids to Devotion you find a very good Table of Sunday Lessons for one year, constructed on this plan, and taken, if I mistake not, from the Liturgy of the Reformed (Dutch) Church in America. I need scarcely add that the Lessons to be read in Church should not only be selected, but carefully studied beforehand.

It is well also to have a suitable and simple form of words for giving out the chapters, such as: "Hearken to the Word of God as it is written in," &c.; or, "The Lesson from the Old Testament, or from the New (as the case may be), is in the —— chapter of —— at the —— verse." Whatever is superfluous in such formulas is objectionable.

There is one important prohibition of the Directory which is laid down in absolute terms, and which should never be transgressed: "When the minister shall judge it necessary to expound any part of what is read, let it not be done until the whole chapter or psalm be ended." The practice which is thus forbidden interferes greatly with the devotional reading of Scripture. What is still worse, it helped very much to banish the simple reading of God's Word from His own House. It was the most melancholy feature in the degradation of Scottish worship, that for a long period the simple reading of Scripture by the minister was everywhere given up, and would not have been tolerated in many parishes. Leighton speaks of "the foolish prejudice and proud disdain" which the Scottish people had already taken in his time against the Scriptures read without "a superadded discourse;" and later we are told that "the simple reading of a chapter without note or comment was as great an offence as a precomposed form of prayer."[1] It makes one almost shudder to meet with a passage such as the following in a work on the Pastoral Care, by Dr Alex. Gerard, Professor of Divinity in King's College, Aberdeen, published in 1799 by his son and successor: "Reading the Scriptures seems to be so necessary and essential a part of Christian worship, that the omission of it is the most faulty defect in the present practice of our Church. Yet so great is the perverseness and weak bigotry of many, that in some places it would almost create a schism to attempt to introduce it, and even the authority of the Directory, framed in the revered ages of the Church, would not be sufficient to secure from blame the person who introduced it. I know nothing, however, which better deserves a man's running the risk of giving offence than restoring the public reading of the Scriptures. In some places it might perhaps be attempted without offence, and there it should be attempted."[2] It is said that an Aberdeenshire clergyman, who was taken to task by his parish-

[1] Memoirs of Dr A. Webster, &c., p. 344.
[2] P. 367. About the same period Principal Hill accounts for and excuses the omission by the spread of education and the fact "that every person has a Bible, which, from his childhood, he is taught and exhorted to use."—Institutes, p. 330.

ioners for making such an attempt, tried to silence their objections by pointing to the words on the title-page of the Bible, "appointed to be read in churches." I do not know whether he was one of Gerard's students or not, but certain it is that the Synod of Aberdeen has the credit of having taken the first step towards remedying this shameful defect. At length, in 1856, the Assembly enjoined all the clergy to read both from the Old and New Testaments at each diet of worship; and in Aids to Devotion, a portion of the Psalter is prescribed in addition to the two chapters, as required by the Directory.

3. *Psalms and Hymns.*—We come next to the Psalms and Hymns of praise which follow the Lessons, or are intermixed with them. The singing of psalms and hymns and spiritual songs is enjoined as part of the worship of God in the New Testament, and it was the Genevan branch of the Reformation that restored this exercise to its due place in Divine Service. Congregational singing was regarded as the responsive part of the Reformed ritual, and it was nowhere more popular than in Scotland, where the greatest care was taken to make the church music effective and attractive. Besides the Psalter, of which large sections were sung in a great variety of metres,

always concluding with the Gloria, the Church provided metrical versions of the Magnificat, the Veni Creator, and other hymns. The new Psalter adopted at Westminster, and which in Scotland superseded the old Psalm-Book, contained no hymns, but the General Assembly of 1647 appointed Zachary Boyd to revise those previously in use, with the view of adding them to the Psalms. This could not be carried out, however, owing to the Disruption of 1651, and the new leaven from the South, which made such rapid progress. Some of the English sects held that the singing even of the Psalms in metre was unlawful, there being, they said, neither precept nor example for it in Scripture. Others objected to prescribed praise, as they objected to prescribed prayer, no doubt quite consistently, and allowed only singing prophets to extemporise such rhapsodies as came into their disordered brains, while the congregation listened in silence to their effusions. By some of these sects praise was given up for a long period altogether. In Scotland the force of fanaticism never went so far; but it was owing to these influences that the party arose which objected to hymns in public worship, though the Apostolic Christians and the Reformers were so plainly of a different opinion;

and it was to satisfy their Puritanic scruples that the use of the Gloria Patri was given up a few years after the Church had threatened to depose Ministers who discontinued it. In the Assembly of 1649 the subject was discussed, and it would seem that an understanding was come to that the use of it should cease, owing to the importunity of the English; but to the last, Calderwood the historian, who had spent his youth and manhood in fighting against prelatical innovations, and his old age in fighting against those from an opposite quarter, stood out, and that successfully, against a proposal made by the Moderator to lay it aside formally, saying, "Moderator, I intreat that the Doxology be not laid aside, for I hope to sing it in heaven."[1]

From England, too, came the custom of *reading the line*, which contributed more than anything else to the degradation of our Church music. It had previously been the practice in the English parish churches,[2] and the Directory recom-

---

[1] The Doxology Approven, by Mr Edward, Minister at Murroes: p. 70.

[2] "It is a custom generally used in most, if not in all, parish churches of this kingdom [England], as well among Presbyterians as others, that the clerk alone reads aloud every verse, one after another, of the psalm that is sung before and after sermon, and that all the people sing it after him."—Durel: Government and Worship of God in the Reformed Churches

mended its continuance, as a temporary measure, for the benefit of those who were unable to read. Henderson, who was no doubt aware that the Synod of the Reformed Church of France [1] had condemned the practice as unfit and improper, objected at Westminster to this feature of Anglicanism, and it was at first extremely unpalatable to the Scots, who looked upon it as an indignity that such a usage should be imposed upon an educated people like them. But it made way, and in course of time came to be regarded as a venerable Scottish custom, part of the inheritance handed down by the Covenanters,—so that, when it was given up, Ministers had to encounter suppressed murmurings, and in many cases open rebellion. A number of Dissenting congregations in different parts of the country owed their origin, not to patronage, nor to unevangelical preaching in the parish church, but to the introduction of paraphrases and the omission

---

beyond the Seas, p. 183. The practice still prevails among the Wesleyans, who have preserved a number of usages which have been given up by the Church.

[1] In 1579 the Synod resolved as follows: "The congregations which, when they sing Psalms in their meetings, cause the verses to be said aloud before they are sung, shall be warned to give over such their attempt, as being unfit and improper; and a censure shall be passed upon those congregations which use that custom."—Durel, p. 183.

of the reading the line; and others were largely increased from these causes.[1] These determined prejudices were carried by emigrants to the ends of the earth. I remember old Scotsmen in the Colonies who never entered church, because the line was not read out as they had been accustomed to hear it in the Old Country; and it is not surprising that the character of some of those sticklers furnished an illustration of the principle that straining at gnats prepares and predisposes men for swallowing camels.

The Psalms and Hymns that follow the Lessons should be outbursts of joy and praise for all God's mercies, and especially for His Word—the treasure of the faith—and all the blessings of the Gospel. The English Prayer-Book affords fine models in the Te Deum and Benedictus sung after the Old and New Testament Lessons in the morning, and in the Magnificat and Nunc Dimittis in the evening service; and happily these grand hymns, of which people never weary, are to be found in our collections, besides many others scarcely less appropriate. It is advantageous to mark in one's Psalter and Hymnal those portions that are suitable, either as introductory to public worship or for general purposes of praise, and these may be

[1] M'Kerrow's Hist. of the Seces., pp. 16, 60, 79.

given out successively Sunday after Sunday. One can thus furnish the greater part of the Psalms and Hymns for choir practice early in the week. Large portions of the Paraphrases and even of the Hymns, beautiful as they may be as poems, should never be sung in Church at all. It is a too rigid rule that would exclude, altogether, compositions fitted to excite devotional feeling, though not addressed to God; but in our service, where worship is defective, it is best to select, for the most part, Psalms and Hymns of praise or of prayer.

Chanting.—It greatly lightens and brightens the service when, in addition to these metrical selections, the prose psalms for the day are chanted instead of being read. This is the simplest, and at the same time the most perfect, mode of offering praise. Experience shows that it is universally popular. It delights the humblest class, as well as the most refined, and it would have met the scruples even of those sects which objected to metre. Nothing lays hold of a congregation like chanting, or contributes so much to the heartiness of a service. In praise the powers of both body and soul are called into requisition, and the outward volume of song, and the inward tide of devotion, act and react on each other. God's people of old praised Him with mirth and gladness, and rejoiced before Him "with all their might." This is still more requisite in Christian times, when our praises should be a foretaste of the joy of heaven itself; and truly it is not only a good, but a pleasant thing, to celebrate, in this manner, the praises of the Most High.[1]

4. *Second Prayer.*—We come now to the second prayer, which immediately precedes the sermon. This is a modern restoration. For a long period there were only two prayers in the service, but an intermediate one has now become general, in accordance with the Directory and the old Scottish practice. In some of the Reformed Liturgies, and in Aids to Devotion, this prayer is one of thanksgiving as well as for illumination. When Knox's Liturgy was in use, the thanksgiving was often offered in the last prayer, after the intercessions, thus crowning and completing the

---

[1] In the Eastern Churches, the Jewish practice of singing responsively or antiphonally seems to have prevailed from the days of the Apostles. In the West the singing was nothing but chanting with one voice, till the latter part of the fourth century, when S. Ambrose introduced the Eastern practice of singing to each other by turns into the Church of Milan, whence it spread over the rest of Europe.—August. Con., Book ix. chap. 7.

Another mode of singing sometimes followed, was that of a single person beginning the verse, and the people joining with him in the close.—Apos. Con., Book ii. chap. 57.

devotions of the congregation. This was in literal conformity with the words of Scripture—supplications, prayers, intercessions, and giving of thanks,—and it brought the ordinary service into close harmony with that of a Communion Sunday; still, thanksgiving is sufficiently appropriate after the Lessons, which unfold the riches of divine grace; and by introducing it then, the three prayers of the service may be made of nearly equal length.

In giving thanks, the most natural order is to bless the Lord for all His bounties in nature, providence, and grace. You find excellent models of a General Thanksgiving, in the prayer of the Reformed Liturgies,—" O God, Thy glory is great," and in that in Knox's Book, beginning, " Honour and Praise be unto Thee." That in the English Prayer-Book is also admirable, and it is interesting for us to remember that it was introduced at the request of the English Presbyterians, and was composed by one of their eminent Divines —Reynolds, who at the Restoration was offered, and accepted, the Bishopric of Norwich. He did not forget, what should never be forgotten, that there is a *jus divinum* upon giving thanks not only for ourselves, but for all men.

Next comes the short prayer for *illumination*,

in which we ask God for assistance in preaching and hearing His Word, and for His blessing thereon; and it is now the general practice to introduce here the Lord's Prayer.[1]

The Lord's Prayer.—The restored use of this divine and perfect form is one of the great improvements of recent years; and it is encouraging to think that, notwithstanding the aversion with which it was so long regarded, there are few of our people now who would not feel a service defective without it. It was enjoined in the Book of Common Order, and was in universal use in Scotland, as in all the countries and ages of Christendom, till about 1640, when those who had imbibed the Sectarian spirit began, in the language of the time, to "scunner it," and to cáll it a "threedbare prayer." The Directory recommended its continued use; but hostility to it spread rapidly among those who called themselves "the godly party," and in 1649 it was given up in the churches of Edinburgh, and soon afterwards throughout the whole country.[2] Dur-

---

[1] In the Book of Common Order and other Reformed Liturgies, it is introduced at the end of the last prayer. It had the same place in the daily offices of the Primitive Church, but in the Sunday service it was said before Communion.—Bingham, Book xiii. chap. 11.

[2] Wodrow's Analecta, vol. i. p. 274.

ing Cromwell's usurpation, we read of his troopers preaching in Scottish pulpits, casting the stool of repentance out of the churches, fining Scottish ministers for travelling on Sundays on their way to the General Assembly, interrupting public worship when it was not to their liking, and we may be quite sure that with iron heel they stamped out the Lord's Prayer wherever it attempted to raise its head. At the Restoration those who conformed to Episcopacy resumed its use, and it then became a badge of distinction betwixt them and the Presbyterians, as it had formerly been betwixt Presbyterians and the Sectaries. After the Revolution the Episcopalians taunted the Presbyterians with departing from the old usage of the Scottish Church, and disregarding the recommendation of the Directory. They defended themselves by saying that they gave the substance of it, and sometimes used it. But there came a time when other ground was taken; when the use of it was not only denounced by the populace as a rag of Popery, but when grave divines boldly asserted that it was not suitable for Christian devotion. It is extraordinary to find Dr Andrew Thomson, the most distinguished Scottish clergyman of his day, and the first to advocate the revival of sacred music, preaching in St

George's, Edinburgh, in a strain hostile to the use of the Lord's Prayer *simpliciter*, and justifying its omission from the services of the Church. Had he known that the Presbytery of that city, in 1641, three years after the swearing of the National Covenant, issued a solemn warning against this and other Brownist errors, it is not likely that he would have committed himself to such a position. The history of the Church at that period has been far too much overlooked. I once asked the late Dr Laing how it was that no life had been written of Robert Douglas, by far the most prominent man among the Covenanting clergy after the death of Henderson; and by the testimony of all his contemporaries,—Gustavus Adolphus, under whom he had served as chaplain during the Thirty Years' War, included,—one of the greatest men of his age. He replied that he had often urged the biographer of Knox and Melville to undertake it, but that Douglas's principles and career did not suit his purposes. Such a biography would exhibit the Resolutioners and the Protesters in their true colours. The Protesters have been honoured for their sufferings at a later period, but the founders of the party were considered neither good Scotsmen nor good Presbyterians. Many of them were "deep in the interests of the Usurper," and they were essentially tainted with Independency. The first Disruption of the Church lies at their door, and this was the main cause of the restoration of Episcopacy in 1661, with all the miseries that followed.

5. *Third Prayer.* — Passing over the sermon, and the act of praise which usually follows, we come next to the third prayer, which consists chiefly of *intercession*. The Directory tells us "to turn the chief and most useful heads of the sermon into some few petitions, and to pray that it may abide in the heart and bring forth fruit." This is natural and fitting; but we should bear in mind the words "chief heads" and "few petitions," and take care not to pray the sermon over again. After a sentence or two of this import, we should pass to the intercessions—and here, again, order is the first consideration. A good arrangement is to pray, first, for the Church; secondly, for kings and all in authority;[1] and thirdly, for the afflicted. After this the intercessions of a more miscellaneous character may be introduced, as for travellers, sojourners, and strangers; benefactors, friends, and kindred; to

---

[1] The not uncommon notion that we should intercede first for them in authority, rests on a popular misapprehension of the meaning of 1 Tim., chap. ii., ver. 1 and 2.

which may be added thanks for those who have died in the Lord, and are at rest in Paradise. One cannot be too particular, as no class should be neglected, and these varied intercessions are all specially welcome to some who are present. In the second service of the day, our prayers for others are appropriately followed by petitions for mercies, spiritual and temporal, for those who are present, and by asking the divine protection during the night, and that we may see the morning and the day in joy. And the whole should conclude with a prayer to God to receive our offerings, to accept our service, notwithstanding its imperfections, and to follow it with His blessing.[1]

6. *Praise.*—The concluding Psalm or Hymn need not have any reference to the sermon. A dismission is strictly appropriate; but, apart from this, nothing can be more suitable than a Psalm of thanksgiving, or a Hymn in honour of Christ.

7. *Benediction.*—We have now reached the Benediction, which is God's answer to our worship, and its proper close. In it God's Ministers

---

[1] In the Reformed Liturgies and the Book of Common Order this prayer concludes with the Lord's Prayer and the Apostles' Creed. "The Creed was not used to be repeated in the daily service till about the middle of the fifth century in the Greek Church, and not till some time after in the Latin Church."— Bingham, Book x. chap. iv. sec. 17.

put His Name upon the people, and He blesses them. That a blessing is thus imparted from on high, through the channel of an ordained ministry, to those whose hearts are open to receive it, is asserted in all the standards that have at any time been of authority in the Church. This was so well understood formerly, and the blessing was so highly valued, that, in order to induce people to come twice to church, it was sometimes not given till the second service. Not only have the old ideas on this subject died out for the most part, but some of the clergy have been known to denounce them as " involving a blasphemous assumption of sacerdotal power." Many ministers never bless at all, but use a form such as the following, which includes present and absent, saints departed and saints unborn, and which, but for the sacredness of the subject, would deserve to be called a rigmarole: " And now may grace, mercy, and peace be with us, and all the Israel of God, here and everywhere, now, henceforth, and for ever, world without end. Amen."

There are two perfect forms of Benediction in Scripture—the Priestly in Numbers vi., and the Apostolical in 2 Corinthians xiii. 14. To these may be added another no less scriptural, though a compilation: " The peace of God," &c.

As the Church declares that it belongs to the Minister's office to bless the people from God under the Gospel, as it did to the Priests under the Law,[1] those who are unordained only pray for a blessing. Hence the practice, so long rigidly adhered to, of licentiates saying "us," instead of "you," and of their not making use of the sign of blessing—viz., the lifting up of the hands. In the Directory turned into a Liturgy for the use of the laity, this part of the service is headed, "Prayer for a Blessing," which is given as a prayer accordingly. Benediction is so sacred an act, that, at the close of meetings not for worship, it is well always to use the words as a prayer.

SUGGESTIONS.

Having gone over the different parts of the service, I shall now offer a few suggestions as to the filling up of the outline thus sketched. To have a fixed order and sequence of topics in our minds, is itself a great help and a great safeguard. It keeps one from being tossed to and fro like the ship without compass or rudder. Still, order is not enough; thought and preparation beforehand, as well as a devotional spirit at

---

[1] The Form of Church Government.

the time, are necessary to the successful filling in of details. "Be not rash with thy mouth, and let not thy heart be hasty to utter anything before God." Such is the command of Scripture; and it implies that our prayers should be premeditated, both as regards thought and expressions. This is due to God, to our fellow-worshippers, and to ourselves; for prayer is not an intellectual exercise, and it is not favourable to devotion that we should have to think out at the time what we are to say. It is easy to string together texts of Scripture incorrectly quoted, or to extemporise at random a varied and ceaseless round of pious nonsense, some prominent word in the sentence last uttered suggesting the sentence that follows. If variety were one's chief aim, far better no framework at all. A few materials would suffice, and could be presented in new combinations indefinitely, like the bits of coloured glass in a kaleidoscope. But every one who would not be held guilty of carelessness, I might say of profaneness, in addressing the Most High, will shrink from uttering such effusions.

1. First, we should keep in mind in our church prayers that we address God as an assembly of Christians, as His children, members of His house-

hold and family, and nothing should be said inconsistent with this.

2. As church prayers are *common*, not private, we should confine ourselves to expressions which are suitable to all. "Peculiarities are for private, not for public, devotion," and nothing should be said to which every Christian present cannot add, Amen. "We approach God as a society," and we should carefully guard against putting forward mere sentiments of our own, or of a section of the congregation. For example, in times of political strife, when the community is divided as to the policy of Government, one should not imitate the rival American chaplains, who are said to have prayed for and against the measures proposed in Congress.

3. As the Minister is the mouthpiece of the congregation in their common prayers to God, he should shrink from saying anything with the purpose of conveying instruction or reproof to them, or of paying them compliments. The oblique attitude in which the Minister, with one eye on heaven and the other upon earth, pretends to address to God, who is the great listener in His own house, what he really means for the congregation, is above all things to be avoided. Even the common practice of intimating in prayer that

a stranger is to officiate in the afternoon or evening, is of questionable propriety. It reminds one of the story of the revivalist preacher, who was in the habit of praying thus: "And bless Thy humble servant before Thee, who is to preach this afternoon at —— at — o'clock."

4. Again, it should be remembered that our petitions, confessions, and thanksgivings are all *acts* of devotion, to be then and there performed, and not mere purposes to be carried out at some future period; and therefore such phrases as We adore, We repent, We beseech, We praise, should be employed; and not, We desire to do so, or We would desire, which is a different matter, and leaves the thing undone. This reminds me of an opposite vice, by no means uncommon, that of praying for things past, which is an absurdity,—thus, "May the services of a past Communion season have been blessed to many souls."

5. Again, we should guard against those misquotations, misapplications, and what have been called grotesque groupings of Scripture with which the traditional Liturgy abounds. For misquotations, take the examples, "May they kiss the rod and Him who hath appointed it;" "Thou inhabitest eternity and the praises there-

of;" "Be in our midst to bless us and to do us good:" and for misapplications, "Our own hearts condemn us, and Thou art greater than our hearts and knowest all things;" and again, "May our names be written in the Lamb's Book of Life,"—the former of which should be true of no Christian, while the latter is already true of all. Then as a grotesque grouping, there is the well-known and oft-exposed, but still used, specimen, "We come before Thee with our hands on our mouths, and our mouths in the dust, crying out," &c. Equally to be avoided are those accommodations of Scripture metaphors and oriental phrases, which, because of their incongruity with modern life, have become a matter of jest to the thoughtless, such as the following: "We would set up our Ebenezer;" "May his bow long abide in strength;" "May those who tarry at home divide the spoil."

6. Again, it is desirable that our supplications should as far as possible be divided into distinct paragraphs, so that at the end of each the people may breathe an inaudible Amen, or, "O Lord, hear us."[1]

7. Further, we should always remember the rule of Scripture, "God is in heaven, and thou upon

---

[1] Formerly the Scottish people accompanied the prayers with "sighing and groaning."—Bishop Cowper's Works, p. 639.

earth, therefore let thy words be few." None of the three prayers should exceed eight or, at the most, ten minutes, if we would avoid the risk of praying people out of a good frame, after we have prayed them into one, as Whitfield blamed a friend for doing.

8. And lastly, after the Scriptures, and especially the Psalms, which are the great storehouse of devotion, let me recommend you to study Liturgies and the devotional literature of past ages. The Primitive Liturgies are the common heritage of Christendom, and surely the different Churches of the Reformation should borrow what is good from each other. As has been said, "The sense of communion with past ages, and with contemporaries of other lands and tongues, has something of a heart-raising nature which is altogether or in part wanting in the case of new and as yet unwonted forms."

These studies can be combined with your private devotions; and they will not only furnish you with the richest materials for public prayer, but they will educate your taste, and imbue you with a true instinct.

In the Liturgies we have the purest gems of devotion in the choicest settings; the grandest and holiest thoughts and aspirations, clothed in the simplest and most beautiful forms. In prayer, more than anywhere else, simplicity is beauty. Nothing can be more objectionable than the use of tawdry and bombastic phrases, nothing more out of place in our devotions than an oratorical display.

It is an excellent plan to jot down under the different headings to which they belong—such as "confession," or "thanksgiving"—the materials suitable for public devotion which you meet with in the Bible or Books of Prayer, or which occur to your own minds. Thus stores will rapidly accumulate, which you can without difficulty set in order, and make the basis of your public services.

BOOKS OF REFERENCE.

Before concluding, I shall mention a list of books which are useful either as furnishing materials for prayer, or as sources of information on the history of worship in our own and other branches of the Church.

Neale's Primitive Liturgies, with Translations.
Bingham's Antiquities of the Christian Church.
King's Primitive Church (second part).
Ebrard's Reformed Church Books.
Liturgies of Geneva, Lausanne, and Neufchâtel.
Bersier's Liturgy.

Liturgy of the French Protestant Church of Charleston, S.C. (New York).
Liturgy of the [Dutch] Reformed Church in America.
Liturgy of the [German] Reformed Church in America.
⁎ Eutaxia, or the Presbyterian Liturgies (New York).
The Book of Common Prayer as amended by the Westminster Divines in the Royal Commission of 1661, and in agreement with the Directory for Public Worship of the Presbyterian Church in the United States (Philadelphia).
Hall's Reliquiæ Liturgicæ.
Baillie's Letters.
Prayers for Social and Family Worship, authorised by the Church of Scotland.
Order of Public Worship, by Dr Robert Lee.
Book of Common Order (Euchologion).
Knox's Liturgy and Westminster Directory, edited by Sprott and Leishman.
Scottish Liturgies of the Reign of James VI. Sprott.
⁎ Chapter on Liturgics in Van Oosterzee's Practical Theology.
Liturgy and Offices of the Church (Catholic and Apostolic).

LECTURE II.

BAPTISM, AND THE ADMISSION OF CATECHUMENS.

The subjects of Lecture to-day are Baptism, and the Admission of young people to the renewal of their Baptismal vows, and to the participation of the Lord's Supper.

Baptism.

I. BAPTISM OF INFANTS.

The Baptism of Infants falls first to be considered. There can be no question that the form given for that service in the Directory is in substance obligatory, as the General Assembly, so recently as 1870, "earnestly recommended all Ministers to frame their baptismal addresses and exhortations according to the method set forth therein."

1. The first Rubric of the Directory is that

"Baptism, as it is not unnecessarily to be delayed, so it is not to be administered in any case by any private person, but by a Minister of Christ called to be the Steward of the mysteries of God." The first clause originally required Baptism to be administered on the second Lord's Day at furthest. It had been usual from the days of the Primitive Church, as it still is in the Church of Rome, to baptize children as soon as possible after their birth.

An African Synod, which met A.D. 254, and at which sixty-six Bishops were present, decided that it was not to be deferred till the eighth day, as some had held, owing to its having taken the place of circumcision. The Reformers held similar opinions, and remonstrated against delay as "bringing contempt upon the Church, and upon the whole redemption and Communion of Christ."[1] The old custom was continued down to the time of our grandfathers and grandmothers, who, as our old Session Records show, were as a rule baptized in Church the first Sunday after they entered the world. The habit of postponing it unnecessarily, which has since become common, is connected with low views of the ordinance, and should not be encouraged.

[1] Bucer.

With regard to the Baptizers, the Confession of Faith also says that "neither sacrament may be dispensed by any but by a Minister of the Word lawfully ordained."[1] In 1565 the General Assembly acknowledged the validity of Romish Baptism, and ordered that it was not to be repeated. This was necessary to the Christian standing of the Reformers themselves, and is involved in the continuity of the Visible Church. Calvin even said that parents, in cases of necessity, should present their children to Romish Priests for Baptism rather than suffer them to remain unbaptized, as that involved an apparent contempt for Christianity itself.[2] The repetition of Baptism has generally been looked upon as a sacrilegious practice. The Scottish Episcopalians took to it somewhat largely in the case of Presbyterian converts a quarter of a century ago, forgetful that this was to repudiate the Baptism of their own early Bishops and Clergy, and thus to saw off the branch on which they are perched at a point betwixt them and the tree. Some

---

[1] Chap. xxvii. sec. iv.

[2] See Scott's Continuation of Milner's Church History, vol. iii. p. 401. A generation or two ago in some parts of Canada, the Scottish Highlanders, though Protestant, often had their children baptized by Roman Catholic priests in the absence of clergymen of their own faith.

glaring cases of these converts going a step further, and receiving another conditional Baptism on their reception into the Church of Rome, according to a modern practice of that Communion, appear to have had a wholesome effect upon our Episcopal neighbours.

2. The second Rubric enjoins that Baptism "shall not be administered in private places or privately, but in the place of Public Worship, and in the face of the Congregation." In Knox's Liturgy it is said that "Sacraments are not to be used in private corners," but are "necessarily annexed to God's Word as seals of the same," and that, "therefore, the infant that is to be baptized shall be brought to the Church on the day appointed to Common Prayer and Preaching." So strict was the Church at first in this matter, that a Minister of Tranent was suspended, and obliged to make his public repentance, for baptizing children in private houses. One of the five Articles of the Perth Assembly of 1618, which caused so much strife in the Church, for the first time allowed private Baptism, and this only "for a great and necessary cause." King James was bent upon this relaxation of the old law, and one of his smart sayings is recorded in connection with it. A Clergyman, remonstrating against the

change, asked the King if he thought a child dying unbaptized would be damned. "No," replied the British Solomon; "but if you refuse to baptize a dying child you will." The Perth Articles were not all equally objected to, and if they had been proposed singly instead of *en bloc*, some of them would have been generally approved of; but they were afterwards all cast out by the Glasgow Assembly of 1638. Our Commissioners at Westminster took a leading part in carrying the rule which enforced public Baptism, a practice then very uncommon in England. Baillie writes: "The abuse was great over all this land. In the greatest Parish in London, scarce one child in a year was brought to the Church for Baptism." In 1690, the first Assembly after the Revolution passed a very stringent law on the subject, which is still in force. It "discharges the administration of Baptism in private,—that is," it goes on to say, "in any place, or at any time when the congregation is not orderly called together to wait on the dispensing of the Word." This language was probably meant, and at all events was interpreted, to admit of Baptism in a private house, provided intimation was made from the pulpit that Divine Service was to be held in such house, and the people asked to attend. The more conscientious Clergy long strictly adhered to the law thus understood. Boston of Ettrick, one of the ablest divines and most faithful ministers of the Church, in the early part of last century, says, "I never administered Baptism in a private house without previous intimation to the congregation. In eighteen years no child died unbaptized, through adhering to this rule." And he adds, "Glory to a good God for it." If an exception had been clearly made in favour of dying children, as pious Boston evidently wished, the rule might have been kept; but for want of this, it came gradually to be disregarded, till there were Parish Churches in which no one had been baptized within the memory of any one living. Stringent laws and lax practices are too apt to go together, and nowhere can this combination have a worse moral effect than in the Church. Apart from this, it can scarcely be doubted that private Baptism, as often administered, has tended to the degradation of divine ordinances, and to the fostering of irreverence in the land. There is something very unchristian, too, in the class distinctions which are often connected with it. No wonder the poor are indignant when they are told that they must bring their children to church, while those in better circumstances get theirs baptized at home. Most righteously did the First Book of Discipline say concerning Pastors that "whatsoever they do to the rich in respect of their ministry, the same they are bound to do to the poorest under their charge." It is humiliating to think of Church members asking the laws to be set aside, and distinctions made in their favour in the matter of God's ordinances, because they are a little higher in the social scale than their neighbours. There is only one distinction that should be made, and that for modesty's sake. Illegitimate children may well be baptized, not privately, but in church, before a sufficient number of witnesses, after the congregation is dismissed. I am well aware of the great difficulties which Ministers meet with in trying to carry out the law of the Church; but they should persevere in the attempt; and when obliged to baptize in private, without any good reason, it should be done under protest, and the religious exercises should approach as nearly as possible a complete church service. The Church of England, once a warning to our Fathers, is now a model to us in this respect. So do fashions change, and thus the world goes round.

The Book of Common Order enjoined that Baptism was to be administered after the sermon, and this has always been the Scottish custom. Henderson, in his Government and Order of the Church of Scotland — a little treatise published in 1641,—says that it was usually administered at the afternoon service, and this is still the common practice in England.

3. The third Rubric says that "the child is to be presented by the Father, or (in case of his necessary absence) by some Christian friend in his place." The Book of Common Order required the presence not only of the Father, but of a Godfather. In the Scottish, as in all other branches of the Reformed Church, God-parents were joined with Parents as sponsors. Thus one of Knox's sons had for Godfather, Whittingham, Dean of Durham; the other, Coverdale, Bishop of Exeter. The practice was defended as "maintaining a sweet communion among the faithful by a conjunction of friendship," and as a provision for the Christian training of children in case of their parents being removed by death. Opposition to it arose first among the English Sectaries. When Brown, their founder, came to Scotland on a Mission tour in 1584, he "made show," Calderwood tells us, "after an arrogant manner before the Session of the Kirk of Edinburgh, that he would maintain that witnesses at

Baptism was not a thing indifferent, but simply evil. But he failed in his probation."[1] The Directory was not understood to exclude additional sponsors, as after its adoption in Scotland we find Sessions giving instructions as to the number that should accompany the parent. Gradually, however, they came to be regarded merely as witnesses. The Assembly in 1712 passed an Act discharging other sponsors than parents when they are communicants; but this Act was directed rather against taking substitutes for them than against the old practice of allowing others in addition. I may mention that in many of our Colonies our Clergy minister to Reformed Churches of Continental origin, which retain this and other usages which prevailed in Scotland for long after the Reformation. The Act of 1712 also provides that, "if parents be dead, or absent, or grossly ignorant, or under scandal, or contumacious," another sponsor is to present the child, —a relation if possible; and that in the case of foundlings the Kirk-Session is to act in this capacity, so that no children in the land need remain unbaptized.

Any child descended, however remotely, from Christian progenitors, was held by the Reformers

---

[1] Hist., vol. iv. p. 1.

and the compilers of our standards to have a right to Baptism, whatever the character of its immediate ancestors, just as every descendant of Abraham had a right to circumcision; while as to the children of idolaters and excommunicated persons, they taught that they ought to be baptized to competent sponsors. It is quite against the law of the Church—the spirit, if not the letter—and is an absurdity on the face of it, for those who have not accepted their own baptismal covenant, to stand as sponsors for children, to say nothing of such enormities as I have known of—persons allowed to act in this capacity who were not themselves baptized.

THE SERVICE.

To come now to the service. The Directory says the parent or other sponsor is to present the child, "professing his earnest desire that it may be baptized." This does not, of course, mean that he is to make a short address to that effect, but that the Minister is to put a question like that in the Book of Common Order: "Do you here present this child to be baptized, earnestly desiring that he may be ingrafted in the mystical body of Jesus Christ?" and that the sponsor is to give his assent.

The Address.—The Minister is then "to use some words of instruction touching the institution, nature, use, and ends of this Sacrament."

He should begin with the words of institution as given in Matthew xxviii. 18-20, and in the instruction should be careful to adhere faithfully to the doctrine of the Church as set forth in her standards. Baptism, which is the only Christian ordinance that vast multitudes are privileged to receive, is, in the lowest view of it, a great covenant transaction betwixt the baptized person and the Triune God; while, according to all the Reformed Confessions, though the Visible Church is and always will be a mixed community, both Sacraments are effectual means of salvation; and the sensible signs employed in them not only signify and seal — *i.e.*, make sure — but *apply* Christ and His benefits to the heirs of salvation. You will find ample material and suitable models for this address in the Book of Common Order, the Directory, and in the Baptismal Forms which were laid before the Assembly in 1871 by the Committee on Aids to Devotion. For a short explanation of the nature of the ordinance, one can hardly do better than take the words of the Shorter or Larger Catechism.

At the conclusion of this address, the Directory

says that the Minister is also "to admonish all that are present to look back to their Baptism; to repent of their sins against their covenant with God; to stir up their faith; to improve and make right use of their Baptism, and of the covenant sealed thereby betwixt God and their souls." In the Book of Common Order there is also a paragraph to this effect. This is a feature of the service which has fallen into general disuse, and which ought to be revived.

The baptismal address may be shortened or lengthened according to circumstances, but no essential ideas should be left out. Straining after variety for variety's sake, or through fear of awakening the ignorant prejudices of the people, is altogether needless, and is apt to result in omitting things that should be said, and putting in things that should be left out.

Questions to Sponsors.—The Directory does not prescribe any profession of faith to be exacted of Sponsors. In Scotland they had always been made to rehearse the Creed, as required by the Book of Common Order; and the Scottish Commissioners at Westminster earnestly contended for the general adoption of this practice. Failing in this, they urged that questions equivalent should be asked, and assented to. Baillie writes: "The

Belief in Baptism was never said in England, and they would not undergo that yoke; but we have got the Assembly to agree to equivalent interrogatories much against the mind of the Independents."[1] These interrogatories have disappeared from the Directory, and it has been supposed that they were struck out by the House of Commons. In Scotland the old custom lingered on for a time. We find Leighton in 1665 earnestly urging the Clergy of his Diocese to cause parents to repeat the Belief at the Baptism of their children. The practice was then dying out, and the Creed itself was disliked by those who had imbibed the sectarian spirit. Parents had still to make confession of the Faith into which the child was to be baptized, but each Minister imposed whatever creed he pleased. In 1711 the Assembly enjoined Ministers to baptize the children of Foreign Protestants on their "professing their faith in Christ, and obedience to Him," and "engaging to educate them in the fear of God, and knowledge of the principles of the Reformed Protestant religion." This liberal Act was meant to protect strangers from the heavy burdens that were imposed by many of the Clergy upon their own flocks. It had become common to require an

[1] Letters, vol. ii. p. 258.

assent to the Scriptures, the Confession of Faith, the Catechisms (Larger and Shorter), and in some cases to the Solemn League and Covenant. Among the older Dissenters even this was not enough. A Clergyman told me that in Egypt some years ago he was present at the baptism of a child of an Arab Fellah connected with the American Presbyterian Mission there. This common labourer from the banks of the Nile was obliged to declare his adherence, not only to the above creed, but, in addition, to the Act and Testimony of the Seceders as drawn up in Scotland in such a year, and as amended and accepted in America in another. My informant belonged to the straitest sect of our religion, but even he thought that this was rather too much of a good thing. Another friend told me of a case at home of quite a different sort, where the Minister said to the parent, he had but one question to ask, and it was this —"Was he a saved man?" His idea, of course, was that the man should be able to give a categorical answer, and that the efficacy of the Sacrament depended upon its being in the affirmative. I have myself heard the following form used : " I need not ask you if you believe the Christian faith : your presence here is a sufficient guarantee for that."

Equally varied and extraordinary are the *obligations* which are sometimes imposed. Henderson describes the old Scottish usage thus: "He that presenteth the child promiseth to bring him up in the faith into which he is baptized, and in the fear of God." The Directory also orders that the Minister shall require the Sponsor's solemn promise "to bring up the child in the knowledge of the grounds of the Christian religion, and in the nurture and admonition of the Lord." But this promise grew in many cases to portentous dimensions. A late eminent Clergyman of our Church used to tell of an incident which he witnessed, and which he said filled him with horror. The Minister at a baptism went on imposing burdens in the most minute and stringent manner, thus: "And do you promise to have family worship in your house, and that not merely occasionally, but regularly twice a-day?" and so on, till the poor father turned pale, and staggered as if about to faint. There was a painful pause as he hesitated in giving his assent, but in a little he rallied, and swallowed the draught that was presented to his lips. No wonder that one of our Clergymen should have said, "It appears intolerable that in the same Church, and that recognised and established by law, one Minister shall demand of candidates for Baptism or the Lord's Supper, a different profession of faith from that which another demands,"[1] or we may add, impose different obligations. The presiding Minister at an ordination might as well be allowed to impose an extemporised profession of faith, and to exact any promises he pleased. Some years ago there was such a strong feeling on this subject that on an Overture from a number of leading men in the Church, the Committee on Aids to Devotion was instructed by the General Assembly to "prepare a form consistently with the rules in the Directory, in which the professions and engagements of Christian parents may be expressed." In obedience to their instructions the Committee prepared two forms for Infant, and one for Adult, Baptism. The Assembly approved their diligence, ordered the drafts to be printed, and copies to be sent to all the Ministers of the Church. These forms, to which I have already made reference, you will find in the volume of Assembly Reports for 1871. In two of these the belief imposed is the Apostles' Creed.

1. This is in accordance with the practice of the Primitive Church, and of a great part of Christendom, and should be followed in all cases. The

[1] Lee's Reform of the Church of Scotland, p. 177.

Creed is but an expansion of the baptismal formula, and is the common faith of the Universal Church into which the child is to be baptized. Such a change has come over our countrymen that it would be very difficult to get them now to rehearse it, as they did for the first century after the Reformation; but the next best course is for the Minister to introduce it thus: "Do you receive the Articles of the Christian faith whereof we make our confession, saying, 'I believe in God,' &c.?"

2. Different views are entertained in the Church as to the *engagements* which should be entered into by the Sponsor on behalf of the child. Stuart of Pardovan, whose book on the law and practice of the Church, published early in last century, has been the great authority since, and whose attachment to Presbytery was above all suspicion, says: "In the baptismal engagement the parent or Sponsor is, in name of the child, to renounce the devil and all his works, the vain pomp and glory of this wicked world, and all the sinful lusts of the flesh." That these views were prevalent at the time, appears also from what are called the Larger Overtures, which are printed with the Acts of Assembly of 1705. These Overtures, the significance of which has been too much overlooked, were virtually the draft of a new Book of Dis-

cipline, on which the leading men of the Church were employed for many years after the Revolution. They were printed by order of Assembly in 1704, and were sent down to Presbyteries and Synods, who had them long under consideration; but they were never sanctioned, as a whole, on account of differences of opinion on some of the many points which they embraced. In them it is said that "young communicants are to be put in mind of their parents' engagements made for them in their baptism." Such ideas did not originate with the indulged Episcopal Clergy, who, though they remained Parish Ministers, did not sit in the Courts of the Church, and had no influence on its legislation. In more modern times both Moderatism and revived Puritanism have agreed in rejecting them, while the latter has even strongly denounced them. This hostility finds expression in the Report of the Committee on Aids to Devotion, anent Baptismal professions and obligations, presented to the Assembly in 1870.

In the Savoy Liturgy, drawn up by the English Presbyterians at the Restoration, an attempt is made to reconcile these different views, and probably a form such as the following would satisfy all parties: "Do you dedicate this child unto God to be baptized in this faith, and to be thereby engaged to renounce the devil," and so on? No one doubts that the child is thus engaged, though one would scarcely discover it from many baptismal services. Indeed, one test of a rightly constructed service is that the child, and not the Sponsor, figures most prominently in it.

3. All are at one as to requiring a promise from the Sponsor to train up the child in the doctrines and duties of our holy religion. This should be expressed in general terms, like those which I have already quoted from the Directory. To go into details is to run the risk of involving people in the guilt of breaking vows made to God in the most solemn circumstances. Whatever you do in the matter of imposing creeds and obligations, make them the same to all classes,—high and low, gentle and simple. All are equal in the Church, and to modify a sacramental service, with the view of suiting people of superior rank and intelligence, is a gross violation of the great law of Christian brotherhood, and, to put it upon lower ground, nothing can be more essentially vulgar.

In the Reformed Liturgies it is appropriately added here: "The Lord spare you and your child, and give you grace to fulfil your promise."

Prayer before Baptism.—Prayer is then offered

to God to sanctify and bless His own ordinance, and to bestow upon the child all the blessings signified by it. For this prayer you will find suitable models in the Book of Common Order, the Directory, and in the volume issued by the Church Service Society. The Directory says that this prayer is "to be joined with the Word of Institution for sanctifying the water to this spiritual use." The probable meaning is that Our Lord's command should be incorporated with the prayer, thus: "Almighty God, whose dearly beloved Son, Jesus Christ Our Lord, gave commandment to His apostles that they should go and teach all nations, baptizing them in the name of the Father, and of the Son, and of the Holy Ghost, we beseech Thee," &c. The injunction of the Directory to pray for the sanctifying of the water is in accordance with the practice of the Primitive Church.

I was once present at a baptism when no prayer was offered before the administration of the rite, and, I regret to say, this was not a solitary instance of such a serious omission. In a letter which I had recently from a friend, he says: "The last bit of progress I hear of is, that the Minister of —— last Sunday christened children in —— Church without one word of prayer before or after; and when spoken to, said—'The hymn sung did as well.' Such things," my friend adds, "are a just retribution on the Church for not having something of liturgical form— enough to make such imperfect rites impossible."

The Rite.—"The Minister is then to demand the name of the child, which, being told him, he is to say, calling the child by his name, 'I baptize thee,' &c. As he pronounceth these words he is to baptize the child with water."

You may have seen, as I have, a Minister first baptize the child, and then after a pause add, "The child's name is M. or N.," as if to show his disregard of a custom which has been continued in the Church of God from the days of Abraham, whose name was changed when he received the rite of circumcision. Such novelties indicate both a want of sense and of reverence. It may hardly seem credible, but I was once reproved by a dissatisfied parent for not giving the surname as well as the Christian name, and was told that the Minister who had baptized the rest of the family had given them all "baith their names." Some Ministers make free even with the words of Institution, adding "one God" after the name of the Blessed Trinity, and you will find this form even in Ministers' Directories. I remember hearing an Elder compliment a young Clergyman for making this addition to Our Lord's words. The worthy man said he liked it, and thought it a great improvement. The Clergyman, who had never thought of the matter before, was naturally somewhat taken aback at such a compliment, and did not repeat what, in his case, was simply a blunder.

The Directory further recommends "pouring or sprinkling of the water on the face of the child," as "not only lawful, but sufficient and most expedient." The essential thing is the application of water to the body, and the quantity does not affect the validity of the sacrament, any more than the quantity of bread and wine partaken of in the Lord's Supper affects the validity of that ordinance. At the same time, one should not overlook the fact that immersion was the mode practised in the Primitive Church, and that this form of administration symbolises most perfectly the death and burial of the old nature, and the resurrection of the new. Though pouring or sprinkling is preferred, immersion is not forbidden by the Directory; and I have known this mode followed by Clergymen of our Church abroad, when requested by persons brought up among the Anabaptists, who attached importance to it.

Trine aspersion, in accordance with the trine immersion of the Primitive Church, is practised in the Dutch and some other branches of the Reformed Church, while in others a free application of water is enjoined. Some Ministers seem anxious to use no more than the smallest drop; and, on good authority, I have heard of some who were careful to let this fall, not upon the child's face, but upon its garments. There is a well-known English story of an ultra-evangelical Clergyman, whose proper place would have been among the Quakers, asking a neighbour if he really used water in Baptism, as he himself had long since given up that piece of superstition. Water is of the same importance in the one sacrament as bread and wine are in the other; and one of the chief characteristics of both is their bodily reference. Baptism, as has been said, takes infeftment not only of the soul, but of the body for Christ, and this is renewed at each participation of the Holy Communion. If water were put on the dress instead of the face, it would be no Baptism; and perhaps it was to guard against the possibility of such a thing that the Book of Common Order requires the Minister to lay it on the child's forehead.

When a number of children are to be baptized

together, it is foolish not to respect the old custom of baptizing those of the male sex first, and each according to age. Some absurd prejudices used to be connected with this; but there is reason in what the old wives will tell you, that " Adam was first formed, then Eve."

The clause in the Directory, " without any other ceremony," refers to the use of the sign of the Cross.

The practice of the Minister blessing the child with imposition of hands immediately after the application of the water, is an innovation, I believe, of comparatively recent origin in our Church; but it is in conformity with Our Lord's example, who took the little children in His arms, and put His hands on them, and blessed them; and it was a usage of the early Church to which great significance was attached. When it is done, it is important to make use of the Apostolic Benediction, on account of the distinct reference to the Holy Ghost, rather than that from Numbers, which is often given.

It is quite in accordance with old practice, for the Minister, after the Act of Baptism, to make a declaration such as the following, which is shortened from that in the Savoy Liturgy: " This child is now received by Christ's appointment into His Church, and is engaged to confess the faith of Christ crucified, and to continue Christ's faithful soldier and servant unto his life's end."

Concluding Prayer.—The Prayer that follows should embrace the following topics: (1.) Thanksgiving for God's mercy in receiving the child into His household and family, with supplications that its life may be prolonged, that "it may not fall short of or walk contrary to the grace of Baptism," that it may be faithful to its engagements, persevere to the end, and finally receive the crown of life. (2.) Prayer for the Sponsors, that they may discharge their obligations aright. (3.) Thanksgiving for the mother's deliverance in time of trouble. (4.) Prayer for the congregation, that the administration of the Sacrament may be sanctified to them, with thanks for our own Baptism, for parents, pastors, and teachers; an acknowledgment of our backslidings, with petitions that, as we have been once washed every whit, we may be washed from daily transgressions, and have grace to be faithful to our vows, and to walk in brotherly love, as becometh those who have been baptized by the One Spirit into the one Body.

This is one of the ways in which, as the Larger

Catechism teaches, we are to discharge the much neglected duty of improving our own Baptism.

These petitions should be followed by the General Intercession, and the whole service be concluded in the usual way.

For a post-baptismal Hymn nothing can be more appropriate than the 47th Paraphrase.

Here I may notice one or two expressions from the traditional Liturgy which ought to be carefully avoided. "Bless the engaging parent" is one of those which affords food for merriment in the streets of Gath and Askelon, especially when the man's appearance is not in his favour. Then, again, the petitions, "Ratify in heaven what in Thy name we do upon earth," and "May his name be written in the Lamb's Book of Life," are suitable for the prayer before Baptism, but not in that after, where one usually hears them.

BAPTISM OF ADULTS.

This most solemn service has frequently to be performed in the mission-field, and, I am sorry to say, there is now too often occasion for it at home.

All the reasons for public Baptism in the case of Infants apply here with equal force, with this in addition, that to the Adult himself no such opportunity can again occur of confessing Christ before men. Those who have seen adults publicly baptized, and who have witnessed the solemn impression produced on the congregation, cannot but regret the way in which this service is too often performed in this country. At the very least, it should take place in church before a sufficient number of witnesses, if it be impossible, in the present state of things, to get candidates to come before the assembled congregation.

There is no provision for this service in the Directory, or in the early editions of the Reformed Liturgies. The Dutch Church, as it was the first to enter the heathen mission-field, was the first to provide such a form, the present excellent service in its Liturgy having been added in 1604, shortly before it began those noble missionary enterprises in the East, which are now forgotten or condemned as having been too much an affair of the State, but which form one of the brightest pages in the history of the Reformed Church at that time.

The form for Adult Baptism should closely resemble that for the Baptism of Infants, only such changes being made as are absolutely necessary.

Thus, instead of the first question to the Sponsor, the Minister should ask the candidate "If it is his desire to be baptized, and thereby ingrafted into the Body of Christ."

The instruction, in so far as it relates to the institution, nature, and ends of Baptism, may be the same in both cases; but at the close there should be a paragraph such as the following, borrowed partly from the Dutch service, and given in the form printed by authority of the Assembly in 1871: "And though the infant children of Christian parents are not to be excluded from this token of the covenant of promise, yet we are not warranted to baptize those of riper years until they profess their faith in Christ and obedience to Him. Forasmuch, then, as you are desirous of receiving the Holy Sacrament, it is necessary that you sincerely give answer before God and His Church to the questions I have now to ask."

The questions which follow in this form are unexceptionable; and as they have the *quasi*-sanction of the Church, it is well to ask them verbatim.

It is in accordance with the practice of our own and other branches of the Reformed Church, and is both reverent and convenient, that an adult should kneel during the act of Baptism. From the discussion about kneeling at the Lord's Supper which took place after that gesture was enjoined in 1618, it appears that parents also formerly knelt in presenting their children for Baptism.[1]

The solemn *blessing* which follows may appropriately and conveniently be accompanied with the imposition of hands, as in the case of infants.

In the *declaration* which is next made, it should be stated that the person baptized is now admitted to the participation of the Lord's Supper, and to all the privileges of the New Covenant.

After the post-baptismal prayer a suitable *exhortation* should be given. As there is a close connection between Adult Baptism and the renewal of the baptismal engagement by Catechumens, and as both admit to full communion, the same blessing, prayer, and exhortation, with a few verbal alterations, are suitable for both services.

In some cases one has a difficulty in knowing whether to baptize young people as infants or as adults. Perhaps, as a general rule, the age of twelve should mark the dividing-line.

[1] Gillespie's Dispute against the English Popish Ceremonies, p. 106.

Admission of Catechumens.

We come now to the service for the renewal of baptismal vows, and the admission of Catechumens to the Lord's Table. There is no more curious history than that of Chrism, out of which the rite of Confirmation is usually regarded as having arisen. "All learned men," as Bingham says, "who have exactly considered this matter, as well Papists as Protestants, are agreed that this was the ancient and general practice of the Church — to confirm infants as soon as they were baptized." The first Confirmation or *Complimentum baptismi* seems to have consisted of blessing, with imposition of hands, and prayer for the graces of the Holy Spirit. About the beginning of the third century, anointing with oil was introduced to represent the unction from above, and hence the rite came to be called Chrism. In the Eastern Church, which preserves the usages of the early centuries almost unchanged, infants are still anointed immediately, or within a few days, after Baptism, — the Priest being the minister of the rite, not the Bishop, though the oil is now previously consecrated by him. For the first 1300 years infant chrism was the practice of the West, as well as infant communion, which is still universal in the Eastern Churches. You see from all this how little confirmation has to do with the Apostolic laying on of hands for the impartation of the miraculous gifts of the Holy Ghost, with which an attempt is sometimes made to connect it. In the Romish Church, Confirmation or Chrism is now administered to children usually when about twelve or fourteen years of age, and not till after they have received their first Communion. Formerly the rite was not accompanied with imposition of hands; but it would appear that in some countries the Bishop, in addition to the prescribed ceremonies—namely, making the sign of the cross on the forehead with oil, and giving a blow on the cheek, emblematic of the Christian warfare—now lays his hand on the head of each candidate.

There was no form for the Reception of Catechumens in the Book of Common Order, or in the early editions of other Reformed Liturgies—a defect in them which has been since supplied,—but the First Book of Discipline says: "None are to be admitted to this mystery (*i.e.*, the Lord's Supper) who cannot formally say the Lord's Prayer, the Articles of the Belief, nor declare the sum of the Law." There are notices which show that candidates were carefully instructed, and their admission no doubt took place in church at the public examination of the congregation before communion, which was long universal.[1]

Episcopal Confirmation, or Bishopping, as it was called, was enjoined by one of the Five Articles of the Perth Assembly; but it was not practised during the next twenty years in which Episcopacy was continued in the Church, nor was there any attempt to introduce it between 1661 and 1688, when that form of Government was reimposed.

The Scottish Episcopalians did not begin it till last century, and their tendencies being then towards Eastern rather than Anglican usages, some of their Bishops confirmed infants.[2] I may mention that Episcopal Confirmation was not introduced into the Channel Islands till 1829, though for more than two centuries the connection of the inhabitants with the French Reformed Church had given place to union with the Church of England; and also, that a generation ago, in some of our Colonies, Episcopal Presbyters had authority to confirm in the absence of Bishops.

[1] Sir H. Moncreiff says this practice was kept up in some parishes in 1818.—Life of Erskine, p. 72.

[2] Life and Times of Bishop Torry, p. 34.

There is nothing in the Directory bearing on the reception of Catechumens, and that this has been felt to be a serious omission wherever the Westminster Standards have been received, is evident from the many attempts that have been made to supply what is wanting. A paragraph on the subject was prepared, which it was proposed to introduce as a rubric before the form for the administration of the Lord's Supper; but on all questions affecting the qualifications for Church membership, and the exercise of Christian discipline, the Presbyterians had to encounter the opposition, both of the Independents and the Erastians, and the paragraph, if adopted by the Assembly, was rejected by the House of Commons. Henderson describes the Scottish practice as follows: "None are admitted to the Lord's Supper but such as, upon examination, are found to have a competent measure of knowledge in the grounds of the Christian religion and the doctrine of the Sacraments, and are able, according to the Apostle's commandment, and profess themselves willing, to examine themselves and to renew their covenant made with God in Baptism; promising to walk as becometh Christians, and to submit themselves to all the ordinances of Christ." And we find Leighton, whose great desire was to restore old Scottish usages, both as a minimum admitting of no reduction, and as less likely to give offence than any Episcopal ceremonies, urging his Clergy in 1668 to cause young people at their first admission to the Holy Communion, "expressly to declare their belief of the Christian faith into which, in their infancy, they were baptized, and reminding them of that their baptismal vow, and the great engagement it lays on them to a holy and Christian life; to require of them an explicit owning of that vow and engagement, and their solemn promise accordingly to endeavour the observing and performance of it in the whole course of their following life."[1]

The section on the Reception of Catechumens in the Larger Overtures of 1705, to which I have already referred, is as follows: "At the first admission of any to the Lord's Supper, Ministers should put the persons to be admitted in mind of their parents' engagement for them in Baptism, and put them explicitly and personally to renew their baptismal covenant to be the Lord's, and to live unto Him, and serve Him all the days of their lives." In 1706 the Assembly passed an Act of this import, and there has been no legis-

[1] Synod Register, pp. 63, 64.

lation on the subject since. The Act recommends Ministers "to take as strict a trial as can be of such as they admit to the Lord's Supper, especially before their first admission thereto; and that they diligently instruct them particularly as to the covenant of grace, and the nature and end of that ordinance, as a seal thereof, and charge upon their consciences the obligations they lie under from their baptismal covenant, and seriously exhort them to renew the same." During last century faithful Clergymen attached great importance to such a service, and many of them were in the habit of putting formal questions to the Catechumens, and receiving them with suitable prayers and exhortations in the presence of the Session, and such of the congregation as chose to remain. Boston moved in the Church Courts with the view of having a form of admission sanctioned by authority, but without success. He condemns the general practice as faulty; but for himself he tells us that after sermon he "called in his new communicants, and, before the Session, put them explicitly to consent to the covenant whereof they desired the seal, and that he proposed to them" a series of questions, preserved in his Autobiography, "to which they consented by bowing their heads."[1]

[1] Autobiography, p. 429.

And Gerard of Aberdeen, speaking for a different part of the country, and a different style of churchmanship, after recommending the Clergy, "not only in private, but in as public a manner as they found convenient," to require Catechumens "to make solemn profession of their embracing the Christian faith for themselves, and to vow that they will live suitably to it, renouncing the sins which they have formerly indulged, and promising to live henceforth as becomes Christians," adds, "This is practised by some Ministers with good success, and a very great effect."[1] The whole practical system of the Church is based on the baptismal covenant entered by the child, and accepted by the young person, and the acceptance should be as formal and explicit as the engagement itself. This has been so generally neglected, that I fear even the idea of it is lost in many cases, and that the results have been very injurious to the interests of the Church, and of religion itself. I have frequently heard members of the Church in different parts of the world speak with dissatisfaction of the way in which they had been prepared for and admitted to the Communion, and of their surprise and disappointment at the absence of those solemnities which they had ex-

[1] Pastoral Care, p. 381.

pected in connection with it. Thanks be to God, the better practice, which in some districts never went out, is reviving and extending, and the admission of young communicants is now receiving something of the prominence which is assigned to it in other Reformed Churches, among whom it is regarded as a matter of great interest, not only to the applicants themselves, and to their families, but to the whole community. The Reformed Liturgies all contain prescribed forms for the service; while in several of the offshoots of our own Church in America and the Colonies, the questions to be asked have the sanction of the highest ecclesiastical Courts, and are put in all cases.

Instruction beforehand.—It is the Minister's first duty to train the candidates until satisfied as to their religious knowledge. As it is of great importance that Catechumens should be under special instruction for a lengthened period, it is not advisable to admit them more than once or twice a-year, however frequently the Lord's Supper may be administered. In Geneva the special instruction lasts for a year, the classes meeting twice a-week. Boys usually enter these classes at the age of sixteen, and girls at fifteen, and they are admitted before the Easter and September

Communions. For a long period after the Reformation it was usual to admit young people to the Lord's Supper at an earlier age than is common now, or than we would think advisable. The French Church, which in the days of its glory and prosperity was a standard to the rest of the Reformed, fixed twelve as the earliest age at which it was suitable to receive them; and in Scotland we find that James Melville and John Livingstone became communicants about that age, in accordance, apparently, with what was customary among the children of pious families.

No pains should be spared to impress Catechumens with the solemnity of the step they are taking, and the necessity of their giving themselves wholly and heartily to the Lord. This is the best, and unfortunately almost the only, opportunity which the Clergy now have of personal spiritual dealing with many of those who are under their pastoral care, and a solemn responsibility rests upon them to improve it to the utmost. The influence of a first communion usually tells powerfully for good or for evil throughout life. We ought not, however, to forget that one of the points of difference betwixt the Church and the Sect is, that the former admits to the Lord's Supper on credible evidence of the sincerity of the profession made, while the latter professes definitely to separate " the precious from the vile," and only receives those of whose spiritual regeneration it is certain. Nothing can exceed for strength of language the terms in which the Reformers and our leading Divines of former days denounced this principle of judging the heart. Calvin said it broke up the Church into "little sects of a few hypocrites." Luther said, "May God preserve us from a Church in which there are none but saints"—*i.e.*, which lays claim to absolute purity of communion; while Rutherford, in discussing the same subject, goes the length of asserting that there might be a true Church without a true Christian in it.

It is also necessary, especially in these times, when there are so many unbaptized persons in the community, and so much moving to and fro, to make particular inquiries as to the Baptism of the candidates. Not a few cases have occurred within my knowledge where young people were on the verge of being admitted to the Communion without having been baptized, and I have known instances where this has actually taken place. Should such an unfortunate circumstance occur, it would be the Minister's duty to treat as null what had been done in ignorance, and to administer the initiatory rite of Christianity with the least possible delay. Justin Martyr says: "It is not lawful for any one to partake of the sacramental food except he be baptized." And in the Apostolic Constitutions it is enjoined that "if any one should be a participator in ignorance, he should be immediately instructed and baptized, that he might not go away a despiser." Yet, to my knowledge, several cases have recently occurred where young people who had been admitted to the Communion unbaptized, and who afterwards came to their Pastors in much anxiety of mind to ask their advice, were assured by them that Baptism was quite unnecessary in such circumstances; that the greater included the less; and that, being already in the Church, it was absurd that they should go out for the sake of coming in again. I need hardly say that the Church, as a whole, and our own Church through the greater part of its history, would have regarded such advice as subversive of the first principles of Christianity.[1]

The Minister, after instructing the young com-

[1] The general principle is not affected by the fact that there are one or two cases on record where the early Church, on discovering that communicants of long standing had received heretical baptism, the validity of which was doubtful, did not insist on the repetition of the ordinance.

municants, should submit their names to the Session, and inquire of those whose duty it is to assist him in discipline, whether their character and conduct, so far as known to them, are such as becometh Christians.

THE SERVICE.

Their formal reception should take place if possible in Church after sermon on the week-day of preparation for the Lord's Supper. This gives them an opportunity of confessing Christ before men, and of receiving the benefit of the united prayers of the congregation, both of which they will esteem high privileges if their hearts are right with God. It is also their public introduction to the congregation, and in this aspect it is alike full of interest to themselves and to those in whose ranks they then take their place.

Their names having been read out by the Minister, they should come forward, and stand in front of the pulpit or Communion Table.

Vows.—After a short introduction, referring to the circumstances in which they are placed, and to the service in which they are about to take part, the Minister should ask such questions as the following:—

"Whether they believe the Articles of the Christian faith into which they were baptized? Whether they own and accept their baptismal covenant, consecrating themselves to Father, Son, and Holy Ghost, and promising to submit to all the ordinances of Christ's appointment, and to serve Him in holiness and righteousness all the days of their life?"

The questions in the form for Adult Baptism printed by authority of the General Assembly, with a few verbal changes, serve for this purpose also.

When they have given their assent by bowing their heads, or by verbal answer, the Minister should, in the Name of the Lord Jesus Christ, admit them to the participation of the Lord's Supper, and to all the privileges of the new covenant.

The Blessing.—This may be accompanied by a solemn blessing, such as the following: "The very God of peace sanctify you wholly; and I pray God your whole spirit, and soul, and body be preserved blameless unto the coming of Our Lord Jesus Christ."[1]

[1] Among the Reformed in some countries the Blessing is given with imposition of hands. Calvin, speaking of Confirmation, says, "This laying on of hands, which is done simply by way of benediction, I commend, and would like to see re-

Prayer.—The Minister should then commend them to God in prayer, giving thanks on their behalf that they have been spared to own their baptismal covenant, and on behalf of the Church to which He has given the joy of receiving them into full communion; and beseeching Him to forgive all their past sins, graciously to accept them now dedicating themselves to Him, and to shed down upon them the sevenfold gifts of the Holy Ghost, that they may be enabled to fulfil their vows, and remain faithful to the end.

Exhortation.—A short exhortation, very similar to that given in cases of Adult Baptism, should be added. Suitable materials for these prayers and exhortations are furnished by the Reformed Liturgies, and by the Book prepared by the Church Service Society.

Such a service is fitted to have a most solemnising effect upon the Catechumens, and upon the still younger members of the congregation who look forward to it as awaiting them in due time; while it also serves to remind older people of their obligations, and to encourage them by the prospect of help in their Christian labours.

stored to its pure use in the present day."—Inst., Book iv. chap. xix. sec. 4.

It is almost certain, too, that if such observances had been common throughout the land in time past, and had been regarded as the rule of the Church, that most unchristian state of things which exists in some parts of the Highlands, where none but a few old people are communicants, and where those who have not accepted their own Baptism act as Sponsors for children, could not possibly have arisen. Bunsen somewhere says, that in times of irreligion and unbelief Confirmation saved the German Church; and most assuredly the more attention that is paid to the training of Catechumens, and the more solemn their admission to the renewal of their baptismal covenant, the better will it be for the Church, and for religion in our land.[1]

[1] It is now becoming common to give young Communicants First Communion Cards, containing the name of the Church, their own name, and date of admission, with a suitable motto-text which they may recall throughout their whole lives.

LECTURE III.

THE HOLY COMMUNION.

THE subject of Lecture to-day is, The Administration of the Lord's Supper, that chief ordinance of the Church, in which, united with Christ in His work of Intercession within the veil, we represent and plead before the Father His Sacrifice once offered on the Cross, make "a spiritual oblation of all possible praise for the same," feed upon Him risen and glorified, and witness for Him before the world. This holiest of services has been celebrated by the faithful, from age to age, with great delight; and around it the choicest treasures of devotion have been gathered.

Frequency of Communion.—The Directory says that the " Communion is frequently to be celebrated," so frequently, it is implied, as to supersede the necessity of a previous intimation.

The greatest Protestant Divines have always favoured a more frequent celebration of the Lord's Supper than they have been able to carry out. Calvin says: "We ought always to provide that no meeting of the Church is held without . . . the dispensation of the Supper," and that "most assuredly the custom which prescribes Communion once a-year is an invention of the devil."[1] Bucer says: "I could wish that all would communicate at the Table of the Lord every Lord's Day." It would be easy to multiply testimonies to the same effect. Thus Baxter, who on such subjects may be taken as a fair representative of the English Presbyterians in his time, says: "The Lord's Supper is a part of the settled order for Lord's Day worship, and omitting it maimeth and altereth the worship of the day." There can be no doubt that the Apostolic Church observed it every Sunday; and that it was regarded as the chief feature of Public Worship, is evident from the expression of Scripture, that the believers came together—not to hear sermons, or offer prayers—but to "break bread." This long continued to be the practice of the Church, and the Primitive Liturgies are simply forms for its administration. There can be little doubt, too, that infrequent

[1] Institutes, Book iv. chap. xvii. sec. 44, 46.

communion, and the withholding the cup from the laity, had very much to do with the development of other forms of absolution which have no foundation in Scripture. No feature of the Apostolic Church can be defaced or displaced without the danger of its avenging itself in general derangement and disproportion; and therefore, one should always testify for what is primitive and apostolical, even when obliged to submit to an imperfect order. There is every reason to think that it was meant that Christ's death should be commemorated at a Communion Table as frequently and regularly as it had been foreshadowed in the sacrifices of the altar during the former dispensation.

After the Reformation, the Lord's Supper appears, from a Rubric in the Book of Common Order, to have been celebrated in Scotland at first monthly. In 1562 it was ordered to be observed in the Country at least twice, and in Towns at least four times in the year. This, however, represented much more than two or four annual celebrations, as it was long the custom to have separate administrations on the same day,—the first sometimes as early as five o'clock in the morning,—and to continue this for several Sundays in succession, as is still the practice in

Holland. After a time, notwithstanding all injunctions to the contrary, what Calvin called the invention of the evil one prevailed, and even this low standard was not always reached. During the troubles of the Commonwealth, the Lord's Supper is said to have been neglected for years in many Parishes of the three Kingdoms.[1] After the Restoration there was little or no improvement in Scotland. Anderson of Dumbarton states that in his Presbytery it was celebrated three times oftener within the twelve years previous to 1714 than it had been during the twenty-eight years of the Second Episcopacy.[2] After the Revolution, attempts were made to bring the practice of the Church into greater conformity with its own regulations, but they were neither generally successful nor lasting. One section of the Clergy seem to have regarded the Lord's Supper very much in the light of a service, in which Christians made a public profession that they

[1] Durel's Government and Public Worship in the Reformed Churches beyond the Seas, p. 44.

"The Blessed Sacrament now wholly out of use in the Parish Churches."—Evelyn's Diary, Dec. 18, 1649.

In July 1655, the Communion was administered in Edinburgh the first time after an interval of six years. — Nicol's Diary.

[2] Defence of the Church Government, &c., of the Presbyterians, p. 318.

were the people of God, and they naturally enough concluded that it was not necessary to repeat this except at considerable intervals. Others regarded it with such superstitious awe that they shrank from frequent celebration. A story is told of a Clergyman in the North who spent seven years in preaching on the subject, by way of preparing his people for it; and, after it was over, other seven years in improving it. Scott, in his 'Fasti,' mentions the case of a Clergyman, so late as the early part of this century, who "had never witnessed the dispensation of the Communion till he was called to officiate in his ministerial capacity."[1] The best of the Clergy all along mourned over the prevalent disregard of our Lord's last command; and in 1748 the Synod of Glasgow and Ayr, on the motion of one of the most eminent and faithful Ministers of the time — Dr John Erskine, afterwards of the Greyfriars' Church, Edinburgh,—overtured the Assembly to enjoin that it should be observed four times, at the least, annually in every Parish; that preparation services should be held only on one week-day; and that it should be administered on the same Sunday in all the Parishes of each Presbytery. After a century and a quarter, we are now approaching

[1] Part ii. p. 443.

this standard, and every Clergyman should do his best to reach it. All experience shows that the commemoration of the Lord's death is the most effective preaching of the Cross; and if the Communion conveys spiritual nourishment, and is needful for the increase of holiness, as all Christians believe, infrequent participation must necessarily involve loss of grace. It is the general practice of the Reformed Churches to have it at least quarterly; and wherever this has been restored in our own Country, it is greatly appreciated by the most devout members of our flocks. The matter is entirely in the hands of the Clergy, as the Assembly so late as 1878 decided that " The administration of the Sacrament of the Lord's Supper, according to the settled order and practice of this Church, belongs to the Minister of the Parish, subject only to the control of his Presbytery, upon sufficient grounds shown."

Preparatory Services.—The Directory says that where the Lord's Supper cannot " be frequently administered, it is requisite that public warning be given the Sabbath-day before the administration thereof; and that either then, or on some day of that week, something concerning that ordinance, and the due preparation thereunto and participation thereof, be taught." From Henderson we learn that, according to the previous Scottish practice, "The doctrine of preparation was taught the last day of the week,—at least towards the end of the week;" and in the Act supplementary to the Directory passed by our Assembly in 1645, it is ordered "That there be a service of preparation delivered in the ordinary place of Public Worship upon the day immediately preceding the Communion." This injunction has not been revived since 1690; but it is important, as expressing the mind of the Church during the Covenanting period, and it is also in harmony with the practice of the Reformed Churches. A service of preparation is suitable in all circumstances; and it affords an opportunity also for the admission of young communicants, and making other preliminary arrangements.

There is no authority for Fast Days before the observance of the Lord's Supper in the legislation of the Church, though the practice of receiving the Communion fasting is almost as old as Christianity, and was common in some parts of Scotland till a generation ago. The extra days—first Monday, and afterwards the Fast Day, with multiplied services—were introduced by the Protesters during the anarchy that prevailed in the time of the Usurper, and were strongly disap-

THE HOLY COMMUNION. 105

proved of by the Resolutioners as "a clear violation of the order unanimously established in the Church," and as occasioning " great animosity and alienation of simple people against their Ministers who would not imitate those irregular courses." [1] It is to be borne in mind, however, that daily prayers in Church, with sermons twice a-week, had previously been common in all the towns and villages, and that it was also usual to assemble the people for examination before the Communion. For this purpose they came to the Church in relays during the days of the preceding week. This was quite a different thing from the ordinary diets of Catechising throughout the year. It had taken the place of confession before Easter in the Pre-Reformation Church, and there was a general feeling that unless people underwent this examination they were not to participate in the Communion. Calvin, indeed, had been anxious for a private examination, and for a time partially succeeded in carrying it out. "I have often told you," he writes to Farel, "that I should have thought it unwise to abolish confession in our churches, unless the rite which I have lately in-

[1] For notices of pamphlets by Resolutioners on this subject, see Dr John Erskine's Dissertation on Frequent Communicating, pp. 310, 311 ; also, Book of Common Order and Directory, by Sprott and Leishman, p. 349.

troduced be established in its place"—viz., "a personal and private interview with the Pastor previous to each sacramental occasion."[1]

For a long period after the Reformation, a special meeting was also held in our Churches on one of the days of the week preceding the Communion, for the removal of offences and the reconciliation of Church members who had been at variance. All these extra services have been discontinued. As we have now so few meetings for worship, and as Fast Days before Communion are almost the only public recognition left of Fasting as a divine institution, I see no good reason for giving them up, although better arrangements might be made for their observance. Fast Days are only kept before one, or at most two, Communions during the year, and when retained, they render any other day of preparation unnecessary. On such days both the devotions and the sermon should be strictly appropriate to the occasion, and should be helpful to people who are anxious to make a worthy approach to the Holy Table. The practice of Ministers from a distance preaching their most popular sermons at such times, without any regard to their suitableness for seasons of penitence and humiliation, has,

[1] See Eutaxia, p. 19.

I think, had no little to do with emptying our Churches on Fast Days. Here, as in everything else, and most of all in ministerial duty, there is no rule like that of seeking first the kingdom of God and His righteousness.

Relation to the ordinary Sunday Service.—The Communion service, according to the Directory, is to follow the Morning Sermon and Prayer. The Westminster Divines, for two days, discussed the question whether the Benediction should be pronounced at the close of the ordinary service, and non-communicants then be dismissed. The Scottish Commissioners defended the custom of their own Church, which was the same as at present, but no decision was come to. It is very important to follow, as closely as possible, the order of the Primitive Church, according to which the Communion and preceding services were regarded as one, and the whole as the normal worship of the Lord's Day. And as thanksgiving is so prominent a feature of the Communion that it came to be called the Eucharist, and as the Lord's Prayer should be used at the close of the Consecration prayer, it is best to omit both before the sermon, and to retain only the short intervening prayer for illumination. This has the further advantage of shortening the services of a Communion Sunday, which were formerly prolonged to a most unedifying length. It is now coming to be felt that devotion, rather than instruction, should be the great feature of such days, and that even the action sermon should be shorter, rather than longer, than other discourses. I need not remark further on the ordinary service, except that special Psalms and Hymns should be chosen, and that all should bear on the great theme with which the hearts of devout communicants are full. Those sacramental Psalms and Paraphrases which have been long in use in particular localities, come to be associated with the most sacred personal and family recollections of the people, and it is wise and edifying to choose them in preference to others not less suitable.

Exhortation to the Congregation.—Before commencing the Communion Service, "the Minister," says the Directory, "shall make a short exhortation," setting forth the inestimable benefits conferred by that holy ordinance, the necessity of coming to it with right dispositions, and the danger of partaking unworthily. He is then, in the name of Christ, to warn all those who are living in any sin against their knowledge or conscience, that they presume not to approach the Holy Table; and on the other hand, he is, in an especial manner, to invite and encourage the truly penitent to draw near, assuring them of the richest blessings.

The compilers of the Directory, when they said *short*, meant it. It was their intention that the words indicated by them, which are partly taken from the English Liturgy and the Book of Common Order, should form the basis of a few sentences of instruction, warning, and invitation. In Knox's Book, as in other Reformed Liturgies, this exhortation formed part of the address after reading the words of Institution. Calderwood, in the minute description which he has given in the *Altare Damascenum* of a Scottish Communion, as observed for the first sixty years after the Reformation, says,—"The Minister, when the sermon is finished, reads the words of institution, gives a short exhortation and admonition, then blesses;" but Henderson, writing twenty years later, describes the practice as similar to that prescribed by the Directory. This address came to be popularly known as the *Fencing of the Table*. Under the new spirit which entered the Church in Henderson's time, it soon ceased to be short, the invitation was in a great measure lost sight of, and its most prominent feature came to be a series of debarrations beginning thus: "I debar from the Table of the Lord " such and such a class. A number of years ago, when what had been long called the consuetudinary law of the Church began to break down, and when the spirit of innovation assailed even the written law, some Clergymen discontinued this part of the service altogether. I do not know how far this has gone, but it is not uncommon to hear men say that they fence the Table on the previous Sunday, and that they consider it unreasonable to introduce such an exhortation after the communicants have taken their places at the Lord's Table. In point of fact, formerly they never did take their seats till they were invited, in the name of Christ, to do so; and these Ministers have overlooked the original idea of this address, which was more that of an invitation to the Lord's Table than of a debarration from it. The biographer of an eminent Dissenting Minister gives the following account of "fencing" the Table: " The history of this unseasonable interruption is simply this,—At the origin of the Secession great multitudes left the Established Church who could not obtain the necessary certificates of Church membership, and the resort of the conscientious Seceding Pastor was to this practice."[1] If the writer

[1] Life of Dr Lawson of Selkirk, p. 81.

had looked into the Directory, he would not have resorted to this method of making history.

The exhortation before the Communion was considered of importance by all the Reformed Churches, both as a warning to the unworthy, and still more as including an invitation, in the name of Christ, to all the faithful to draw near to His Table. Moreover, it was regarded as a notable example of a binding and loosing service; and hence the warnings and invitations were usually prefaced by our Clergy in former days, with such words as these: "By virtue of the Keys of the Kingdom of Heaven committed to His Ministers," &c.[1]

The omission of such an exhortation is contrary to the law and practice of the Church; and the reasons assigned for it would tend to the cutting down of all religious services, and to a very irreverent mode of celebrating them. Even the modern practice of people taking their seats at the Lord's Table at the commencement of Public Worship is unknown in the other Reformed Churches, and would have been considered highly objectionable by our own Church in former days. They should wait till they are

---

[1] See, *e.g.*, Spalding's Communion Sermons and Services, p. 192.

invited by Christ's Ambassador, in His Master's name, to do so.

In the Directory and Knox's Liturgy you will find suitable material for this short preliminary address. The first part of the exhortation in Knox's Book is also given verbatim in the English Prayer-Book; and these memorials of the days when the English Church was considered one with the rest of the Reformed, have an interest for all who regret the subsequent alienation, and who would rejoice to see it removed.

When this exhortation is finished, the Minister gives out a Psalm or Hymn, and intimates that while it is being sung the communion elements will be brought forward, and the first company of communicants will take their places at the Lord's Table. It is also usual for those who do not intend remaining to the close then to retire, and it would be well if it were the custom for all intending communicants to come as near as possible to the Holy Table,[1] so as to join the more heartily and unitedly in all the parts of the service. The 35th Paraphrase is commonly

[1] This is the name used in the early Liturgies, and in the Greek Church.

sung at this time, and nothing could be more appropriate.

The Communion Service.

1. *Words of Institution.*—Having taken his place at the Holy Table "decently covered," with the communion elements before him, "the bread in comely and convenient vessels," "the wine in large cups," the Minister begins the service by reading the Words of Institution out of the First Epistle to the Corinthians, Chapter xi., verses 23, 24, 25, 26. These words St Paul received from the Lord Jesus, Who, not content with allowing this Apostle, who had been born out of due time, to receive instruction as to the Sacrament from St Peter or St John, made it the subject of special revelation to him, after He was risen and glorified. Hence the Church has always regarded these as the Words of Institution in their "perfect form," to use an expression of the First Book of Discipline. In Knox's Liturgy the 27th, 28th, and 29th verses are also ordered to be read. This was because the call to self-examination did not form part of a preliminary address, but followed the Words of Institution according to that Order. But the

Directory very properly omits these verses, because they are St Paul's words, not our Lord's, and because they have already been considered in the previous exhortation from the pulpit.

Explanation of the Words of Institution.—After reading the Words of Institution, "the Minister," says the Directory, "when he seeth requisite, may explain and apply them." Such an address, though optional, is customary, and a few sentences on the topics indicated are highly appropriate. They serve to bring out the most striking and beautiful characteristic of our Communion Service—viz., that it is so eminently scriptural. Our Lord bids us do as He did. His Ministers are but the instruments He employs to repeat His actions, to pronounce His blessing, and to speak His words, and that form must be the most perfect which is in most complete accordance with His example.

2. *The first Action.*—The first Action is taking the elements to be consecrated. This consists in the Minister's putting his hands on them, or, as was formerly the practice, taking and elevating the cups and the patens, or a part for the whole. In the Book of Common Order, it is said, "Then he *taketh* bread and giveth thanks." This is not mentioned in the Directory, but great significance

was attached to it in our Church, and the old rule was long scrupulously observed. Boston says, "Nothing is more distinctly mentioned than this;" and he, in common with our older Divines, held that it represented the Father setting apart the Son to the office of Mediator. *Lifting*, as this Action was called, began to be given up in some of the Churches of Edinburgh about 1740; and the innovation infected the Seceders, among whom it gave rise to a violent controversy betwixt Lifters and Antilifters—the former holding the Action essential, the latter regarding it as indifferent. The dispute ended in a schism and the formation of a new sect; but the basis was found too narrow to exist upon, and the Lifters soon disappeared as a separate community. A friend of mine used to tell of a visit which he paid to one of the last representatives of this sect. Having asked him, Why he went to no place of worship? and Whether he did not think that there was still a Visible Church upon earth? the venerable confessor drew himself up with a mixture of dignity and indignation, and replied, "There's ae auld man here, Sir." Though practically left an open question in the Church, the best school of the Clergy retained the custom on principle, and down almost to our own day, were careful to recommend it to young men admitted to the Ministry. Probably a majority of the clergy still adhere to the old practice, simply from the force of example, and some hold the cup and a piece of the bread in their hands during the consecration prayer. This was also an old usage, as appears, for example, from the funeral sermon of the celebrated Dr Webster, the leader of the Evangelical party in the last century, in which it is said, "Follow him next to a Communion Table, holding in his hands the sacramental pledges of the broken body and shed blood of the Redeemer, and by prayer and supplication with thanksgiving, setting them apart from a common to a sacred use." This practice is recommended, I may add, in the American revision of our Directory. I have frequently met with clergymen who thought that lifting meant the elevation of the elements after the consecration immediately before distribution, and that it was upon that point the controversy turned. Some years ago I was present at the Communion in a very old-fashioned Church, where several old-fashioned and decidedly anti-innovating Ministers assisted a young man who had temporary charge of the Parish. When he proceeded to *take* the elements before the consecration prayer, having learned the usage from his father, and having never known of any other way, quite a panic seized the venerable assistants, and one of them stopped him, supposing that he had forgotten the prayer, and was about to distribute without it.

As we cannot adhere too closely to our Lord's example, this Action should not be omitted, but it is best not to do more than touch the elements, or raise them for a moment.

3. *Consecration Prayer.*— The Minister then offers the Consecration Prayer, which is so called from one of its most essential features. According to our order, this prayer embraces the following topics,—a profession of our faith; confession of sin and unworthiness, with prayer for pardon and peace; the great thanksgiving; and last of all, the consecration. In the Directory the profession of faith forms the second section of the prayer; but it is now not uncommon to begin with this, and to use, for the purpose, the Creed, introducing it thus: "With Thy Holy Church throughout all the world we believe in Thee, the Father Almighty, Maker of heaven and earth;" or, "Strengthen us, O Lord, in the Christian Faith, whereof we make confession, saying, I believe," &c. The profession of faith in the Directory, like some other features in that work, is apt to be lost sight of, from not

being sufficiently emphasised. Indeed, in all our Standards, there is a great deal between the lines, and one requires to know the history of the time and its theological literature to be able to read them aright.

In our Church, as in other branches of the Reformed, the repetition of the Creed formed part of the ordinary Sunday Service down till the adoption of the Westminster documents; and "this was not only or mainly meant as a help to the memory of the people, but as a solemn profession of their believing the Articles of the Christian Faith, and a quickening of their affections towards the same." The recital of the Nicene Creed was introduced into the Communion Service of the Church A.D. 471, and in the Eastern Liturgies it precedes the Eucharistic prayer.

The prayer that follows should be one of intense devotion, and the greatest care should be taken to make it as perfect as possible. That given in Euchologion is a compilation from many sources, but it is based ultimately upon the Eastern Liturgies, like the American (German) Reformed, and Catholic Apostolic Services, from which it is largely borrowed. It embodies some of the richest materials of Christian devotion, and the arrangement is sufficiently in harmony with our traditional service. It begins with a prayer of access, which is more than becoming in the special approach which we then make to God's presence.

This is followed by the great thanksgiving for all His bounties in creation, providence, and redemption, which ends, like those of the Eastern Liturgies, with the Trisagion or Seraphic Hymn, "Holy, Holy, Holy."

Then comes the Invocation of the Holy Ghost, or Prayer of Consecration proper, in which, to follow the words of the Directory, we should "earnestly pray to God, the Father of all mercies and God of all consolation, to vouchsafe His gracious presence, and the effectual working of His Spirit in us: and so to sanctify the elements both of bread and wine, and to bless His own ordinance that we may receive by faith the Body and Blood of Jesus Christ." If the Holy Ghost, by whom the whole body of the Church is governed and sanctified, should be honoured in all acts of worship, this is peculiarly essential in the Holy Communion. Such an invocation, together with the recital of the words of institution, have both been widely regarded in the Christian Church as essential to the consecration of the elements. The Church of Rome has indeed long taught that the words of institution alone make the Sacrament, but this was not the primitive doctrine. The Greeks maintain that in the Latin Church, as well as in the Eastern, the invocation of the Holy Ghost was formerly considered the principal thing; that it was, after a time, said in secret, in order that heretics might not learn how to consecrate, and that it fell out of use in the dark ages. They admit that there are passages in the Fathers which seem to attribute the consecration to the words of institution, but say that these only mean that had not our Lord given command to administer the Communion, there would have been no authority for it, and that it would be no Sacrament at all.

To the form for the administration of the Lord's Supper in Knox's Liturgy, a note is appended disclaiming the idea that the repetition of the words of institution makes the Sacrament; but that form, like those of the other Reformed Churches at the time, and like the Church of England Liturgy now, wants a distinct invocation of the Holy Spirit. This defect was probably remedied in practice; at all events we find the antiprelatic section of the Clergy complaining that in it "there was not one word of Lord bless the elements or action," and there is ample evidence that our greatest theologians have held both the invocation and the words of institution to be essential. George Gillespie strongly defended the primitive and Eastern view. The English Presbyterians complained that in the English Liturgy the manner of consecrating the elements was not explicit and distinct enough. The Confession of Faith, in harmony with the Directory, asserts that Ministers are "to declare the word of institution, to pray, and bless the elements, and thereby to set them apart from a common to an holy use." Boston says: "The elements are consecrated by the word of institution, thanksgiving, and prayer." "The Popish consecration," he adds, "hits not the mark; for these words, 'This is My Body,' were uttered by our Lord after the consecration." This part of the service is of cardinal importance; and though we may not think the grace and blessing of the Sacrament dependent on our using an absolutely correct form of words, it is surely best, as it is easy, to use a form which unites the suffrages of Christendom, and which no one can point to as unsatisfactory or insufficient.

The Lord's Prayer.—Here, as I have already intimated, the Lord's Prayer should be introduced — that perfect form which supplies the defects of our own, and which in the shortest compass includes everything for which we ought to pray. St Augustine says, "Almost every Church concludes the Canon with the Lord's Prayer;" and the practice had probably been handed down from the days of the Apostles. The fullest application of the words, "Give us this day our daily bread," is to the bread of life, and they have always been said here with a reference to Christ's body and blood, as exhibited in the Communion to be our meat and drink unto life eternal.

4. *The Declaration.*—This finished, the Directory orders "that the Minister is, in a few words, to show that these elements, otherwise common, are now set apart and sanctified to this holy use by the word of institution and prayer." As an illustration of the way in which such Rubrics were meant to be obeyed, I may quote the form of this declaration given in the Savoy Liturgy: "This bread and wine being set apart and consecrated to this holy use by God's appointment, are now no common bread and wine, but sacramentally the body and blood of Christ." Such a declaration is now seldom if ever made. The omission probably dates from the latter half of last century, when there was so much Socinianism in the country, and when so many emptied

the Sacraments of their true meaning. Not without reason did Edward Irving, in a famous charge which he delivered at an ordination by the Presbytery of London, of which he was at the time Moderator, tell the newly appointed Minister to read nothing that had been written on the Sacraments for the preceding hundred years. Going back beyond that period to a better age, we find Boston writing thus of a Communion Service: "The elements, after consecration, being declared to be no more common bread and wine, but sacred symbols of the body and blood of Christ, I felt in my spirit a sensible change accordingly. I discerned the sacramental union of the signs and the thing signified, and was thereby let into a view of the mystical union. I saw it, I believed it, and I do believe it this day. I do not remember myself ever to have been so distinct in the view and faith of this glorious mystery. . . . This is the second time I have most remarkably felt that change on my spirit upon the declaring as above said. May I never omit to declare as said is in the administration of that ordinance."[1] There is much to be said for a practice enjoined by the Church, and thus proved by experience to be so

[1] Autobiography, p. 296.

valuable. The great sin of the Corinthian Church was their not discerning the Lord's Body in the Sacrament; and with such a warning, communicants cannot be too carefully guarded against like irreverence and unbelief.[1]

5. *Commemoration and Communion.* — "*The Minister,*" says the Directory, "*is to take the Bread in his hand, and say in these expressions (or other the like used by Christ or His Apostles upon this occasion*"):—

"According to the holy institution, command, and example of our blessed Saviour Jesus Christ, I take this Bread, and having given thanks, break it, and give it unto you.

"*Then the Minister, who is also himself to communicate, is to break the Bread, and give it to the Communicants* (saying) :—

---

[1] The Reformed Doctrine as to the Lord's Supper is no longer held by many of the Evangelical School. Views are prevalent which are more negative than those which Calvin characterised as profane. Some years ago at an Irish Episcopal Synod there was a great outcry against Sacramentarianism, whereupon the Bishop said he would like to hear the views of those present on two statements referring to the Lord's Supper, which he would read. The first was received with exclamations of horror, the second met with the heartiest approbation. "Gentlemen," said his Lordship, "The extract which you repudiate with so much abhorrence is from the writings of one of our most illustrious Reformers; and the latter, which you so enthusiastically applaud, is from the works of that Christ-denying heretic Socinus."

"Take ye, Eat ye: This is the Body of Christ which is broken for you : Do this in remembrance of Him.

"*In like manner the Minister is to take the Cup, and say:* . . .

"According to the institution, command, and example of our Lord Jesus Christ, I take this Cup, and give it unto you.

"*Here he giveth it to the Communicants* (saying):

"This Cup is the New Testament in the Blood of Christ, which is shed for the remission of the sins of many : Drink ye all of it."

Calderwood describes the old Scottish practice thus : "The blessing or thanksgiving ended, the Minister says—Our Lord, on that night on which He was betrayed, took bread, and gave thanks, as we have already done, and break, as I also now break, and gave to His disciples, saying (then he hands it to those nearest on the right and the left) This is my Body," &c.[1]

Gillespie gives the same form with a somewhat important addition. "Besides the common blessing of the elements in the beginning of the action," he says; "we give thanks also in the several actions of distribution, saying after this or the like manner: The Lord Jesus, the same night He

[1] Altare Damascenum, pp. 777, 778.

was betrayed, took bread; and when He had given thanks, as we also give thanks to God who gave His Son to die for us, brake it," &c.; and with the Cup, "as we also give thanks to God who gave His Son to shed His blood for us."[1] He defends this form as an imitation of the example of Christ, who gave thanks severally, both at the giving of the Bread and the giving of the Cup.

In Henderson's description of the Communion it is said: "The elements being sanctified by the word and prayer, the Minister sacramentally breaketh the Bread, taketh and eateth himself, and delivereth to the people, . . . saying: Take ye, eat ye; This is the Body of the Lord which is broken for you: Do it in remembrance of Him. After all at the Table have taken and eaten, the Minister taketh the Cup, and drinking first himself, he giveth it to the nearest, saying," &c.

Henderson's form more closely resembles the Directory, in many parts of which his hand

---

[1] English Popish Ceremonies, p. 200. Gillespie's form implies that the Words of Institution are to be recited as a prayer, as is done in all Catholic Liturgies; and that the showing forth of Christ's death is an act done towards God. "In the Eucharist we unite ourselves with that showing forth of His death which Christ is now making in heaven." This is the central fact of Christian worship; and it was not overlooked by our older Divines, who were in the habit of saying, in their Communion services, "We make the remembrance unto God."

appears; but Calderwood's has always been generally followed.

The Fraction.—Though the whole service shows forth the Lord's Death, which is the primary end of the ordinance, and though partaking is necessary to the commemoration, still it is the Fraction which specially symbolises the sacrifice of the Cross, as the slaying of the victims on the altar had foreshadowed it from the foundation of the world. This, as Boston says, is an essential rite of the Sacrament; and he adds the important remark, that " There is not one word of pouring out the wine, though no doubt it was done, because the shedding of Christ's blood is sufficiently represented by the breaking of His Body." It was one of the exceptions formerly taken by the English Presbyterians to the Book of Common Prayer, that in it the breaking of the bread was not mentioned. This was added at the last revision, but it is inserted before what, according to that form, is the consecration, so that it is the breaking of bread merely, not of Christ's Sacramental Body, and is therefore no proper commemoration of His death. In a different way the Scottish Episcopal Office, strange to say, after all the attention that was bestowed upon it, has the same fundamental defect. In all ancient

Liturgies, as in our service, the Fraction follows the consecration.

After this central Action, the Minister, as in the Primitive Church, is to communicate first. This is implied, rather than stated explicitly, in the Directory; but the old Scottish accounts show that the Minister always partook of each element before distributing it. Of all the innovations of the present day—innovations properly so called and not restorations—there is none so extraordinary, and so utterly subversive of all the old ideas of the Church, as the practice in some congregations, where simultaneous communion has been introduced, of Elders giving the elements to the Minister. Such a thing would certainly have shocked all Reformed Churchmen in other days. The Minister, as representing his Master, gives to all; and what Elders, acting here in the capacity of Deacons, whose proper work it is,[1] do, is at most merely to pass on what has been given.

In distributing, the Minister should adhere scrupulously to our Lord's words, whether he

[1] "When the Bishop or Presbyter has offered, the Deacon distributes to the people not as a Priest, but as one that ministers to the Priest."—Apost. Const., Book viii. chap. 28. At Alexandria the people were allowed to take the bread from the paten.

follows the narrative form, which appears to be best, or that of the Directory, and should add nothing of his own, whatever he may take from the Liturgies.[1]

The Scottish Commissioners at Westminster defended the practice of giving the Cup immediately, against the Independents, who argued that it should not be given till all had received the Bread.

It appears, also, that they had some difficulty in preventing the insertion of a clause forbidding private devotion before and after receiving the elements. Baillie tells us that this was regarded by the Church of Scotland as a custom both "lawful and laudable," and that it was "the ordinary practice of most, if not all, pastors and people" he was acquainted with. Our best clergy have always represented the Lord's Table as a place of special request, where we come into the immediate presence of the King; and the godly in our land have been wont to consider beforehand what mercies and blessings they should ask from their Lord and Saviour when admitted to

---

[1] Nothing can be meaner or in worse taste than expressions such as the following, which one has heard: "I have much pleasure in putting into your hands," &c.; "Let no words of mine disturb your meditations."

His banqueting-house, and to the greatest nearness to Him out of heaven.

Table Addresses.—In the Directory there is no reference to what are called Table Addresses. The supplementary Act of our Assembly of 1645 orders " That there be no reading in the time of communicating, but . . . a short exhortation at every Table; that thereafter there be silence during the time of the communicants receiving, except only when the Minister expresses some few short sentences . . . that they may be incited and quickened in their meditations in the action."

Down till that period there had been no address previous to giving the elements to the separate companies; but while the action of eating and drinking lasted, the Minister either addressed those at the Table, or caused the Reader to read the history of the Passion, according to the Rubric of the Book of Common Order. This was usually read from St John's Gospel, beginning at the 13th chapter; and when the Table was emptying and filling, the 103d or 34th Psalm was sung; and so " by this intercourse of reading and singing, the people were kept in holy exercises till all had communicated." This was the old Scottish Order—one Table, many companies, and no superfluous addresses. All the descriptions show that there was no speaking except while the eating and drinking lasted. As soon as this was finished, the company rose from the Table, and others took their place at once. The communicants thus passed on in procession, and no more time was taken up than was absolutely necessary for their receiving the elements; but after the Westminster Assembly, our Church enjoined one short address before each distribution.

Simultaneous Communion was left an open question by the Directory, much against the wish of the Scottish Commissioners. The discussion turned on the point whether all were to receive at the Table, or whether the elements might be handed to people sitting in pews around it. The debate was long, and sometimes violent. Baillie says: "To come out of their pews to a Table they (the English Puritans) deny the necessity of it; we affirm it necessary, and will stand to it." And Henderson, in his speech during the discussion, said: "We, sent from the Church of Scotland, are all of one mind on this point. We can hardly part from it—nay, I may add, we may not possibly part from it." They not only thought simultaneous communion, as then practised by the Independents, very irreverent, but they felt their distinctive principles to be involved in the question, and that to allow the pew system was to fall from Churchism into Sectarianism. On this and other points that divided them from the Independents, they felt that they were within the lines of organised Christianity, but that, to use the words of a friend, "they were on the outermost edge of it, and that beyond them there was nothing but a waste howling wilderness."

Our Assembly, in its Act approving the Directory, settled the question for Scotland, by declaring that the clause "sitting about the Table or at it" was not to be "interpreted as if, in the judgment of this Kirk, it were indifferent, and free for any of the communicants not to come to and receive at the Table." The innovation of receiving in pews was first introduced about 1825; and having been brought to the notice of the Church Courts, the Assembly in that year condemned the practice, and pronounced it to be the law and immemorial usage of this Church "to dispense the sacrament of the Lord's Supper to the people seated at or round a Communion Table or Tables." Notwithstanding this decision, the pew system has latterly become common, and I am told that even receiving in the galleries is not unknown. If the champions of our Church usages in former days were to come to life again, there are few things at which they would stand more aghast than to see the sectarian practice, against which they fought so stout a battle, supplanting the old order in which they gloried. This change is partly to be accounted for by the decay of Church principles, and consequent tendency to Independency all along the line; but it was greatly furthered by the two long addresses which, till recently, were given at each Table. The one short exhortation of the supplementary Act of 1645, itself a novelty, seems to have been all that was usual till the early part of last century. When we read of men like the father of Principal Carstairs serving fifteen Tables in succession, it is a relief to find that this did not involve the more than Herculean task of delivering thirty lengthy discourses, but merely a few sentences before each distribution. But in course of time the addresses were doubled or even trebled in number, for in some quarters an extra one was inserted betwixt the giving of the Bread and the giving of the Cup,[1] and they were often drawn out to a great length. The result was that the continuity of the Communion was broken. People began to regard the service at each Table as com-

[1] Brichan's Sermons and Sacramental Addresses, p. 337.

plete in itself, and to adopt the most unseemly practice of going home after rising from it, without waiting to give God thanks, and to join in the great Intercession which follows, and which has always been regarded such an essential feature of the Communion. To retire in this way after receiving the elements was forbidden by the old rules of the Church, and is obviously to offer a maimed and imperfect service.

It appears to me that no arrangement could be more suitable and impressive than that of successive Tables, with no addresses, except a few words before each distribution, as enjoined by the law of the Church. With more frequent Communions, and, in large congregations, several celebrations on the same day, or even on successive Sundays, according to the old usage, the matter would be further simplified, and less Table accommodation required.

The supplementary Act of 1645 enjoins, "That, while the Tables are dissolving and filling, there be always singing of some portion of a Psalm, according to the custom." The 103d Psalm is indicated in the Form for the Administration of the Lord's Supper in the Book of Common Order, and it has always been sung at Scottish Communions from the time of the Reformation. The practice of singing during Communion is certainly primitive, and probably Apostolic. In the Ethiopic Liturgy, which Bunsen regarded as the primitive form, the Rubric after consecration runs thus: "Then they uplift the Hymn of Praise, and the people enter in to receive the medicine of their souls whereby sin is remitted." So in the Apostolical Constitutions [1] it is ordered that the 34th Psalm, there called the 33d, shall be sung while the people are partaking. In the Church of England it was the custom in 1621, as appears from Wither's Poems, to sing as the successive companies approached and withdrew from the Table, and this practice is still kept up among the Wesleyans in Canada, and probably elsewhere.

6. *Call to Thanksgiving.*—A call to Thanksgiving naturally follows. Accordingly, the Directory says, "After all have communicated, the Minister may, in a few words, put them in mind of the grace of God in Jesus Christ, held forth in the Sacrament, and exhort them to walk worthy of it." A sentence or two of this import was all that was intended, and all that had previously been common in Scotland. Henderson describes the old practice thus: "After the last company hath received, the Minister . . . goeth to the pulpit, where, after

[1] Book viii. chap. xiii.

a short speech tending to thanksgiving, he doth again solemnly give thanks to God." Till recently it was usual to address the last company after receiving, and for the Pastor then to ascend the pulpit and deliver a long exhortation to the whole body of Communicants, but these innovations of a later period may well be departed from in favour of the simpler order prescribed not only by the Directory, but by the Reformed and the Primitive Liturgies. For models of the one brief address required, I refer you to the Genevan and Dutch Services, and to the still more beautiful form given in the Apostolical Constitutions: "Now we have received the precious Body and the precious Blood of Christ, let us give thanks to Him who has thought us worthy to partake of these holy mysteries, and let us beseech Him that it may not be to us for condemnation, but for salvation, and to the advantage of soul and body; to the preservation of piety, to the remission of sins, and to the life of the world to come. Let us arise, and, by the grace of Christ, let us dedicate ourselves to God, to the only unbegotten God, and to His Christ."

7. *The Post-Communion Prayer* is then offered. The form in the Directory is very short; the topics indicated being thanksgiving, prayer for

pardon for the defects of the service, and for grace to live as becomes those who have received so great pledges of salvation. The prayer in the Book of Common Order is of the same import. In both, Intercession is wanting, because it had been provided for in the earlier part of the service. From Henderson's account, however, we learn that the Minister concluded, as on other Sundays, with petitions for the Church, the Authorities, and the Afflicted. In all the early Liturgies the Intercession precedes the Act of Communion. It is introduced either before the Words of Institution, or between them and the Invocation, or between the Invocation and the Lord's Prayer; but it has long been the practice of our Church to introduce it in the concluding prayer. This is scarcely less appropriate, and indeed our Lord's example may be pled for it, as it was after Supper that He offered the great intercessory prayer recorded in the 17th chapter of St John's Gospel.

According to our usage, this prayer should embrace the following topics: Thanksgiving for God's grace vouchsafed unto us in the Sacrament, with petitions that we may be enabled to walk worthy of it. The dedication of our souls and bodies anew to the Lord is the proper response to Christ's giving Himself a sacrifice for us, and should never be omitted here; then follows the Great Intercession for the Church, for all ranks and conditions of our fellow-men in the Body of Christ, with thanks for the righteous departed, and prayers for the second coming of the Lord. If there is no reference to this great hope, which is so prominently associated with the Communion, the service, as has been said, is essentially defective. The prayer cannot more appropriately close than with aspirations after the fulness of joy that awaits us at His coming, when we shall be like Him, and see Him as He is.

8. *Concluding Hymn.*—The Directory makes no mention of a concluding Hymn of Praise, or of the Benediction, but they are obviously taken for granted. For praise we have the example of our Lord and of His Apostles, who sang a Hymn at the close of the first Communion; no doubt the last part of the great Hallel (Ps. 115-118) which, in the Jewish Church, was sung after the fourth cup in the Passover meal. It has been the general custom of the Reformed Churches to sing at this time the Nunc Dimittis, or Song of Simeon, of which we have a version in the 38th Paraphrase, the 8th, 10th, and 11th verses. The 9th verse is an addition to the original text, and,

both on this account and because it contains a distinct prayer for death, it is well to omit it.

The closing Rubric of the Directory is that "the collection for the poor is so to be ordered, that no part of the Public Worship be thereby hindered." This implies that a special Communion offering should be made. This has been the practice of the Church in all ages, and in Scotland, what is given on these occasions is usually devoted to the poorer brethren whose names are on the Communion Roll. It is well to give prominence to these "gifts of love" in the intimations made beforehand, so that the speciality of the offering, and the associations connected with it, may not be overlooked. After the Reformation it seems to have been taken as people went to the Table. Thus, in an account of the Communion at Perth in 1580, we read that the celebration took place in the Chancel, which was railed off, and that the people gave their tokens and their alms as they entered.[1] It afterwards became more common for the offering to be made as they left the Table. In 1618 the Kirk-Session of Aberdeen ordered that the alms of the Communicants should be taken at their rising from the Table, "according to the form

[1] Scott's History of the Reformers, p. 191.

observed by Reformed Congregations in the South part of the Realm."[1] This custom is still observed in some parts of Aberdeenshire, and instead of its being abolished, which a new Minister is very likely to attempt, especially if from the South, whence the usage came, it would be better if it could be restored where it has been given up. This could be done easily, and without any interruption of the service, by simply placing an alms-dish at the end of the Table by which the Communicants retire.

Pardovan remarks that it would be better to demand Tokens of Communicants at their entry to the Table rather than after they are seated. This is a most reasonable suggestion, and it could easily be carried out, and without the loss of time involved in the present practice, by placing a box for the purpose at the end by which they enter.

The whole service concludes with the Benediction, "before which," as Henderson says, "none are to depart unless in case of necessity."

From the same authority we learn that the Communion Services in his time were closed by the Doctrine of Thanksgiving, taught by the Minister on the Sunday afternoon. The Directory is silent on this point, but the supplementary

[1] Selections from Records, Spalding Club, p. 86.

Act of 1645 orders that "there be one sermon of Thanksgiving after the Communion is ended." It is usually said that the Monday Service was introduced after, and as a fruit of, Livingston's celebrated sermon preached at the Kirk of Shotts in 1630, on a Monday following the dispensation of the Communion in that Parish; but there is no evidence of its having become common till many years later.

No one who has been familiar with the Scottish Communion Season of a later day can be insensible to its solemnities. In many parts of the country, down to our own time, religious exercises were kept up from Thursday till Monday, and were scarcely regarded as complete till followed by special family devotions. After dinner in the Manse on that day, when the cloth was removed, the Books were usually brought in, prayer offered, and a concluding Hymn of Praise, such as the 2d Paraphrase, sung by the assembled guests. All in whose memory these prolonged services are associated with revered Pastors and beloved kindred now with God, must ever think of them with tender and hallowed feelings, and may be disposed to regard the former times as in some respects better than the present.

Still, the additions to the older practice and rules of the Church, owed their origin to influences which lowered the standard of worship, and were condemned by her greatest and wisest Ministers. For generations they proved an insuperable hindrance to the frequent celebration of the Lord's Supper; and as this was certainly a far greater evil than the good they accomplished, we ought not to regret the return that has taken place in our time to a practice still older, and in stricter conformity with the laws of the Church.

LECTURE IV.

THE SOLEMNISATION OF MATRIMONY—THE BURIAL OF THE DEAD—PUBLIC SOLEMN FASTING—DAYS OF PUBLIC THANKSGIVING.

FOLLOWING the Order of the Directory, the next Service that falls to be considered is—

The Solemnisation of Matrimony.

Proclamation of Banns.—The first Rubric on this subject which it is necessary to notice is that enjoining that "Before the solemnising of Marriage between any persons, their purpose of Marriage shall be published by the Minister three several Sabbath Days in the congregation, at the place or places of their most usual and constant abode respectively." The Assembly of 1690 passed an Act rigidly enforcing Proclamation on three Sundays, and this continued to be the law of the Church till 1879, subject to the same right of Presbyteries to dispense with Banns in emergencies, which Bishops had exercised in Episcopal times. This right was referred to as inherent in Presbyteries by the Glasgow Assembly of 1638. It does not appear that they have ever used their dispensing power since the Revolution Settlement; but we learn from Pardovan that the Act of 1690 was not understood to interfere with it, and all our greatest legal authorities on the law of Marriage acknowledge that they possess it. Instead of conforming to the law—proclamation on three Sundays the rule, with a licence from the Presbytery in exceptional cases—Ministers took the matter into their own hands, and for a long period allowed the three proclamations to be made ordinarily on a single Sunday. The First Book of Discipline says: "That if the persons are so known that no suspicion of danger may arise, then the time may be shortened at the discretion of the Minister:" and this is no doubt the foundation of the practice which, notwithstanding rules to the contrary, has generally prevailed in the Church when under Presbyterian Government. By a recent Act of Parliament, a secular substitute for Banns has been legalised, and the General Assembly in 1879 authorised

Ministers, "if they see fit, to receive, as a valid notice of Marriage, a registrar's certificate." At the same time, it modified the old regulations of the Church, by enacting that "Proclamation of Banns shall, in ordinary cases, be on two separate Sabbaths," instead of three; and that "it shall be in the power of the Minister to complete the proclamation on a single Sabbath," when he is satisfied that there is no impediment. This Act, like the Directory, requires the Proclamation to be made by the officiating Minister.

With regard to the persons to be married, the Directory contains some regulations as to age and consent which I pass over; but as they who "marry should marry in the Lord," I may remark that it is involved in the idea of a Christian marriage, that both parties should be baptized. Formerly the Church ordained that none were to be admitted into that holy estate till they could repeat the Creed, the Lord's Prayer, and the Ten Commandments; and from the Reformation till the times of the Covenant, we read of marriages being postponed by the Clergy till these fundamentals of the Christian Faith were mastered by the candidates for connubial bliss. Certainly at that time no Minister would have given the blessing of the Church to those who were not within its pale. I have been in the practice of insisting upon the parties, if unbaptized, preparing for and receiving Baptism, before uniting them in Marriage; and I have always found that this was not only willingly acceded to, but that it was expected.

Time and Place of Marriage.—The Directory orders that " The Minister . . . is publicly to solemnise Marriage in the place appointed by authority for Public Worship, before a competent number of credible witnesses, at some convenient hour of the day, at any time of the year, except on a day of public humiliation." It is added, " and we advise that it be not on the Lord's Day."

The Book of Common Order had enjoined that it should take place in Church during Divine Service on Sunday, and the First Book of Discipline also says that Marriage should only be solemnised on Sunday after sermon; but in 1579 the Assembly resolved that the ceremony might be performed on any day of the week, on the understanding apparently, for the Records of that period are imperfect, that "preaching should be joined thereto." The practice of marrying in Church on Sundays prevailed, however, for the greater part of a century, and a Marriage pew was often one of the articles of furniture in Churches when other pews had not yet been erected. Baillie speaks of marrying as one of the ordinary Sunday duties of the Scottish Clergy in his time. The service seems to have been usually performed at the close of the sermon. Thus, Sir Thomas Hope the Lord Advocate, and founder of the Scottish family of that name, mentions in his Diary the marriage of his son in 1638 in the Grey Friars' Church, Edinburgh, " on Sunday immediately after the preaching." After this time, more Puritanic views of the Lord's Day, and perhaps also less sacred and Churchly views of the marriage ceremony, became prevalent; and accordingly we find the Kirk-Session of Edinburgh forbidding Sunday Marriages in 1641, and that of Glasgow following their example in 1643. The reason alleged for this, however, was not that the practice was objectionable in itself, but that the preparation of the wedding feast involved so much work on the Lord's Day.[1] At Westminster the extreme Puritans would have allowed Mar-

[1] On the 1st of January 1635, the Presbytery of Glasgow ordered that the Sabbath be kept from 12 o'clock on Saturday night to 12 on Sunday night.—Register, Maitland Club Miscellany, i. p. 67. This change was then generally adopted, and had, no doubt, something to do with the opposition to marriage on Sundays.

riage in private houses, and some of them thought a civil contract sufficient, but Baillie writes: "Thanks be to God, we have gotten the Independents satisfied, and a unanimous consent of all the Assembly, that Marriage shall be celebrated only by the Minister, and that in the Church, after our fashion." The advice of the Directory, not to marry on Sundays, was often disregarded in Scotland, as we find references to Sunday Marriages in the Session Records many years afterwards;[1] and in some parts of the country, persons who were married on that day during Divine Service, according to the old custom, are remembered by people still living. In the Church of England the practice is not unknown even at the present day.

Down till about 1700 there was no marrying in private houses in Scotland, but this fashion was then introduced among the upper classes. It was not allowed, however, at first, except under penalties, and for many years after that date a very common entry in Session Records is that such and such parties were "fined for being married out of Church." Dr Somerville of Jedburgh, in his Autobiography, says that Marriage in Church was still the rule among the humbler classes in the middle of last century. After that

[1] See Notes and Queries, Aug. 1880, p. 144.

time the law was generally disregarded, but in some districts it still continued to be observed; and there are Parishes where, down till the present day, the service has been commonly performed in Church. A few years ago when the tide turned, and the old Scottish practice began to be resumed in quarters where it had been for some generations in disuse, it was commented on as an unheard-of innovation, or denounced as an aping of Episcopacy. An English Ladies' Newspaper, which devotes much attention to fashionable Marriages, in chronicling that of a Scottish nobleman which took place not long ago in a private house, stated that "the ceremony was conducted according to the Presbyterian Form, which *does not admit of celebration in Church.*" This is but one instance out of many where what were formerly the characteristics of our Church have been relinquished to Episcopacy, and we have fallen into those usages of the Independents from which our Clergy in the seventeenth century shrank with much more aversion than they did from the ceremonies of the Church of England. We are now returning to the law and old custom of the Church, and the Clergy should further the movement, both by precept and by example, when they have the opportunity.

The manner in which the ceremony has been conducted for generations past has not tended to impress the community at large with its religious character, but has rather lowered its sacred associations, and this may possibly have contributed, among the lower classes, to a diminished abhorrence of one of our great national sins. It could scarcely fail to have a wholesome effect, if it were understood that all virtuous Marriages were to be solemnised publicly in God's House, and if those parties were relegated to the Session-room for the ceremony who have to compear there at any rate for purposes of discipline.[1]

THE SERVICE.

It has often been said that no service is so difficult of construction as a proper form for Marriage, and that none of the Liturgical Offices are in all respects satisfactory. The traditional Scottish service is a compromise betwixt those given in the Book of Common Order and in the Directory, both of which contain excellent materials. In some points the one is usually followed, in some the

[1] In the Reformed Churches of Bohemia and Moravia, it is ordered that such persons shall "be married in the presence of no more than two witnesses without public ceremonies."—Cath. Pres. for Sept. 1881, p. 236.

other. In practice the order varies, but the following seems to be the most natural and complete; and it is most in accordance with the Reformed Liturgies. 1. Exhortation, concluding with charge as to impediments; 2. Prayer; 3. Vows; 4. Declaration and Marriage Blessing; 5. Prayer; 6. Psalm 128, said or sung; 7. Benediction.

When the celebration takes place in Church, a Marriage Hymn is usually sung as the Wedding party enter; and the Bride and Bridegroom take their places in front of the Communion Table—the man on the right hand, and the woman on his left.

Exhortation.—The address, according to the Rubric of the Directory, should consist of a brief declaration out of the Scripture of "the institution, use, and ends of Marriage," and the duties of husband and wife towards each other.

On the first point it is proper to speak of its institution in Paradise, its having been honoured by our Lord's presence, gift, and miracle, at Cana in Galilee, its having been commended by St Paul, and consecrated as setting forth the mystical union betwixt Christ and His Church; and then, after a short statement as to its use and ends, to proceed to the mutual duties which it imposes. These cannot be so well declared as in the words of Holy Scripture, and it is usual to read here Ephesians v., from the 22d verse to the end.

The Minister is then solemnly to charge " the persons to be married, before the great God who searcheth all hearts, and to Whom they must give a strict account at the last day, that if either of them know any cause, by precontract or otherwise, why they may not lawfully proceed to Marriage, that they now discover it." In Knox's Liturgy this charge is given in the same words as those in the English Prayer-Book; and it also requires the Minister, if no impediment be offered, to take those present to witness, and, as in the English Office, to charge them that if any of them know of any lawful impediment to the Marriage, that they declare the same.

Prayer.—If no such hindrance be alleged, the Minister then engages in prayer. That given in the Directory is admirable so far as it goes. Indeed it would be difficult to find in any service a better form of words than the following: "We earnestly entreat Thee, O Lord, whose presence and favour is the happiness of every condition, and sweetens every relation, to be the portion of these Thy servants, who are now to be joined in the honourable estate of Marriage, and to own and accept them in Christ: and as Thou hast brought them together by Thy Providence, we beseech Thee to sanctify them by Thy Spirit, giving them a new frame of heart fit for their new estate, enriching them with all grace whereby they may perform the duties, enjoy the comforts, undergo the cares, and resist the temptations which accompany that condition, as becometh Christians."

It is well, however, to supplement this with a petition that they may enter upon their solemn vows as in God's sight, and faithfully perform the same according to His Holy Word.

The Minister is then to cause the Man to take the Woman by the right hand—which may be appropriately done in these words: "As a seal to the solemn vows which you are now about to take, give each other the right hand."

"Join hands," which one sometimes hears, hardly meets the necessities of the case, and is somewhat wanting in dignity.

The Vows.—According to the Directory, the Minister is to cause both Man and Woman to repeat the vows which it definitely prescribes. In the Book of Common Order the vows are the same as in the Continental Reformed Liturgies, and differ from those in the Directory. They are put in the form of a question, and the parties answer, "Even so I take her or him before God, and in the presence of this Congregation." It is usual to put the vows of the Directory in this way also, and merely to require the parties to assent, by bowing the head, or in the words, "I do." But it would be much better to adhere strictly to the rule, and to require the words to be repeated, as in oaths taken in Civil Courts. There is no difficulty about this, and it adds to the solemnity of the Service. Ministers neither gain respect for their office nor for the Church, nor do they improve her services, by reducing still further that minimum of form which she has enjoined. In fact, people like a little, and some a good deal, of ceremony on such occasions. It is not only common to dispense with the repetition of the words, but Ministers are sometimes guilty of the grave offence of mutilating them; as, for example, substituting *dutiful* for *obedient*, by the way of making things smoother for the fair sex than Scripture has done. It is worse than bad taste to take such liberties. The vows prescribed by the Directory are as nearly perfect as anything of the kind can be, and should in no case be departed from. It is perhaps not unnecessary to mention also, that they require the simple use of the Christian names N or M., whatever the rank, titles, or age of the happy pair.

Use of the Ring.—The words of the Directory, "without any further ceremony," evidently refer to the use of the ring. Notwithstanding this prohibition, it is fast becoming part of the "consuetudinary" law of the Church to put it on during the service, and the time chosen for this is immediately after the vows have been taken; just, in fact, when the Directory forbids it. The ring was given in betrothals in the Primitive Church, but its use in the marriage service itself has not been traced higher than the tenth century. Neither in our own nor in any other branch of the Reformed Church, except the English, was it introduced at first into the service, although, of course, as the ancient and accepted sign of wedlock, it was always put on afterwards. The main reason for this departure from Pre-Reformation custom was their dislike of ceremonies during Public Worship (when Marriage was then celebrated), which were not of divine institution. It was chiefly among the English Puritans, however, that objection to the ring was made a matter of principle, and scruples on the subject seem now to be everywhere dying out. When it is to be given, the simplest method of introducing it is for the Minister to say: "In token of fidelity to these vows the wedding-ring will now be given and received." There is no good reason for his making an announcement such as the following, which was made some time ago at a fashionable Marriage in Church, to the astonishment of the Episcopalians who were present: "The ring may now be given, but it must be distinctly understood that this forms no part of the religious service."

The Minister is then, "in the face of the Congregation, to pronounce them to be Husband and Wife, according to God's Ordinance;" and it adds to the solemnity, and is in conformity with the best liturgical examples, to make this declaration, "In the name of the Father, and of the Son, and of the Holy Ghost." It is usual to add our Lord's own words, as in Knox's Liturgy: "Whom God hath joined together, let not man put asunder."

A Blessing should then be pronounced upon the newly wedded pair. That given in Knox's Book is as follows: "The Lord sanctify and bless you, the Lord pour the riches of His grace upon you, that ye may please Him, and live together in holy love to your lives' end."

This is the proper place to introduce any words of counsel which the Minister may wish to address to them, or short sermon, should the old practice revive among us, as in England, of "preaching being joined thereto." The addresses given in the Genevan and other Reformed Liturgies are very suitable and touching, as are also some of the Marriage Sermons which you find reported in English religious Newspapers.

Prayer.—The concluding prayer given in the Directory is very short, and there is none at all in Knox's Liturgy, perhaps because the service would be followed by the usual prayer of Intercession. It is common, however, in our Church, as in most others, to offer here a prayer of some length. That given in Euchologion is taken partly from the Marriage Service of the Greek Church, which is very rich and beautiful, and partly from the Book of Prayers, compiled by the late Dr Robert Lee. Though somewhat artificial, it is as suitable as any that I am acquainted with. Either this or the previous prayer should conclude with the Lord's Prayer, without which no public religious service should be regarded as complete.

Knox's Book, in conformity with the usage of the Continental Churches, directs that at the close of the service the 128th Psalm, or "some other pertaining to the purpose, be sung." Among the Scriptural Chants recently published by the authority of the General Assembly, you find two for the Marriage Service in addition to this Psalm. When there is no music, the Minister should recite it, introducing it thus, as in the Dutch Liturgy: "Hearken now to the promise of God from Psalm 128." The usual Benediction is then pronounced.

The greatest care should be taken with the Marriage Service, both because of the danger of erring in matters of taste and propriety, and because Marriage is always a great event in the lives of the parties united, as well as to many of the witnesses, however common it may be for the Minister to tie the knot. People are on their best behaviour at such times, and it brings discredit upon the Church if the religious solemnity is wanting in dignity and propriety. I have heard of some very unfortunate exhibitions on such occasions in the presence of large companies; and you all know how common it is, or was a few years ago, for members of our Church belonging to the higher classes, to pass by their own Clergymen and repair to the Episcopal Chapel for Marriage rites. Attached members of the Church who take this course, so dishonouring to their own Clergy and Communion, are in the habit of defending it, on the ground that we have no prescribed Marriage Service—that they were at the mercy of the Minister, and did not know what he might say. Certainly there are some things in the English Service which are very far from being in accordance with modern taste, but people will bear the evils they know of rather than risk others, possibly worse, which they know not of. However much we may dislike to hear or read of it, it is perhaps not greatly to be wondered at that the more refined members of the Church shrink from intrusting this delicate piece of duty to the hands of some of the Clergy, and that they prefer being married according to a prescribed form. Soon after my ordination, I was unexpectedly called, for the first time, to unite a happy pair who could brook no delay, as the Steamer which landed me at the place of their residence was, in an hour or two, to carry them off to a distant station. When the ceremony was over, I had grave doubts whether they were married at all or not, and felt no little ashamed at the appearance I had made. On another occasion I happened to be present at a Marriage, when the service was performed, in the presence of a large and respectable gathering, by a College friend who had also been recently ordained. My friend, who was a distinguished student, and who has since risen to professional eminence, floundered hopelessly on that occasion, and lost the thread of his discourse, if he had any to lose. When at length, to my great relief, he came to an end, I turned round, partly to avoid meeting his eye, and partly to hide my diminished head, for I felt anything but reassured by this representation of the Church among strangers. Our host, an Englishman, was standing by, and, apparently somewhat bewildered, said to me, "Ah! that is the Scottish Marriage Service, is it?" I was obliged to give a qualified assent, whereupon he said that "he had never heard it before;" and he certainly looked as if he wished never to hear it again.

In drawing up a Form—for this is obviously not an occasion for an extemporaneous effusion, however gifted with fluency any of you may be,— it is much the wisest course to take your materials from the Directory, Knox's Book, and other Liturgical sources, and the less you vary it the better. One Form is surely enough for one Scottish Parish during an incumbency, when, in other parts of the Christian world, the same service satisfies whole nations for many centuries.

Concerning Visitation of the Sick.

The Visitation of the Sick forms the next section of the Directory; but as this is not part of the public service of the Church, it does not fall within the scope of these Lectures. I may merely remark that the introduction of such a service, containing many minute and wise rules, into the Directory (as into all Liturgies), shows the different ideas which the Church formerly held as to Ministerial Visitation of the Sick from those prevalent now. It is not uncommon to hear the poor condemned for the peculiar value which many of them still attach to the prayers of an ordained Minister of Christ in times of sickness by those who think it a proof of enlightenment to place such devotions on the same level with their own, or those of other private Christians. Private Christians are often more gifted and more godly than their Pastors; but as the Compilers of the Directory state in the Form of Church Government, "It is the office of the Elder—that is, the Pastor—to pray for the sick in private," and that to his prayers "a blessing is specially promised."

I also take this opportunity of recommending to your notice a very useful work on the Visitation of the Sick, compiled by the Rev. Dr Lees of St Giles', Edinburgh, one of the Clergy who have of late years taken an active interest in the improvement of the Service of the House of God. This movement will doubtless, in course of time, bear much similar fruit, and add largely to the devotional literature of the Church, which has hitherto been deplorably meagre as compared with its libraries of controversy.

We pass to the next Section—

Concerning Burial of the Dead.

Among all the Reformed Churches there was at first a feeling against religious services at Funerals, because of the old practice of praying and offering masses for the dead. Though in later times it has often been said that because the Pope prays for the dead, the Scot refuses, at Funerals, to pray for the living, the objection to Funeral Services in our early Reformed Church was not very decided, nor was it universal. Nor is there any foundation whatever for the common assertion that it was a principle with our Reformers to do the opposite of what had been done in the Pre-Reformation Church. In the common editions of the First Book of Discipline, it is said that it is "judged best," on account of prevailing superstition, that there should be neither singing, nor reading (that is, of Scripture or Prayer), nor preaching of sermons at funerals. But in what is considered the most authentic edition of that Book—that given in Knox's Works—a sentence omitted in the common editions is added, which leaves it to particular Churches to use their liberty in the matter; and there can be no doubt that this formed part of the original copy. Archbishop Spottiswoode gives it in his version, and its genuineness is proved by the fact that the Summary of that Book, drawn up for the instruction of Ministers and Readers in their office, after repeating the opinion against singing and reading, adds: "But this we remit to the judgment of particular Kirks, with advice of the Ministers." The Book of Common Order says that when "the corpse is . . . brought to the grave, . . . the Minister if he be present, and required, goeth to the Church, if it be not far off, and maketh some comfortable exhortation to the people, touching death and the resurrection." This implies that the exhortation might be given at the grave, if the Church was not at hand. At least Wodrow, who did not like the permission, so understood it. "I know not," he says, "how the direction to make an exhortation when the corpse is laid in the grave has been inserted in the Book." Among the traces left by the use of the English Prayer-Book for some years by our first Reformers is a "Form of Burial as used in the Kirk of Montrose" about 1580. It consists of a homily on death, a prayer from King Edward's Liturgy, and a funeral hymn,—the whole of which were to be said or sung when the body was brought to the grave. After the Reformation, it was common to have not only singing and reading, but the preaching of sermons at funerals, particularly in the case of eminent men. Thus we find Knox, notwithstanding the part he had in drawing up the First Book of Discipline, preaching at the burial of the Good Regent; and many other instances might be mentioned. After a time, however, the practice of singing, reading, and praying at funerals, seems to have fallen into general disuse. In the Liturgy drawn up about 1616, under King James's auspices, which was taken partly from the English Prayer-Book and partly from Knox's Liturgy, which it was designed to supersede, it is said "we do not dislike" the reading of Scripture, singing of Psalms, and Prayer, used in some Reformed Churches, at funerals; "but our Church, not being accustomed therewith, doth leave it to the discretion of the Minister, who, being present at the burial, and required, ought not to refuse to make some comfortable exhortation to the people touching death and resurrection to life."[1] This last clause is taken from Knox's Book. There was a revival of funeral services and sermons before 1637, but the Covenant proved fatal to them.[2]

Henderson tells us, in 1641, that there was no religious service at all at funerals—even the address had disappeared; and this continued to be the case till a generation ago. There are traces, however, of devotional exercises of what was considered the superstitious order in the house of mourning during the interval betwixt death and burial. Thus, in 1643, the Aberdeen Town Council forbade the people to ask the Doctors of the Music School and the Readers to read or sing hereafter at Lykewakes, which had no doubt been the custom down till that time. The practice, still known in many parts of the country, though now dying out, of asking Ministers to be present and conduct a religious service at the coffining of the dead, must be of old standing, and is apparently a relic of the Lykewake service.

[1] Scottish Liturgies of the Reign of James VI., p. 89.
[2] See Chambers's Domestic Annals of Scotland, vol. ii. pp. 74, 78, 299.

The Directory forbids prayer, singing, and reading at the house, on the way to the churchyard, or at the grave; but, like Knox's Liturgy, it allows the Minister, if he be present, to deliver an address at the grave: and the records of the discussion on the subject show that the Rubric was not meant to forbid the use of such words of committal as "We commit this body to the ground," &c. However, for long after its adoption in Scotland, there was no religious service of any kind at funerals, and even the preaching of funeral sermons was objected to by an extreme party. Many interesting old customs were continued till last century, some of which are being now revived,—such as strewing the mortcloth with flowers, and the attendance of women at funerals, which was kept up in Scotland after it had ceased in England. One is surprised to find that *incense* was used at Scottish burials so late as the early part of last century,—not, of course, as a symbol of prayer, but because of its fragrant and purifying properties. Thus, in 1705, the Aberdeen Town Council "appoints that in all time coming the Master of Church Works shall receive from each person who shall burn incense or perfume at the burial of their friends in the Church, £4 Scots; and in the Churchyard, 40 shillings Scots."[1] All these usages, however, died out in course of time, and a generation or two ago nothing was left but smoking and drinking—and often hard drinking—with many toasts, including sometimes, it is said, before the festivities were over, not only the *memory*, but the *health* of the deceased. An eminent Clergyman informed me that at the funeral of one of his clerical neighbours, when he was a young man, it was proposed by the members of Presbytery that one of their number should engage in prayer in the house. The son of the deceased, who was himself a Parish Minister, objected, saying that "he would allow no innovations of that kind, but that it should be just an old-fashioned funeral." It is not above fifty years since the first prayer was heard at a funeral among the Puritans of New England, and the same thing may be said of some of the Reformed Churches on the Continent. About that time prayers came in in Scotland, in the form of a grace and returning of thanks for the refreshments, which previously would seem to have been partaken of unblessed. This was the thin end of the wedge, and now we are back to where our forefathers were in the days of the early Reformed Church. Toasts are a thing of

[1] Records, p. 333.

the past, or nearly so—for it is only a few years since I heard a venerable Clergyman at a funeral propose "The memory of the deceased," and "Consolation to the mourners,"—and religious exercises have now a place even in the absence of refreshments.

Though an address at the grave was always legal, prayer and reading of Scripture, whether there or in the house, are, as I have said, forbidden by the Directory, but the Church has now virtually sanctioned both.

Service at the grave has long been common in our colonies, and in some of them where I have been, our Clergy, in gown and bands, head the funeral processions on their way to the place of interment. Prayers in the house are now almost universal in this country, and they are becoming common also at the grave. In a Parish in the South with which I am acquainted, a generation ago the Minister, on one occasion, ventured to have a service in the churchyard; but it created a terrible commotion in that part of the country. The worthy man's Elders all left him, and declared that he was going post-haste to Rome. One used to hear stories, in that quarter, of the consumption of enormous quantities of whisky on such occasions, but a prayer at the grave was not to be endured. Some of my own contemporaries were dealt with by their Presbyteries for introducing the practice, five-and-twenty years ago; but all opposition to it seems to have ceased, and it is not uncommon for people to request it. Even the singing of Hymns at the grave has been introduced in some cases, in accordance with the practice of the Primitive Church, and the General Assembly has gone the length of providing Chants for the purpose. Surely it is most Christian to make such services expressive not only of our sorrow, but of the feelings of joy and triumph which the great hopes of the Gospel inspire, even at the grave's devouring mouth; and who would not heartily join at such a time in a hymn like that beginning—

> " Jesus lives ! No longer now
> Can thy terrors, Death, appal us " ?

The idea of asking a grace and returning of thanks still lingers, but is very fast disappearing. I was present some time ago at a funeral, when a chapter was read and a prayer offered by a clergyman seated at one end of the dining-room table, and the same thing repeated by another divine at the other end. The prayers seemed to me to be objectionable, as they consisted mainly of encomiums on the deceased; and on my saying to a clergyman who was present that I did not like the service, he answered, "No; it was a great mistake that the cake and wine had not been handed round *between* the prayers." That was all my friend saw to find fault with.

THE SERVICE.

In the House.—In the house or the church, where there is sometimes service, the most suitable Scriptures to be read are, by common consent, the 39th and 90th Psalms, part of the 15th chapter of 1st Corinthians, and the 4th chapter of 1st Thessalonians, from the 13th verse to the end. It is advisable to read both a Psalm and part of one of these chapters.

The prayer which follows should consist of the following topics: An acknowledgment of God's sovereignty, and submission to His will; petitions for consolation to the mourners according to their varying circumstances, and that the bereavement may be sanctified to them, and be a warning to all; supplications for pardon, acceptance in, and union with Christ, who is the resurrection and the life; for the aids of the Holy Ghost, that we may walk in holiness and righteousness all our days, and that, living or dying, we may be the Lord's; thanksgiving for life and immortality brought to light by the Gospel, for the righteous departed, and all God's goodness to them in life and in death; prayers that their memory may be sanctified to us, and quicken us to holy and righteous living, so that we may meet them again in glory and in joy. And the whole may conclude in some such form as this: "And now be with us as we follow, to the house appointed for all living, the body of our dear brother or sister here departed,—not sorrowing as those who have no hope, but believing that, as Jesus died and rose again, even so them also which sleep in Jesus shall God bring with Him."

At the Grave.—If there be a service at the grave, it should be short, and of a more general character, as it is offered by the whole company, and not merely by mourners and immediate friends.

After the body has been lowered, the Minister, standing at the head of the grave, may repeat one or two verses of Scripture as to the great victory which Our Lord hath purchased for us by His death and resurrection. Nothing can be more congenial to Christian feeling than this triumphant proclamation of immortality made by

Christ's ambassador in the presence, as it were, of the great destroyer.

The prayer may begin with the words of committal, thus: "Almighty God, who hast been pleased to call out of this sinful and dying world the soul of our brother here departed, we commit his body to the ground, earth to earth, dust to dust, till that great day when earth and sea shall give up their dead, and when the Lord Jesus shall change our vile bodies, and make them like unto His own glorious Body, according to the mighty working whereby He is able to subdue all things to Himself." This is appropriately followed by earnest petitions for mercy and grace, that we may be faithful to the end; by thanksgiving for Christ's victory over death and the grave; and a prayer for the hastening of His Second Coming, when saints departed shall be raised, and those alive shall be changed, and so shall we ever be with the Lord. And the whole should close with the Benediction.

Suitable material for the prayers is to be found in those authorised by the General Assembly, in Dr Robert Lee's Book, Euchologion, the Reformed Liturgies, and the English Prayer-Book.

Let me strongly recommend you, in the prayers, to avoid everything of the nature of a eulogium of the deceased. Some localities are very much more guilty in this respect than others. Principal Hill says that Ministers, in conducting religious services, usually follow the customs of that part of the country where Providence has cast their lot. Thus it is that an objectionable practice is continued even by those who may not approve of it. I have often heard prayers at funerals which were beautiful pieces of composition, but which should have done duty as part of a funeral sermon, or of an obituary notice in the newspaper. These eulogiums are usually introduced thus: "We thank Thee," or "Thou knowest" that he was so and so, or did so and so; and if any excellence of which the public was not aware is to be touched upon, it is sometimes added, "And as some of us here know very well," he was this or that. "Thou knowest" is a phrase always to be suspected in a prayer, as it too often indicates that what is to follow is to be addressed not to the Most High, but to those who should be presenting their supplications to Him. Compliments are also occasionally paid to the surviving members of the family thus: "We thank Thee for," or "Thou knowest their faithfulness and devotion," and so on. And there are people who can hardly help criticising, and drawing comparisons as to the ability shown by different Ministers in this department of work. "Clever man, Dr ——," said a City Lawyer to me; "I had a good deal to do with him in connection with the funerals of old ladies—clients of mine —who were members of his flock. He used to take me aside, and ask me a few questions as to their habits and circumstances, and in the prayer, a few minutes afterwards, he brought in with great skill all that I told him about them." Better no funeral service at all than such eulogiums, at a time when we are brought face to face with the fearful wages of sin, and where all should be humbled in the dust before God. It is quite enough, even in the case of the eminently good and great, to give thanks for the Divine goodness to them in life and death, and for the holy example which they have left. Anything beyond this should be reserved for the funeral oration or sermon. Except in the matter of personal allusions, I have seldom heard anything objectionable in funeral prayers; but I have often been struck by the want of thanksgiving for the Lord's victory over death, and for the great hope of the resurrection of the dead. The different circumstances of the mourners obviously call for variety in petition for them, and in this matter you will find valuable help in the funeral prayers given in the General Assembly's Book. It was a very doubtful compliment that was paid to an old Minister whom I remember, who at a funeral complained to a Parishioner that his memory was failing. "Oh, I dinna think that, Sir," was the reply. "Your memory is just wonderful; for I heard you gie that same prayer which you gied us just now, word for word, thirty years ago." There are few occasions in which one feels the value of free prayer more than when called upon to commend a bereaved family to the compassion of Our Father in heaven.

The next two sections of the Directory are on Public Solemn Fasting and The Observation of Days of Public Thanksgiving; and on each of these subjects I shall offer a few remarks.

Public Solemn Fasting.

The only fixed Fast of universal obligation in the early Church was at Good Friday, "when the Bridegroom was taken away," and in obedience, as it was supposed, to His command. It usually lasted for forty hours—from 12 o'clock on Friday till Sunday morning, when Our Lord rose from the dead, and the sorrow of His disciples was turned into joy. This was called *quadragesima*, and it grew into the forty days of Lent; but originally the sole reference was to the period during which Our Lord was under the power of death, and not to His fasting in the wilderness. There were also the partial Fasts of every Wednesday and Friday, in remembrance of His betrayal and sufferings, but these were not obligatory; and Occasional Fasts appointed by the Bishops of particular churches, when circumstances called for special services of humiliation before God.

Our Church early took up the position, that to prescribe fixed anniversaries, as Fasts and Festivals, was contrary to the nature of sorrowing and rejoicing, and interfered with Christian liberty. This was the reason urged for the objections made to the keeping of the great Christian Anniversaries in common with the rest of the Reformed Church. It was held that days of Public Fasting or of Thanksgiving should be all occasional, and should be appointed from time to time by the Courts of the Church, or by Civil authority.

Again, our Church differed from the rest of Christendom as regards fasting on the Lord's Day. Sunday had always been considered a day of rejoicing, and the primitive Christians thought it sinful to fast upon it, so much so that any of the clergy guilty of this offence were to be deprived;[1] but our early Assemblies seem to have preferred it for this purpose, because the people could then most conveniently meet for worship.

In the Book of Common Order you find a treatise called "The Order of the General Fast," drawn up by Knox in 1565, at the request of the Assembly. This treatise contains regulations, prayers, psalms, and lessons for a fast of eight days, which was observed by the Church in the spring of that year, and frequently for forty years afterwards. No doubt this looks very like a substitute for Lent, which ceased to be observed religiously at the Reformation, though for many years after the Privy Council forbade the killing of cattle at that time. The Assembly, in enjoining the observance of this Fast from time to time, usually added that Knox's Order was to be followed. Strict abstinence from food, and from playing any kind of games, was required on only two days out of the eight, but moderate diet and the laying aside of

---

[1] "If any one of the clergy be found to fast on the Lord's Day or on the Sabbath Day, excepting one only (the Saturday before Easter), let him be deprived; but if he be one of the laity, let him be suspended."—Apost. Con., book viii. sec. 47.

gorgeous apparel was ordered for the rest of the time. In cities and towns the people were enjoined to assemble in Church for special religious exercises twice every day, while the Fast lasted; in the forenoon, when the Common Prayers were accustomed to be read—and in the afternoon, at three o'clock, or later. There were other annual Fasts at that period, such as those which were always kept at the opening of the General Assembly in the city where it met.

The Directory of Worship deals only with National Solemn Fasting, which is necessarily exceptional; but, as the section on this subject shows, as well as the other Westminster Standards, it was meant that there should be other Fast days throughout the year, appointed by the Church Courts. The Assembly of Divines regularly observed monthly fasts for seven years, and these were only finally put a stop to by Cromwell. Fasting, according to their ideas, involved not only abstinence from food, but from rich apparel, ornaments, and suchlike, at other times lawful. For long after this period Fast days were frequently appointed by the General Assembly and subordinate Courts of the Church; and in addition, as the biographies of the most godly people in our land show, family and private Fasts were quite common till a generation or two ago. But any time is proverbially no time, and all that remains publicly of this exercise is a National Fast at rare intervals, and what are called Fast days before the Communion. Not only so, but some of the Clergy have no scruples in preaching and in publishing sermons directly contrary to the standards of the Church on this subject. The Christian Church in all ages has regarded fasting as a divine institution, connected both with humiliation for sin and with bodily sanctification; and perhaps these divines might be better employed in considering whether the general neglect of this exercise has not something to do with the prevalence of intemperance and other sins of the flesh, and with the superficial views of repentance which are so common.

The public religious services on a Fast day should obviously be all of a penitential character. The prayers should consist more largely of confession than at other times. Even the thanksgiving should be mingled with acknowledgment of our unworthiness, and with earnest petitions that God's goodness may lead us to deeper penitence; while, as the Directory suggests, in the prayer after sermon it is highly proper that the

Minister should for himself and the congregation renounce the sins and shortcomings which they have confessed, and engage themselves to reform whatever is amiss in their conduct. Special Psalms and Chapters bearing upon the great work of the day, such as you will find indicated in Knox's Order of the Fast, and in other Tables of Lessons, should be selected, and the sermon should be a special one in harmony with the occasion. Anything more unseasonable, as I have already said, than a Minister airing some popular discourse which has nothing to do with penitence or forgiveness, when he and his hearers are professedly humbling themselves in the dust before God, can hardly be conceived of. Even the old Moderates, who in their confession on Fast days were said not to go much lower than this—"We acknowledge that we have not lived according to the dictates of reason,"—had sufficient sense of the fitness of things to preach at such times against prevailing sins, and to reserve their more popular and showy sermons for other occasions.

Days of Public Thanksgiving.

The next Section deals with Public Worship on Days of Thanksgiving for national mercies, such as the restoration of peace and deliverance from plague or pestilence, to which may be added plenteous harvests. The directions for such services are, that in prefacing, the Minister should give "a word of Exhortation, to stir up the people to the duty for which they are met;" that after the opening prayer, he should make "some pithy narration of the deliverance obtained, or mercy received;" that suitable psalms and chapters should be selected, and that prominence should be given to Praise, as "of all other the most proper Ordinance for expressing of joy and thanksgiving;" that the sermon should be from a text pertinent to the occasion ; and that, in the prayers, solemn thanksgiving should be given to God for all His former mercies, and especially for that one which has called them together. It is also ordered that a special collection should be made for the poor, and it is suggested that the services should be shorter than on other days, and—though very cautiously—that the people should "eat the fat and drink the sweet," and spend the rest of the day in social intercourse and in testification of Christian love and charity one towards another.

These counsels are all appropriate to our time, though "the pithy narration" is now usually incorporated with the sermon. Days of Thanksgiving are Festivals, not Fasts. This is so little understood in some parts of the country, and religion is so much associated with gloom, that you will hear people speak of a Fast day for a good harvest. Gladness and holy joy should characterise, in a far greater degree than they usually do, our ordinary Public Worship, while the services on a day of thanksgiving should be of an exceptionally bright and cheerful character. The Lessons and Psalms should be appropriate, as far as possible, to the particular mercy for which we give thanks. In many portions of the Church it is usual on such occasions to sing the Te Deum as a special Act of thanksgiving, and happily we can now follow a practice which has been so widely approved. While all the prayers should be full of acknowledgments of God's goodness, it is perhaps best to give the special prayer of thanksgiving after the sermon, when the mercy received has been spoken of at length. The people should be taught that liberality in almsgiving is, like the joyful singing of Psalms, one of the proper characteristics of a thanksgiving service; and also that, when the religious exercises are over, the rest of the day may properly be spent in innocent recreation and in visits to friends and neighbours. Our people have too few holidays, and this is one cause of the desecration of Fast Days. In most other countries, besides New-Year's Day and Christmas, there are days of observance in which religious services are combined with rest and relaxation. Even the United States of America, which are so largely dominated by Puritan traditions, have their annual Thanksgiving Day, when the fatted calf is killed; and this has recently been imitated by the Dominion of Canada. We might, at least, have annually a Harvest Festival in all our Parishes on a week-day, as is universal in England, and also within the bounds of one or two of our own Synods. The subject deserves more attention from the Church than it has yet received.

LECTURE V.

ORDINATION— LICENSING OF PROBATIONERS—ADMISSION OF ELDERS—CHURCH DISCIPLINE.

THE principal subjects of Lecture to-day are Ordination, and Church Discipline. We are now done with the Directory of Public Worship; but there are two other Treatises drawn up by the Westminster Assembly, and usually bound up with the Confession of Faith, which guide us in these departments of Ministerial duty—viz., The Form of Church Government, and The Directory for Church Government, Church Censures, and Ordination of Ministers.

Ordination.

The Form of Presbyterial Church Government, and of Ordination of Ministers, agreed upon by the Synod of Divines, was approved by our General Assembly in 1645, and is "mentioned as ratified in several Acts of Parliament" during the Covenanting era. It has not been revived either by Church or State since 1690. At the Revolution the Scottish Parliament abolished Prelacy, restored the old Government of the Church, as legalised by the Act of 1592, commonly called the Charter of Presbytery. It is to that Act we have to look for the legal Government of the Church as an established institution of the Empire, and anything contrary to it is *ultra vires*. Many of the details, however, are not filled in, and under it the Church enjoys a very large amount of liberty. She can change, for example, the bounds of Presbyteries, limit or extend the representation to the General Assembly, and could, if she thought fit, revive the order of Visitors or Superintendents, as the Assembly of 1593 continued these officers under the Presbyterian system,—an arrangement which might have been permanent, had it not been for the reaction caused by the persistent attempts of King James to introduce Episcopacy.

The Civil legislation of 1690 has been supplemented by various Acts of Assembly bearing upon the Ordination of Ministers and the Government of the Church; and as all these Acts have been based upon the Westminster documents, or taken verbatim from them, we may regard them as expressive of the mind of the Church on the subjects of which they treat. The statements of the Confession of Faith with regard to Ministers, are to be read in the light of these documents, —as, for example, when it is said, they must be "lawfully ordained;" and further, they are in substantial harmony with the Act of 1592.

As to the *doctrine* of Ordination, the leading principles of the Westminster Standards are the two following: 1. No man ought to take upon him the office of a Minister of the Gospel until he be lawfully called and ordained thereto by those who, having been set apart themselves to the work of the ministry, have power to set apart others. 2. Every Minister of the Word is to be ordained by imposition of hands, with prayer and fasting.

THE ORDAINERS.

With regard to the Ordainers, the Form of Church Government declares that the power of ordination belongs to preaching Presbyters, and this is, of course, a fundamental principle of Presbyterianism. At the Revolution Settlement our Church was established on the basis of the Claim of Right, and specially on the clause of it which asserted that this Church had originally been reformed—not by the laity, nor by Prelates, but by Presbyters—viz., Knox, and other Priests, his coadjutors. The General Assembly in 1695 passed an Act, in which they unanimously declare, that they allow no power to the people, but only in the Pastors of the Church, to ordain Church Officers. And in 1701 the Church revived, or, as Pardovan says, ratified an Act of 1647, directed against the errors of sectarianism and separation, which it describes as spreading like a gangrene, and eating as a canker, and in which all the members of the Church are forbidden to converse with persons tainted with such errors, or to circulate their books. So late as 1842, the Assembly, while repealing a former Act, prohibiting Ministers from employing on any occasion to preach, or from holding ministerial communion in any other manner with, persons not qualified to accept a presentation according to the laws of the Church —an Act which excluded all Presbyterian Dissenters from our pulpits,—enjoined, at the same time, " all Ministers to guard against holding ministerial communion with men who are not duly ordained."

It is the doctrine of the Church that Presbyters

are the successors of the Apostles in all the ordinary functions of the ministry, and this excludes the claim of Prelates to ordain as an order above Presbyters, leaving them only the same power of order as that which belongs to all who are admitted to the Presbyterate. All the Reformed Churches held that there are only two orders, in the ministry, of divine appointment —those of Bishop or Presbyter, and Deacon. The first of these was instituted by Christ Himself in commissioning the eleven, and hence we read of no separate institution of this office, as in the case of the Diaconate. When the Apostles originated the Diaconate as recorded in Acts vi., the platform of Church Government was complete as to its essential features; and it may be questioned whether any single Apostle had power to set up a new office. It is fully admitted that there are traces of superintendency in Scripture apart from that of the Apostles, as in the case of Timothy and Titus, and the frank acknowledgment of this should be made alike in the interests of truth and of Christian reunion; but it is held that they and others raised to like posts of eminency, whether called Bishops, as in post-apostolic times, or not, no more belonged to an order of the ministry above that of Presbyter, than did the

Scottish Superintendents after the Reformation, or the Moderators of our Church Courts now.[1] Episcopacy is, in short, according to this view, but a phase of Presbytery; and there never has, nor can be, any ordination to the ministry except by Presbyters, call them what you will.

One reason why these views were so prevalent at the Reformation was, that they had been generally accepted in the Church before. Popes and Reforming Councils had alike committed themselves to the position that a Bishop is by order no more than a Presbyter, and that his pre-eminence is merely of ecclesiastical, not of divine, right. This question was purposely kept open by the Council of Trent, and the old view is still common in the Roman Catholic Church.

In England, Bishops took part in the Reformation, which was not, to any great extent, the case elsewhere, but the English Church was at that time of the same mind on this subject as the rest of the Reformed. In the Book called 'The Institution of a Christian Man,' which was published in 1536, and approved both by the Lords Temporal

---

[1] The whole Episcopal controversy turns upon the *making* of Presidents in the Primitive Church. It is a remarkable fact that while the Apostolic Constitutions enjoin the laying on of hands at the ordination of Presbyters, this is omitted in the directions for the making of Bishops.

and Spiritual, it is declared that there are only two orders in the ministry of divine appointment, and that the pre-eminence of Bishops was of man. The English ordinal contained nothing to distinguish the order of Bishop from that of Presbyter, between the Reformation and the time of Charles II., when it was amended; so that, as has been said, if the former is a superior order, Protestant Episcopacy was a hundred years too late in introducing it.[1] The Minister of a Parish within the bounds of the Presbytery of Haddington having gone to England, was licensed by Archbishop Grindal in 1582, to celebrate Divine Offices and minister the Sacraments throughout the Province of Canterbury; and the Licence bears that, "as he was admitted and ordained to sacred orders and the Holy Ministry by the imposition of hands, according to the laudable form and rite of the Reformed Church of Scotland," the Archbishop approves and ratifies the form of his ordination done in the manner aforesaid. From the Reformation till the passing of the Act of Uniformity there were "scores, if not

[1] It was the case of Gordon, a Scottish Bishop, who in 1704 joined the Church of Rome, which led that Church to give its decision on the question of Anglican Orders. It ordered Gordon to be reordained, as the English form was not valid; also to be confirmed, as he had not received that rite.

hundreds,"[1] of Clergymen in the Church of England who had no ordination except what they had received from Scottish Presbyters, or from the Reformed Churches on the Continent.

In Scotland, though several Bishops became Ministers in the Reformed Church, the Reformation had been mainly achieved by Presbyters, and the sympathy of our forefathers with the Continental Reformed Churches, disposed them to favour the model of Church Government which they had adopted. Superintendents were, however, admitted at first; and although, on the strength of a clause in the First Book of Discipline, it is commonly said that they were not intended to be permanent, this is not borne out by the Records of the Assembly, which continued for many years to urge the Government to provide funds so that they might be planted throughout the whole country. The Superintendent system was regarded as the most effective, and what proved fatal to it was the

[1] Neal's History of the Puritans, vol. i. p. 303. Durel gives many instances of foreign Reformed Clergy preaching in the Anglo-Gallican Churches, when visiting England. Adrian Saravia, Prebendary of Canterbury, from whom Hooker received Absolution and the Holy Communion on his deathbed, was first a Minister of the Reformed Church of Holland, and there is not the slightest evidence of his having received Episcopal ordination.

subsequent controversy betwixt Prelacy and Presbytery.

The survival of some of the elements of the old Celtic Church had also a tendency in the direction of Presbytery. In the early Scottish and Irish Churches, the primitive and apostolic practice of consecrating all Presbyters Bishops seems to have prevailed longer than elsewhere, and when a distinction between these offices was introduced, the Bishops had no jurisdiction, but held a very subordinate place under the Presbyter Abbot of the Celtic Monastery. There were no Parishes nor Diocesan Bishops in Scotland in the days of the Columban Church. The hierarchy was of only a few centuries' standing at the time of the Reformation,—the Archbishopric of St Andrews itself only dating from the previous century, so that it had not the same prestige as in other countries.

But it is of more importance to notice,—what was certainly considered of far greater moment by the compilers of our standards,—the question as to the right or power of the laity to ordain Church officers. Does the principle "non det qui non habet" hold here as in other things?

This subject was thoroughly discussed by the Westminster Divines and Scottish Commissioners, and there are no stronger statements to be found anywhere than in their writings—such, for example, as the "Jus Divinum Ministerii Evangelici" on the necessity of a succession in the ministry. The fundamental difference betwixt them and the Independents was, that they considered all church power to be vested in the office-bearers, not in the body of the Church.[1] Further, they held that our Lord's promises were a pledge that the ministry could never fail; that Ordination makes the Minister as Baptism makes the member of the Church; that, notwithstanding the corruption of Rome, her Ordination was no less valid than her Baptism, and that if this were not so, the continuity of the Visible Church would be destroyed. It was almost one of their commonplaces, that if a person presumed to minister without a valid Ordination, he was to be asked to work a miracle, and if he failed, he was to be rejected as an impostor. Even in their testimonials of Orders, they were careful to state the doctrine of succession. Take the following as an example: "Forasmuch as the Lord Jesus

---

[1] Baillie's MS. Lectures on this subject, preserved in the Library of Glasgow University, have the following heading: "A brief refutation of the doctrine of Independency, wherein it is shown that the power of Church Government is in the Church officers, and not in the body of the Church."

Christ . . . has judged it meet that there should be a succession of pastors and teachers in His Church even unto the end of the world, . . . and hath deputed the care of the continuation of this ministerial office unto such as have been already called thereunto, requiring them to commit the things they have received unto faithful men, who shall be able to teach others also: We, the Ministers of Christ . . . in the City of York, . . . have upon the 23d day of June 1654 proceeded solemnly to set . . . M. N. apart unto the office of a Presbyter and work of the ministry by laying on our hands, with fasting and prayer: By the virtue whereof we do esteem and declare him a lawful Minister of Christ, and hereby recommend him," &c.[1]

But it may be asked, Were they not too late in putting forward these views, or, if the English succession remained unbroken, had not that of Scotland been fatally vitiated? In books of some repute you will find it stated that Knox derived his sole authority to minister in word and sacrament from the call of the congregation of St Andrews; that our Reformers gave up the laying on of hands; that the early Protestant Clergy were mere laymen; and that hence, to quote the words

[1] Calamy's Life of Baxter, p. 454.

of an English Ecclesiastical Journal, "The Church of Scotland has not the shadow of a claim to so much as a Presbyterian succession." Many of the English Clergy believe that we are in the same position as the Independents, who have neither the intention nor the power to ordain; or as the Wesleyan Methodists, who do intend it, but who, unfortunately for their intentions, only began the form of Ordination in 1836, when all the Presbyters who had taken part in originating that movement were dead, and only lay preachers were left.

Now our divines in the seventeenth century would not have taken up the position they did, as to a succession in the ministry, if they had not been perfectly certain as to the ground on which they themselves stood. No one questioned the fact of their having such a succession at that time, and their main controversy was with the Sectaries, who condemned their ministry, not because it had not, but because it had been derived through the Church of Rome. It was not at Episcopalians, but at the Presbyterians, then dominant in England, that Cromwell was hitting when, in 1653, he wrote thus: "I speak not—I thank God it is far from my heart—for a ministry deriving itself from the Papacy, and pretending to that *which is so much insisted on—succession.* The true succession is through the Spirit."[1]

In Scotland there were some irregularities after the Reformation, as indeed there had been before, but these were not sufficient to break the chain. *Nearly all the old Clergy became Reformed* as soon as they saw that a change was inevitable. The first Protestant Ministers, with few exceptions, had been Priests,—some of them ecclesiastics of high standing under the previous system. For example, the six Johns who drew up the First Book of Discipline, had all been Priests, and most of them men of mark in the Pre-Reformation Church. The laying on of hands was probably omitted at first in some cases in the setting apart of new Clergy, as it was in the induction of old Priests to the charge of Reformed congregations. But if so, this ceremony was restored while the ranks of the old Clergy remained almost unbroken by death. We read of its being practised in 1572, five years after the Church was established. Archbishop Grindal speaks of it as the laudable custom of the Church at the time of John Morrison's ordination, which took place some years before his reception into the Church of England; and the Second Book of Discipline,

[1] Carlyle's Letters of Cromwell, vol. ii. p. 353.

drawn up in 1577, asserts it to be necessary. One of the first who wrote in defence of the validity of the Scottish ministry—the illustrious Patrick Forbes of Corse, afterwards Bishop of Aberdeen who was born in 1564—says that their Romish adversaries were more than impudent to deny that the Reformed Clergy had a lawful ordinary calling.[1]

But there is another and conclusive answer to such statements as those I have referred to. In 1612 Episcopal ordination was introduced from England. Spottiswoode and others were consecrated Bishops at Lambeth without reordination, the validity of their previous orders being recognised. From that time till 1638 all who were admitted to the ministry were ordained by Bishops of the Spottiswoode line, *with the assistance of other Presbyters*, as is still the case in the English Church. Any exceptions to this rule were such as that of Dr John Forbes of Corse, perhaps the greatest theologian our Church has ever produced, who, when his father was Bishop of Aberdeen, was ordained by his uncle, the exiled Minister of Alford, and other Presbyters, on the Continent; but there is no evidence of any one being ordained

---

[1] Defence of the Lawful Calling of the Ministers of Reformed Churches: Middleburg, 1614.

to the ministry in Scotland during that period without the laying on of Episcopal hands. It is usually stated in the biographies of Samuel Rutherford that he contrived to become Minister of Anwoth in 1627 without Episcopal ordination; but there seems to be no more foundation for this than there is for the somewhat similar statement in the life of George Gillespie, that on finishing his education for the ministry he could not conscientiously submit to receive ordination from a Bishop, and accordingly became tutor in the family of the Earl of Cassilis, waiting for better times. He did become Chaplain, first to Lord Kenmure, Rutherford's Patron, and, on his death, to the Earl of Cassilis; but he seems merely to have been waiting, as many have had to do since, for a presentation to a parish. The records of the Presbytery of Kirkcaldy show that at the time of the great Revolution of 1637 he had been presented to the parish of Wemyss, and was under trials for ordination prescribed by Archbishop Spottiswoode, and that he would have been ordained by him forthwith had not the government of the Church been changed. His father, "the thundering preacher" of Kirkcaldy, and many relatives, who were among the most distinguished men on the popular side of the Church

—such as the Simsons, and Adamson, Principal of the University of Edinburgh, and an active member of the Glasgow Assembly of 1638—had all acted on the principle that the existence of Episcopacy, as then in force, was no sufficient ground for schism,—and he was doubtless of the same mind. Thus the great body of the Clergy who reintroduced Presbyterian ordination after 1637 were Presbyters who had been Episcopally ordained, and no one disputes the regularity of the succession since. Moreover, they had not been restricted from ordaining by any act of the Church.

Curiously enough, it is scarcely possible for those who hold that Prelacy, as existing in the English Church, is a higher order of the ministry by divine right, to deny that our Clergy share it in common with the Southern Hierarchy. Several of the Bishops of 1638 remained in the Church as Parish Ministers, and we can point to ordinations after that time when a Bishop was the consecrator, and when, in his intention and that of the Church, the whole powers of the ministry were conferred. Those thus consecrated Bishops, in the ecclesiastical sense of the word, consecrated others, and the process has been going on ever since. Like the old Catholic and the Moravian

Episcopates, this rests, so far as I know, on a single link,—that of Fairley, Bishop of Argyle, afterwards Minister of Lasswade; but our English friends, who admit the validity of these other successions, cannot on any good grounds deny that our parish Ministers have received authority from an Episcopal source to discharge all the functions of the Christian ministry,—not only to preach the Word and administer the Sacraments, but to exercise jurisdiction and to ordain.[1]

In 1661, when the State restored Episcopacy, a new bevy of Clergy were despatched to England and consecrated Bishops, and some of them were not only consecrated but reordained, because of the Act of Uniformity, which for the first time made this necessary. On returning to Scotland, they did not reordain others who were raised to the Episcopate, nor the Clergy who during the previous twenty-three years had been ordained by Presbyteries, and who remained on in their Parishes, as the great majority did. After the Revolution, when a section separated and formed the

---

[1] "The Church many times admitted of the ordinations of Bishops that were consecrated only by one or two Bishops."—Bingham, book ii. chap. xi. sec. 5. There was no general form of ordination at first. "Every Bishop used such a form as he thought convenient."—Bingham, book ii. chap. xix. sec. 17.

Scottish Episcopal Communion, two of the three Bishops who carried on the succession were of this number, and several of the first Clergy who adhered to them had no other than Presbyterian ordination. Indeed both parties at that time generally held the old Reformed view,—that, whether Episcopacy or Presbytery might be preferable, they were only different ways of marshalling officers of the same order. Hence it was that, in 1692, 180 Ministers, in the name of the whole Episcopal Clergy of the North, which was their stronghold, addressed the Assembly, asking admission into the Presbyterian Establishment. Hence, too, the somewhat remarkable statement of Dr Calamy, in his Autobiography. During his visit to Scotland in 1709, he attended the sittings of the General Assembly, and was in the habit of meeting every evening with a company of leading Clergymen from all the Synods of the Church. Not one of them, he tells us, "was for the *Jure Divino* of the Presbyterian form of Church Government, though they freely submitted to it."[1]

I have thought it important to put you in possession of these facts as to the derivation of our ministry. The subject is one which many of the most learned and devout men of every age have

[1] Life and Times, vol. ii. p. 153.

regarded as fundamental, and it is no proof of wisdom or enlightenment to make little of it. On the one hand you have men, like our great divines in former days, declaring that it is a greater presumption for any one to usurp the Gospel ministry than it would have been for a person to have usurped the High Priest's office under the Old Dispensation; that there is no hope of Christian union, except on the basis of a ministry derived by succession from Apostolic times; and that the lack of any Divine ordinance involves, possibly at least, the loss of grace. On the other hand you have those who attach no value to ordination of any kind. Thus, John Foster tells us that he had been in the uniform habit of ridiculing dissenting ordination. "It carries," he says, "an appearance, . . . a sort of pretension of conferring some kind of . . . authorisation to perform the duties of a Christian Minister. Now my wish would be that every notion and practice of this kind—in short, everything sacerdotal and ceremonial—were cleared out of our religious economy. . . . In two places where . . . I have sustained the settled ministerial office, I have declined . . . all such formality of appointment."[1] He refers to the celebrated

[1] Foster's Life, vol. ii. pp. 109-111.

Robert Hall as being in the same predicament; but Hall did not go through the ceremony, because the people were opposed to it. When asked, long afterwards, Why he never was ordained, he replied, "Because, Sir, I was a fool." Sentiments which strike at the root of a Divinely authorised ministry are by no means uncommon, even among those calling themselves Presbyterians. I observed some time ago that the following statement was received at a public meeting in Scotland with immense applause: "I am a determined enemy of sacerdotalism, by which I mean any system which invests any order of men with powers which are not common to the great bulk of mankind." About the same time a Parish Minister was reported to have expressed himself thus, amid the cheers of his auditors: "I disdain the title of Clergyman. I am simply a Minister—a servant of the Church. We are in no respect whatever authorised by God more than any other individual member of the Church, from whom immediately we hold our commission." These views and those of the Westminster Divines are wide as the poles asunder. It seems to me evident that either ordination by those already in office is essential to the lawful exercise of the ministry, or that any one can take it upon himself who pleases; and it would be difficult to exaggerate the importance of the questions involved in accepting one or other of these positions.

THE FORM OF ORDINATION.

Turning now to the Form of Ordination, the Directory states that "Every Minister of the Word is to be ordained by Imposition of Hands and Prayer, with Fasting, by those Preaching Presbyters to whom it doth belong." For many years after the Reformation, the form for admitting Superintendents was the basis of the ordinary Ordination service. After 1612, the English ordinal was often used; and in 1620, new Forms were introduced by the Bishops, mainly taken from the English Prayer-Book, but containing some features of the old Scottish service.[1] From 1645 till 1661 the Westminster Directory for Ordination was followed, and it has been practically resumed since 1690. The special Acts founded upon it have been consolidated of late years. The legislation of the Church in this department is, however, less complete than in

[1] For these Forms see Miscellany of the Wodrow Society, vol. i. p. 597.

any other. The service is still to some extent merely traditional. The want of a Directory for ordination with undoubted Church authority is felt all the more that the duty of presiding on such occasions is often settled by rotation. Hence it frequently falls to the youngest man, who, in the case of a translation, may be called upon, after he has been only a few weeks in the ministry, to address solemn counsels on the discharge of pastoral duty to a person who was ordained before he was born. This is like a subaltern on the parade-ground counselling a General on the art of war, and is obviously not in strict accordance with the eternal fitness of things.

In drawing up an Ordination Service, one requires to consult the directions given in the Form of Church Government and the Acts of Assembly passed on the subject since 1690. It is important also to refer to the Larger Overtures of 1705, as they contain a Directory of Ordination based on that of Westminster, and meant as a substitute for it, though never legalised.

A Fast to be kept.—The Directory enjoins that on the "Day appointed for Ordination . . . a solemn Fast shall be kept by the Congregation, that they may the more earnestly join in prayer for a blessing upon the ordinance of Christ." And the Second Book of Discipline also mentions fasting as one of the ceremonies of ordination. Henderson, in describing the order of the Church in his time, says that on the day of ordination "a Fast is ordained to be kept." The Larger Overtures, which give the practice in the early part of last century, direct that when intimation of the ordination is made by the Presbytery, the people are at the same time to be told that "the day is to be set apart as a Fast unto the parish;" but it seems there was then a difference of opinion as to "whether that or another day should be the day of the Fast." The intention was that the parishioners were to fast rather than the Presbytery; at all events, that the fast should end with the public service so far as they were concerned. I remember asking a venerable clergyman at an ordination dinner, Whether we were not transgressing the old laws of the Church in sitting down to a sumptuous repast? "No," was the unhesitating reply—"the Fast is over now." Fasting at ordinations has not been enjoined since the Revolution; and though common for a time afterwards, in accordance with Scripture and Catholic usage, it has been wholly discontinued, except when a Presbytery has to fast involuntarily. I believe that nowadays the solemn service is not only usually followed by a dinner, but crowned with a soiree.

THE SERVICE.

At the hour for Public Worship the Ministers should enter the church in order, and take their places near the pulpit or Communion Table. In such processions the ancient rule is that the Juniors go first, and the Fathers of the Presbytery last. It is not seemly for them to enter like a rabble, or with less dignity and decorum than are shown by the Judges of the land when they take their places in a Civil Court.

The presiding Minister then conducts Public Worship in the usual manner. The sermon, the Directory says, should be on "the office and duty of Ministers of Christ, and how the people ought to receive them for their work's sake." It would be well if this old rule were always strictly adhered to, as the occasion is one which affords an excellent opportunity for discussing important subjects which many Ministers do not care to bring before their people at other times, and which are far too much overlooked.

Special Psalms and Lessons bearing upon the work of the day should also be selected.

After the sermon, the presiding Minister "narrates the cause of the vacancy, and the steps which have been taken in filling it up." This narrative may conclude thus: "All having accordingly been done in this matter as required by the law and usage of the Church, the Presbytery will now proceed to ordain the said A. B. to the Holy Ministry, and (if he is also to be inducted) thereafter to receive and admit him to the ———— as soon as he shall have answered satisfactorily the questions appointed by the Church."

He then calls upon the candidate, who stands up before the pulpit, and answers the questions prescribed by Act x., 1711.

These questions are founded on those indicated in the Directory of Ordination, but are much more minute. The only creed imposed by the Westminster order is "Faith in Jesus Christ, and persuasion of the truth of the Reformed religion according to the Scriptures;" and this must have guided the practice of the Church after 1645. The Questions in the Larger Overtures are intermediate betwixt this and those of 1711, and are no doubt such as were asked after the Revolution.

The creed imposed is as follows: "If he believe the Scriptures of the Old and New Testaments, and the truths therein contained, to be the Word of God? If he doth own and will adhere to the Confession of Faith and Catechisms of this Church founded on and consonant to the Holy Scriptures?" In other respects the questions are simpler and less rigid than those now prescribed.

Satisfactory answers having been given, a Psalm or Hymn may be sung. By common consent of Christendom, the Veni Creator, composed by King Robert II. of France (996-1031), and of which our 54th Hymn is a translation, is peculiarly appropriate at this time. The most suitable version, which you find in Knox's Psalm-Book, and also in the English Ordination Service, as an alternative to our 54th Hymn, is unfortunately not in our Hymnal.

Act of Ordination.—The presiding Minister then comes down from the pulpit, and, to use the words of the latest Act on the subject, "by prayer and imposition of hands, in which all the Ministers present are to join," "ordains" the candidate, "and sets him apart to the work of the Holy Ministry." In the Larger Overtures it is said the candidate is to kneel, and this has always been the practice in Scotland as throughout the rest of Christendom.

The ordination prayer given in the Directory, and also verbatim in the Larger Overtures, is very short, but the topics suggested are all most appropriate. That in Knox's Liturgy is fuller, and may be consulted with advantage. The prayer in Euchologion is based on these and other Reformed services. The whole ordination service in that volume is the work of the late Principal Campbell of Aberdeen, who from the outset took a deep interest in the Church Service Society, and who, I may take the liberty of saying, was not only one of the most accomplished and learned of Scottish theologians, but was remarkably distinguished for his familiarity with the early history of the Reformed Church, and for his sympathy with its true spirit. He was a genuine representative of that Church in its most flourishing days, before its glory was tarnished by rationalism in some countries, and by ultra-puritanism in others.

The prayer should begin with thanksgiving to God for His great mercy in sending Jesus Christ for our redemption, and specially for that when He had ascended up on high He shed down the Holy Ghost, and gave gifts unto men, Apostles and Prophets, Evangelists, Pastors, and Teachers, that they might, in perpetual succession, feed, and guide, and build up the Church, promising to be with them always till the end of the world.

The prayer should then proceed in such a form as follows: "We further thank Thee for choosing and inclining this Thy servant to take part in this great work. And as we, in Thy Name, do now ordain him a Presbyter in Thy Church, and commit unto him authority to minister Thy Word and Sacraments, and to discharge all the duties of that Holy office, O do Thou, who healest what is infirm, and suppliest what is wanting, receive and strengthen him for Thy service, giving him the unction of the Holy Ghost."[1]

This should be followed with supplications for all needful gifts and graces, that he may fulfil the work of the ministry in all things, and both save himself and the people committed to his charge.

It is at the second paragraph, when reference is made to the candidate, and immediately before the solemn moment of ordination, that the pre-

[1] "It was not thought necessary to express all or any of the offices of a Presbyter in particular, but only in general to pray for grace to be given to the priest then ordained, whereby he might be enabled to perform them."—Bingham, book ii., chap. xx. sec. 17.

siding Minister, and those who assist him, impose hands. One should be especially careful as to the form of words used in this paragraph; and though it is sufficient to admit to the office according to its Divine institution, it is well also to specify its principal duties.

The Christian Church in all ages has held that several ministers should take part in ordination, and that it is irregular, though not necessarily invalid, when done by a single person. Further, I need hardly remind you that the powers of the office are not conferred by the ordainers, any more than is the grace of Sacraments imparted by those who administer them. The powers of the Christian Ministry were conferred by the Head of the Church once for all, and though coming through appointed channels, they descend from Him upon the person ordained, who is admitted to a participation of them in virtue of the office with which he is regularly invested.

According to the Larger Overtures, when the prayer is ended, the Minister who moderates in the action is to take the person ordained by the right hand, saying unto him, "We give unto you the right hand of fellowship to take part of the ministry with us;" and this is the general practice of the Church. In this, as in many other points, Stewart of Pardovan copies these Overtures verbatim, and he has been the great authority with successive generations of clergy.

If the person ordained is also to be inducted to a charge, this should be done as a separate act when the minister returns to the pulpit, and in these words: " In the Name of the Lord Jesus Christ, and by appointment of this Presbytery, I admit you to the pastoral charge of the Parish of ——, and to all the rights and privileges belonging thereto."

Exhortation.—He is then " briefly to exhort him to consider the greatness of his office and work, the danger of negligence both to himself and to his people, the blessing which will accompany his faithfulness in this life and that to come; and withal to exhort the people to carry themselves to him as their minister in the Lord."

Prayer.—He is next " to commend both him and his flock to the grace of God." It is in this prayer that special supplications should be made for the right discharge of their mutual duties, and after this the usual intercession should be offered.

Praise.—A Psalm or Hymn is then sung, such as the 192d in the Hymnal, and the whole service concludes with the Benediction.

In the case of the *Induction* of a Minister already ordained, the presiding Presbyter, after reading the questions of Act x. 1711, " calls on him to declare his adherence to, and renewal of, the answers formerly given." He then passes at once to the words, " In the Name of the Lord Jesus Christ, and by appointment of this Presbytery, I admit you," &c., as before. He then proceeds to the charge and prayer of institution. In a late Act of Assembly on the subject, it is ordered that immediately after the words of admission and before the charge, " the brethren present shall give him the right hand of fellowship." It is usual and appropriate for them to take him by the hand in token of welcome; but, as it is pointed out in the Larger Overtures, the expression both of giving him the right hand of fellowship and taking him to a part of the ministry, "should be omitted, seeing he was received therein at his ordination." Some of these matters have not been so carefully considered in later enactments of Assembly as they were in former days.

There were various other ceremonies long in use at ordinations and inductions in Presbyterian as well as Episcopal times, which have now gone out of fashion in most if not in all Presbyteries.

Thus institution was formerly given by the presiding Presbyter delivering to the newly ordained Pastor the pulpit Bible, and by putting into his hands the key of the Church and the bell-strings.

This was done at the close of the service, as appears, *e.g.*, from the following extract from the Records of the Presbytery of Perth in 1700: " The Moderator having closed the action with prayer and praise, gave the said Mr C. institution by delivering him the Kirk Bible, key of the Kirk doors, and bell-strings; whereupon Mr C. for his part, and J. B., elder, in name of the rest of the elders and parishioners, asked and took instruments in the Clerk's hands."

It is to be regretted that old customs so full of meaning should have been allowed to fall into desuetude. The giving of the Bible is so appropriate that it forms an integral part of the ordination service in many branches of the Church; while the handing of the keys and bell-strings to the new incumbent by the Presbytery, in whose custody they had been during the vacancy, means that they give him full power over them.

The lawyers have already taken possession of the churchyards on behalf of the Heritors, without any authority, I believe, and some of them are now disposed to put forth a similar claim to the custody of the keys of the Church. They might just as well lay claim to the custody of the keys of the Manse or of the Minister's stable. Such claims would not have been thought of if the old custom of handing the keys to the Minister had always been kept up, as it has been in England. It is not creditable to Presbytery that any ecclesiastical right which it inherited from previous and stronger systems of Church government, should be sacrificed through its remissness.

It was also formerly the custom for the Heritors and Elders to take the Minister by the hand in token of their concurrence and assent to his admission, immediately after he had received the right hand of fellowship from his Copresbyters; but the present practice is that they join with the rest of the congregation in doing this at the church-door after the service. It is usual to intimate that the people will have this opportunity, but it should not be done as I have sometimes heard it, thus: "As you leave the church you will have an opportunity of giving your Pastor *the right hand of fellowship.*"

Licensing Probationers.

This can scarcely be considered one of the public services of the Church, as it takes place at an ordinary meeting of Presbytery. The only regulations on the subject are, that after Students of Divinity have completed their trials, the questions prescribed by the Assembly of 1711 are to be put to them, and upon satisfactory answers being given, "the Presbytery are to appoint their Moderator to license them to preach the Gospel." Licentiates were formerly called Expectants, and there is no legislation of any importance with regard to them till after the Revolution Settlement, when the Church enacted that they were only "to preach within the bounds, or by direction of that Presbytery which did license them." It was also "expressly provided and declared that probationers are not to be esteemed by themselves or others to preach by virtue of any pastoral office, but only to make way for their being called to a pastoral charge." It is the practice in Presbyteries for the Moderator to address some counsels to young men when licensed to make trial of their gifts in public; but prayers are not offered on such occasions. If they were, there might be some danger of confounding probationership for the ministry with the ministry itself. In many of the Continental Reformed Churches candidates for the ministry, on completing their trials, are ordained without waiting for their appointment to a charge. Practically our licentiate is a substitute for the preaching Deacon of Episcopal Communions; and some of the greatest defenders of Presbyterian Church Government have held that the Diaconate is the divinely instituted nursery for the Presbyterate, and was typified by the Levitical order out of which the priesthood was chosen of old.

Admission of Elders.

The admission of members of Kirk-session takes place during Public Worship on the Lord's Day, but there are no regulations on the subject in the Westminster Standards.

An order for the election of Elders and Deacons was adopted by the Church in Edinburgh soon after the Reformation, and in 1582 was approved by the Assembly for general use throughout the Church. The form consisted of a short address, a prayer to be read, ending with the Lord's Prayer, and the rehearsal of the Belief. After this, part of the 103d Psalm, at the 19th verse, was to be sung, and a short exhortation given to those who were elected. At that time, and for long afterwards, indeed in some parts of the country till the early part of last century, elders were usually elected annually, and held office only for a year. The old form was in general use before 1645, and no other was then substituted for it. Elders were continued under both the first and the second Episcopacy, and were, I presume, admitted to office in the same way as when the Church was under Presbyterian Government. The legislation on the subject after 1690 is defective, and the practice has at times been very irregular. In 1863 an Act was passed professedly consolidating, but also in some respects supplementing, the previous legislation, and this regulates the present practice of the Church.

According to it the Minister is to put to the persons chosen for the office certain questions "implied" in previous Acts of Assembly. He is then to set them apart to the eldership by prayer, accompanied with an exhortation to them, and an address to the people. After the congregation is dismissed they are to receive the right hand of fellowship from their brethren in the Session.

The most authoritative statement we have as to the nature of the office is that contained in the Form of Church Government, where they are referred to, not as elders in the New Testament sense of the word, but as "other Church Governors," and as "officers" whom "Reformed Churches commonly call Elders."

The Westminster Assembly definitely rejected what is called the Presbyter theory of the office, and regarded them merely as laymen representing the laity in the government of the Church.

The old form of 1582 long served not only for the admission of Elders, but of Deacons. There were formerly Deacons in almost every parish, and the Assembly of 1719 recommended all Ministers to appoint them as well as Elders; but the office is now almost extinct.

There are no regulations in the Westminster documents or in the Acts of Assembly since the Revolution, as to the creed to which they have to give their assent, or the mode of their admission. You find all this supplied in some Ministers' Directories, but these services have no higher ecclesiastical authority than that of their compilers.

In these matters the Church cannot be considered fully equipped or completely organised.

The Doctrine, Worship, and, as we shall see, the Discipline set forth in the Westminster standards have all been virtually revived since 1690; but the Government of the Church rests on a different footing, and there are questions still left open, and defects waiting to be supplied.

Discipline.

I now come to the subject of Church Discipline, which formerly imposed very trying public duties upon our Clergy, but from which they have now in a great measure emancipated themselves.

There are three treatises on the subject which deserve attention. 1. The Order of Excommunication and of Public Repentance, drawn up by Knox in 1567. This formed part of the old Liturgy, and the Assembly ordered it to be observed in all points. 2. The Westminster Directory for Church Censures. 3. The Form of Process in cases of Scandals and Censures, approved by the General Assembly in 1707, and which still embodies the law of the Church on these subjects. There are also some special Acts passed since the Revolution, which are still in force.

In all these treatises public repentance is expressly held to be an ordinance of God. This was practised in all parts of the country till a generation ago, and is still kept up in some remote localities. Formerly those under discipline had to appear in sackcloth, and sometimes with their heads clipped, and head and feet bare, at the door of the church, or on the stool of repentance, from three to fifty-two Sundays, according to the heinousness of their offence.[1] The use of the stool and of sackcloth has only disappeared in some parts of the country within the last few years. A clerical friend told me that he had seen a penitent in a white sheet in a Caithness church shortly before the Disruption; and another friend, who spent a Sunday in the same county when a boy, only missed a similar spectacle by not going to church. And an old parishioner of mine in Aberdeenshire, told me she remembered having seen it in her youth. These externals had formed part of the discipline of the Pre-Reformation Church, and were continued alike under Presbytery and under Episcopacy. In England, public penance and the white sheet were kept up in some parishes till the latter half of last century.[2] Not only have they now dis-

---

[1] See Act of Assembly 1648, sess. 38.
[2] See 'Notes and Queries,' May 1880, p. 353.

appeared from our Church, but I am told that, in some of our cities, Sessional discipline has been given up also, and that Ministers content themselves with dealing with offenders in private. The Form of Process allows great liberty in ordinary cases, but this is certainly to disregard not only the rules but the principles of the Church.

Without entering minutely into the subject, I shall make some remarks on the three modes of dealing with offenders, which the laws of the Church provide for, and which are still in the main adhered to by the clergy, though the practice differs from the law in some important respects. They are alluded to in the 30th chapter of the Confession of Faith as follows: "For the better attaining of the ends of Church Discipline, the Officers of the Church are to proceed by admonition, suspension from the Sacrament of the Lord's Supper for a season, and by excommunication from the Church, according to the nature of the crime, and demerit of the person."

1. There is, first, the case of simple admonition before the Session. In this case, offenders acknowledge their sin, declare their repentance, and their resolution to sin no more. " This being done," the Minister, " after prayer to God

for the penitent, is to admonish him to walk circumspectly."

2. There is next what is called the Lesser Excommunication or Suspension of Offenders from the benefit of the Holy Communion, till such time as they give satisfactory evidence of repentance. In this case the person appearing and confessing his sin is suspended, and is solemnly exhorted to repentance. By laws still in force, but not observed, the names of those who are under this censure are to be publicly read out the Lord's Day immediately preceding that on which the Sacrament of the Lord's Supper is to be administered.[1] When such persons appear again, desiring to be restored, the Minister should ask them, If they are truly penitent, and are resolved to live holily in the time to come? On their answering in the affirmative, he is to absolve them from the sentence of suspension, and to restore them, in the Name of Christ, to the participation of the Sacraments. After engaging in prayer on their behalf, he should exhort them to holy and righteous living for the time to come.

Those who are not communicants, and who cannot, strictly speaking, be suspended, should be kept under discipline till their admission to

[1] Act IV. of Assembly, 1705.

the Lord's Supper, for which, on professing penitence, they should be exhorted to prepare. In connection with this second class of offenders, there are cases, as you find pointed out in the Form of Process, which require to be reported to the Presbytery, and without its consent the Minister cannot proceed to Absolution.

Another case, in which the Minister is only to act under direction of the Presbytery, is in administering the oath of purgation. This peculiarly solemn act is of rare occurrence; but when it takes place, it is due to all parties that it be intimated to the congregation. You will find no forms for these two methods of dealing with offenders, but in some of the Reformed Liturgies there are directions on the subject.

3. There is the Greater Excommunication, and the Order of proceeding to Absolution. For these most solemn services there are minute directions, with appropriate prayers, and formulas for the sentences both of Excommunication and of Absolution in the Form of Process. These are taken almost verbatim from the Westminster Directory for Church Censures, which has thus been virtually sanctioned by the Church. These services are now almost obsolete, the broken-up condition of the Church having made Christian discipline

almost impossible; but should any one be obliged to perform them, it would have to be done under orders from the Presbytery, in presence of the congregation, and it would be his duty to adhere strictly to the form of words authorised by the Church, alike in the exhortations, prayers, and sentences. It is not necessary that I should do more than refer you to them, as given in the Form of Process.

LECTURE VI.

CHURCH ARCHITECTURE—INTERNAL ARRANGEMENTS OF CHURCHES, FITTINGS, AND OTHER REQUISITES FOR DIVINE SERVICE—LAYING OF A FOUNDATION-STONE, AND DEDICATION OF A CHURCH—CONCLUDING OBSERVATIONS.

We have now come to the concluding Lecture, and the subjects which are to be noticed to-day are of a somewhat miscellaneous character. I shall make some remarks, first, on Church Architecture, on the internal arrangements of Churches, the fittings, and other requisites for Divine Service; next, on the Services which are usual at the laying of foundation-stones, and the opening of new Churches; and shall conclude with some observations on the decline and revival of worship in the Church of Scotland.

Church Architecture.

There is no need whatever of my making any apology for discussing the mere externals of Divine Service. They were of sufficient importance to be regulated from heaven under the former dispensation, and whatever their intrinsic importance now in the eyes of Him Who "hath made everything beautiful in His time," it is certain that we are required to serve Him with our best, and that suitable arrangements for Public Worship have very much to do with order, reverence, and heartiness in our devotions.

Churches are the monuments of a nation's piety. "Who does not feel," as has been said, "that man would be debased if he should erect palaces for himself and barns for the Godhead?" Nothing tends more to the degradation of worship than dilapidated Churches and the want of those external appliances and instrumentalities which are requisite for order and decency; and whenever a true revival of religion blesses a community these things receive attention.

The wretched state of many Parish Churches has affected most unfavourably the character of our worship, and though the Church is not blameless in this respect, she has been more sinned against than sinning. Indeed, insult has been added to injury, and she has been habitually blamed for a state of things which she has striven earnestly to prevent or remedy. Thus she has often been charged with the destruction of the great Churches which adorned our country at the time of the Reformation. Not long ago, a Nobleman, who was asked to subscribe towards the erection of a monument to John Knox, suggested, somewhat sarcastically, that Melrose, Dryburgh, and other ruined Churches, sufficiently served the purpose. It was perhaps pardonable in his Lordship not to be aware that the great Churches to which he alluded had been destroyed in an English invasion before the Reformation; but he should not have forgotten that his own title is associated with a suppressed Religious House, and that people who live in glass houses should not throw stones. "What you speak of Mr Knox preaching for the pulling down of Churches," wrote Baillie more than 200 years ago, "is like the rest of your lies. . . . Knox in person . . . went out to save the Monastery of Scoon . . . from all violence. Some few Monasteries and two or three Cathedral Churches were cast down by the idle provocation of some

Popish priests. . . . I have not heard that in all our land above three or four Churches were cast down."[1] The Monastery at Scoon, I may add, to which Baillie refers, was afterwards pulled down by Lord Scoon to build a house for himself, and a good many more shared a similar fate.

In so far as Churches were destroyed at the Reformation it was done either by the neighbouring lairds in order that they might the more easily seize the lands that were attached to them, or by the "rascal multitude" (as Knox calls them) much against the will of the Reformed Clergy. So far from being to blame for the destruction of Churches, they urged, as you find in the First Book of Discipline, that they should be with expedition repaired, "lest that the Word of God and ministration of the Sacraments, by unseemliness of the place, come into contempt," and that they should have "such preparation within as appertaineth . . . to the Majesty of the Word of God."

The early Assemblies, year after year, protested against their neglected and ruinous condition, and pressed upon the Government the necessity of making provision for their repair and upkeep; while the Clergy on all hands complained that

[1] Baillie's Histori. Vindica. of the Church of Scotland, p. 40.

through the "sacrilegious avarice of Earls, Lords, and Gentlemen," they were "like sheep and cattle folds, rather than places for Christian Congregations to assemble in." The law at length imposed the obligation of upholding them on those who had got possession of the property which had previously kept them in repair, but it was constantly evaded in spite of the remonstrances of the Clergy. Since then our Churches have been meaner than those of any other country in Christendom. "The dog-kennel at Osbaldistone Hall," Sir Walter Scott makes Andrew Fairservice say, "is better than many a House of God in Scotland;" and certainly in many cases the Gentleman's stable, with its clock-tower, puts the Parish Church to shame. In some parts of the country, within living memory, umbrellas had to be raised in Churches in rainy weather. One of the commonest remarks of strangers visiting Scotland, when they see an old Church with any pretensions to architecture, is, "Of course this was built before the Reformation." All this is mortifying enough of itself, and it does not improve matters to hear Heritors coolly attributing to the genius of Presbyterianism what is due to their own *genius*, or to see them leaving the Parish Churches because of discomforts, and even horrors, which they are bound to remove.

The Pre-Reformation Churches, in a more or less dilapidated condition, generally stood till last century. After the Act of Annexation (1587) the chancel was usually taken possession of by the layman who then became the representative of the Rector or Religious House that had been despoiled, a gallery was erected in it, and the place where the high altar stood was appropriated as the family burying-place. A corresponding gallery was put up at the West end, and a transept with gallery was thrown out opposite the pulpit. When new Churches had to be built this was the model often followed at first; but in the end of last century, when the population had greatly increased, and many Churches had to be rebuilt, the problem to be solved was how to get the most accommodation at the least expense, and the village mason or carpenter was the person to whom it was submitted. The result was the erection in many parts of the country of huge square barns with immense galleries, and seats crowded close to the pulpit. In some cases noble Pre-Reformation Churches, Archidiaconal and Monastic, were pulled down, and the stones used for erecting " hideous buildings, the very sight of which is debasing." Dunbar and Morebattle Churches shared this fate, and the Abbey Church of Paisley, since partially restored, was doomed to it, but the Heritors were prevented by the Minister from carrying out their scheme. In our own day a new and better spirit has arisen. Many old Churches have been restored, some, such as St Vigeans and that of Biggar, most successfully, and many new ones of a better type have been built. The plans adopted have not, however, always been very satisfactory. The Scottish intellect in such departments is apt to show an excess of vigour, and styles of architecture have been invented which were never before heard of. Beauty of outline and proportion, which is the highest style of beauty, has been too little regarded, and much stupid and expensive ornamentation has often been lavished upon misshapen structures, the effect being to remind one of a deformed figure heavily laden with jewellery and rich apparel. The interior of some of these Churches resembles a circus, class-room, or music-hall. If the last, on entering you see a stage or platform, with a reading desk and sofa in place of an ecclesiastical pulpit, while behind there is a huge organ—the principal object in the building,—and you tremble for the Clergyman in front, who reminds you of those unfortunate Sepoys who, after the Indian Mutiny, were lashed to the mouths of cannon, and blown into a thousand fragments. Strange devices, too, one sometimes hears of for the administration of the Sacraments, such as a font on the top of which a board is screwed to do duty as a Table at times of Communion. In these matters the Church should not be allowed to drift at the mercy of such absurd notions as may enter the head of the village carpenter or self-taught architect. It is the business of a Presbytery, and of every Clergyman in it, to encourage a proper style of ecclesiastical architecture, as the Clergy have done in all ages; and to insist at least upon the internal arrangements of Churches being such as to make the devout and orderly celebration of all the ordinances of religion a possibility. There is nothing in our system inconsistent with the noblest style of architecture—nothing to prevent our utilising all the parts of a Gothic Cathedral; though perhaps the earliest form of the Christian Church, the Basilica, suits best our worship, the means at our disposal, and our traditions. The finest Reformed Churches in the world are the old Swiss Cathedrals, such as that of Basel. In Holland there are also many noble and stately cruciform Churches, the chancel, or head of the Cross, being used for the Communion, as was the case in Scotland after the Reformation.

The parallelogram or simple nave, which is all that we can look for in many parishes, is capable of being treated in a churchly way by devoting the East end to the pulpit, Communion Table, choir seats, organ, and vestry.

Internal Arrangements of Churches, Fittings, and other Requisites for Divine Service.

With regard to the internal arrangements which chiefly affect the worship, I remark—

1. That the seats should all, as far as possible, face the clergyman. Nothing could be worse, for purposes of worship, than the old-fashioned square pew, which obliged half the people to sit with their backs to the pulpit. The pews should be light, and come as near the open bench as possible. Book-boards are useless, except for sleepers. An open back with a bar across is preferable, and the best place for depositing books is on a shelf under the seat in front. The pews should be uniform, for a distinction betwixt the accommodation for rich and poor in God's House is not merely objectionable, but anti-Christian. This is, in fact, the gold-ring principle which is so

emphatically condemned by St James. It is little wonder that we so often hear complaints of the unwillingness of the poor to attend our churches, after they have been taught for centuries that the worst seats, in some out-of-the-way corner, are the proper place for them.

2. Again, if the posture of kneeling during prayer is to be introduced, the seats should be roomy enough to admit of it. Sitting is, in the highest degree, irreverent, and to revive it is to return to a posture out of which Scottish Presbyterians were shamed by Episcopalians in the early part of last century. So much is to be said for standing that it would probably be everywhere adopted were it not for the trouble of maintaining this position both during praise and prayer; but, if we except the weak and infirm, there is no good reason why people might not stand at both. The House of God is no place for the indulgence of laziness, and those who are inclined to lounge and take their ease should remember the clergyman, who has to stand when others sit. In the Primitive Church the people stood, not only at prayer and praise, but during the reading of the lessons. Standing at prayer on the Lord's Day, as every one now knows, was universal among the early Christians. It was

regarded as symbolical of the Resurrection of our Lord. It was believed to have been handed down from the Apostles, and so much importance was attached to it that it was even considered sinful to kneel. The 318 Bishops who assembled at the Council of Nice ordered that the standing posture on Sundays, and on the week-days betwixt Easter and Whitsuntide, should everywhere be continued; and throughout the Eastern Church this rule is still observed. The Scottish custom of standing at prayer was not adopted, however, out of deference to the ancient usage, nor, as is sometimes said, because the Roman Catholics knelt. Kneeling was the usage for nearly a century after the Reformation, and was enforced by injunctions of the Church Courts. This was the practice even during the prayers of the Communion Service, much as kneeling when receiving the elements was objected to. It was during the irreverent time of the Commonwealth that sitting became the fashion. After the restoration of Episcopacy in 1661 this was denounced as indecent, and those who conformed introduced standing. The subject is frequently referred to in the pamphlets of the Revolution period, and from them it is quite clear that the Episcopalians then stood and the Presbyterians sat. Some of the former objected to conformity with the Revolution Church on this, among other grounds—that they might have to give up their more reverent attitude of standing at prayer. It was owing to their denunciation of sitting, and to the fact that the great body of the Episcopalians accepted the Revolution settlement and continued their custom of standing, that this posture in later times came to be considered a characteristic of Presbytery.[1]

3. Again, a Church should be fully furnished and equipped for all the sacred purposes to which it is devoted, and there should be at least sufficient space for the decent celebration of all divine ordinances. At present the pews are often so contiguous to the pulpit that a public Marriage or Baptism is scarcely possible, to say nothing of the want of room and facilities for the Communion and for Ordination. Even the passages are sometimes so narrow that two people could not pass in them unless, like mountain goats, one were to lie down and let the other walk over him. These matters deserve attention, not only for the sake of convenience and seemliness, but for still higher reasons. The form of the House was of old prescribed by God Himself, and it is impossible to

---

[1] See Book of Common Order and Directory, pp. lviii, lix, 329, 330.

avoid impressing upon the minds of the people views, either wrong or right, of divine truth, and of the relative importance of the different features of Divine Service, by the way in which our churches are arranged, and by the provision made for the administration of ordinances.

The rusty iron hoop stuck in the side of the high pulpit to hold the battered pewter basin, to which the parent has to ascend, with his child in his arms, by a staircase used for no other purpose, is an appalling and even perilous arrangement for Baptism. How mean, too, are the cups which we sometimes see on the Lord's Table! while the patens and flagons are often such as would not be tolerated in a respectable kitchen. Indeed some parishes have not yet got the length of the pewter flagon, and the black bottle may still be seen, and the popping of corks be heard, at the Holy Table.[1] It is strange that people of means so seldom think of presenting the necessary equipments for the service of the Lord's House.[2] In Holland the Communion plate is

[1] A friend tells me that this was the case also a few years ago in some of the Irish Episcopal churches.

[2] Formerly, many churches had no Communion Cups at all, but were in the habit of borrowing from their neighbours who were fortunate enough to possess them. A charge of from ten to thirty shillings was made for the use of them.

generally of massive silver, and in some cases of solid gold,—the gifts, in many cases, of those whom God had blessed with abundance. Every minister should do his best to have the church in which he officiates provided with, at least, decent Baptismal and Communion vessels; and, if he can do no better, even a few shillings spent in smoothing and electroplating the old ones may effect a great improvement. Let me say, also, that flagons should be procured at all hazards when they are wanting, and that they should be placed on, not under, the Communion Table.

4. *The Communion Elements.*—In the North-East of Scotland the Communion bread is usually cut into *dice*, with the exception of a few pieces for the Minister to break. This saves unnecessary handling, and has the further advantage that one can provide, almost to a single piece, beforehand the quantity required. In the Central Counties it is usual to have slices cut in the loaf—the crust below and thick pieces at the ends being left as a framework. It is not easy under this system to avoid setting apart to a sacramental use much more than is actually required, and indeed some people have the very vulgar and irreverent idea that there should be a sumptuous board—as at Corinth. In Dumfriesshire, and part of Galloway,

THE COMMUNION ELEMENTS. 241

shortbread is used in many parishes, or at least was so till a few years ago, for I understand the usage is now dying out. This kind of bread was chosen because of its being unleavened. Having held clerical appointments in all the districts where these different usages prevail, I have a decided preference for the Northern custom, or a near approach to it, mainly because there should be as little as possible consecrated beyond what is required.[1]

In some parts of the country it seems to have been the custom formerly reverently to consume in the vestry any of the Bread and Wine left from the Lord's Table. I have met with this practice in quarters where it had been evidently handed down; and indeed the warnings against the superstitious habit of communicants carrying away crumbs in their napkins, which are met with in the writings of our older divines, show that handing over large quantities to the beadle or the poor must have been in their time quite

---

[1] In Geneva, wafer-cakes continued to be used long after the Reformation. The Oriental Church uses leavened bread; the Roman, unleavened. The Catholic and Apostolic Church follow the Western use, because "the Holy Eucharist was instituted by Christ in unleavened bread," and because this was "symbolical of truths applicable to all times."

Q

unknown.[1] It has often been said that the Rubric of the English Prayer-Book on this subject has tended greatly to increase reverence among Episcopalians. Again, it would surely be well if we followed the practice of other countries, Roman Catholic and Reformed, in using a wine for the Communion which contains no more spirit than is necessary for its preservation. This would be right in itself, and would meet the views of all reasonable Teetotallers.[2]

---

[1] "Then go your way . . . not a bit of this bread in your napkin, as the old superstitious custom of some is, but with Christ Himself" (Spalding's Sermons and Table Addresses, p. 200). The custom survived till within the memory of people still living.

[2] The late Dr Bisset of Bourtie informed me that some of the older clergy whom he knew as a young man, were very particular about continuing the use of the mixed cup which had been handed down to them. The Synod of Aberdeen, during the Covenanting period, attempted to stop this early Christian usage, but without success. In the visitation of parishes, one of the questions put at that time was, "Is your wine for the Holy Communion mixed with water or not?"—See Davidson's Inverurie, &c., pp. 308, 311.

Boston speaks of the usage in a way that leads one to believe that it was common in the South of Scotland also. Had the primitive custom been retained, we would never have heard of the substitutes for wine now proposed. Even if such experiments do not desecrate the Sacrament, no one knows where they may end. A friend who has been present at the services of the agents of the London Missionary Society in the Islands of the Pacific, tells me that, instead of bread and wine, they make use of yam and cocoa-nut milk!!

5. *Clerical Robes.*—I notice further that he who guides the public devotions of the Church should not only be in his right mind, but be decently and suitably clothed. One obvious advantage of an official costume in Church or State is that it "sinks the individual and the man of the passing age," and is a reminder of the authority with which those who wear it are clothed. Apart from the idea of a distinction betwixt the secular and the sacred, there is something in official garments which it is idle for people to ignore. Those who disbelieve in the Christian ministry as an Order are, however, quite consistent in objecting to ecclesiastical robes; and the eminent Baptist Minister who is said to denounce the Protestant white neckcloth as the last rag of Popery, is no doubt quite right from his point of view. At the Reformation, sacerdotal vestments were given up in the Reformed Churches, and those which were, properly speaking, Academical, were retained for ecclesiastical purposes. Calvin, and the ministers of the Reformed Church generally, wore cassocks as their ordinary costume on the streets.

Calvin mentions, in a letter to Farel, that he had received a rebuff for this from a silly woman, who declaimed against it, saying, "Is it not written, They shall come to you in long garments?"

but he says he left her in despair of convincing such ignorance. The Scottish Reformers were like their neighbours in this respect; and the General Assembly did not think it beneath its notice to issue directions as to the dress of the clergy, till King James, who had a taste for clerical tailoring, took the matter into his own hands. In the meetings of Synod and Assembly down till 1638 the clergy wore gown and bands. This was also the custom of the Reformed Churches abroad, as may be seen from engravings of the National Synod of the Reformed Church of France in Quick's Synodicon. It was noticed as a novelty that at the Glasgow Assembly of 1638 very few of the clergy appeared in their gowns, while many of the elders wore swords and daggers. In old pictures of the Covenanting clergy, and of leading divines of the Revolution, such as Principal Carstairs, they are represented in gowns and bands, some of which would do no discredit to the most correct ecclesiastical outfitter of the present day. Since 1688 the General Assembly has issued no regulations on the subject of ecclesiastical costume, and nowadays it would probably be thought beneath the dignity of that venerable body to occupy its time with such matters; but perhaps, after all, we are not so much wiser than the ancients. Several of the Synods did, however, deal with the question of vestments after the Revolution. Thus, in 1696, the Synod of Dumfries enacted as follows: "This Synod, considering that it is a thing very decent and suitable, so it hath been the practice of ministers in the Kirk formerly to wear black gowns in the pulpit, and for ordinary to make use of bands, do therefore, by this Act, recommend it to all their brethren within their bounds to keep up that laudable custom, and to study gravity in their apparel and deportment every manner of way."[1] Yet in that same Synod a hundred years afterwards, when the late Dr Wightman, minister of Kirkmahoe, a parish close to the town of Dumfries, began to use a gown in the pulpit, there was quite a rebellion in the community, and many left the church, headed by the precentor, who refused to sit and sing under a man clothed with such a Babylonish garment. It is difficult to account for such a change of sentiment in that locality; but one is constantly reminded in such inquiries as these, that both in the Church at large and in particular parishes, it takes a very short time indeed to make an entirely new tradition. One explanation of the dying out of churchly usages after the

[1] See Chambers's Domestic Annals, vol. iii. p. 148.

Revolution is, that the older Dissenters rejected gowns, paraphrases, hymns, and suchlike, under the mistaken notion that they were walking in the footsteps of the Covenanters of 1638 and 1643, when they were really taking a leaf out of the book of the Cromwellian Sectaries; and Church people got infected with these historical delusions, and wished to be as faithful and loyal to the past as their worthy neighbours. There are, I believe, still parishes in the land where gowns and bands are entirely unknown, and where the introduction of them would raise a storm.

One should take care that his pulpit robes are of the proper make, and that however plain the material, they are in decent condition. Some of the new-fashioned gowns invented by enterprising clothiers, and of which you see representations in the advertising sheets of our religious publications, transgress old Acts of Assembly, such as that forbidding the use of velvet,[1] and are hideous enough to corrupt the taste of the communities into which they are introduced. The old Genevan gown is now best represented by what is called the preacher's gown[2] in the English Church. It indicates a singular disregard of decency and pro-

---
[1] Assembly of 1575.
[2] This, however, is disputed. See Harrison on Rubrics.

priety in God's House for a minister to appear in a faded robe all "tattered and torn." I have known men scrupulously careful about their ordinary costume, appear as scarecrows on Sundays, as a testimony against their flocks for not having presented them with a new gown, and as a hint to them to do so without further delay. It would be better to go about the streets in a ragged coat for a similar reason.

Hoods.—Some clergymen now wear not only gown and band, but the hood of their degree, in church, and on other occasions on which they are called upon to do ministerial duty. This was long the English practice, but it is now being given up across the Borders by those who affect sacerdotal vestments. The hood is a purely academical badge. Some leading men of the Covenanting period objected to Degrees in Divinity because of their supposed association with Episcopacy, and this prejudice seems to have blinded them to historical facts. The Church after the Reformation sanctioned such degrees, and directed that an order should be drawn up for proceeding to them; but when in the following century the subject was revived with a view to the encouragement of learning, it was connected with other innovations, and was denounced as contrary to the principles of the Church and even to the express command of Scripture. The Hierarchical Doctor, it was said, was the prelate's eldest son, and the text, "Be not ye called Doctors," was held to settle the matter conclusively; while all the while the Second Book of Discipline, which was the great manifesto of the Antiprelatic section of the Church, made provision for a whole order of office-bearers bearing this appellation. This prejudice long lingered in the country, especially among those who seceded from the Church. The historian of Knox and Melville had scruples about accepting his degree, and to the last would never use it as a member of Church Courts or when acting in his ministerial capacity. Now we have gone off to the opposite extreme, and "Ministers of all Denominations," as the phrase is, not only accept such degrees when they are offered, but there are some who, if the Universities at home fail to appreciate their merits, are ready to import them for a few dollars from some fountain of literary honour in the backwoods of America, which perhaps has no existence save in the fertile brain of the enterprising Yankee, who crosses the Atlantic with his carpet-bag stuffed with parchments, to the sale of which he trusts for defraying the expenses of his European tour.

Laying of a Foundation-Stone and Dedication of a Church.

When Ministers have to perform these occasional services they are often at a loss as to the proper course to follow. A young clergyman who goes to represent the Church of Scotland in the capital of one of our Colonies, and who soon after his arrival has to discharge such duties in the presence of the Colonial Dignitaries, who are curious to see how we manage these things in Scotland, is very likely to wish that the liberty allowed him by the Church had been a little less than it is. In the absence of any rules or direction in our Church Books on these subjects, I shall offer some suggestions, founded on the services used in other Churches, and on the practice of our clergy.

Laying of a Foundation-Stone.

When the people have assembled at the place where the church is to be built, the minister, standing near the Corner-Stone, may say—

1. Our help is in the name of the Lord, who hath made heaven and earth.
2. Psalm lxxxiv. *may then be said or sung.*

3. *The minister may then say*—Let us pray. (*The prayer may be as follows:—*)

Almighty God, Whom heaven and the heaven of heavens cannot contain, but Who dwellest with humble and contrite hearts, look down in mercy upon us who are here assembled to call upon Thy Holy Name, and to begin a House for Thy Honour and Worship, the preaching of Thy Word, and the Administration of Thy Sacraments. Pardon, we beseech Thee, all our sins and shortcomings, and accept our persons and services for the sake of Thy dear Son. Prosper and bless this work which we have undertaken, that by Thy favour it may promote Thy Glory, and the salvation of souls.

O Lord Jesus Christ, be Thou the beginning, the increase, and the ending thereof: Thou Who art the Corner-Stone cut out of the mountain without hands; Who in the beginning didst lay the foundations of the earth, and Who with the Father and the Holy Ghost livest and reignest ever one God, world without end. Amen.

Our Father, &c.

4. *One or both of the following Lessons may then be read:* Ezra iii. 8-11; Rev. xxi. 10, to the end of the chapter.

5. Psalm cxxvii. *may then be said or sung.*

6. *Laying of Stone. After the usual articles, such as records and coins, have been deposited in the cavity prepared for them, the minister (or other person selected for the purpose), assisted by the builder, shall lay the stone in its place. Then the minister, placing his hand on it, may say—*

In the Name of the Father, the Son, and the Holy Ghost, we lay this Corner-Stone of an edifice to be here erected under the name of —— Church, and devoted to the worship of Almighty God, agreeably to the principles and usages of the Church of Scotland.

Behold, I lay in Zion a chief corner-stone, elect, precious, and he that believeth on Him shall not be confounded. Other foundation can no man lay than that is laid, which is Jesus Christ.

7. Let us pray. (*The prayer may be as follows:—*)

O Lord God Almighty, from Whom cometh down every good and perfect gift, we give Thee hearty thanks for all our friends and benefactors, and for all those through whose charity the walls of this Church are about to arise. Remember them, O Lord, for good, and grant that they and all who may contribute to the furtherance of this work may be preserved both in body and in soul, and may be abundantly recompensed by Thee.

O God, Who art the shield and defence of all Thy people, we beseech Thee to keep the builders of this House from all dangers and accidents, and to endue them with wisdom and grace, that they may perform their duties with skill, industry, and faithfulness, and that the work which through Thy mercy hath now been begun, may be brought to a happy end.

O Almighty God, Who hast built Thy Church upon the foundation of the Apostles and Prophets, Jesus Christ Himself being the chief corner-stone, grant us to be joined together in unity of spirit by their doctrine, that we may be made an holy temple acceptable unto Thee through the Spirit; and so be prepared for that eternal city which hath foundations, whose builder and maker is God: All which we ask, &c.

8. Psalm lxxxvii. *may then be said or sung.*

9. *The customary addresses may then be delivered.*

10. *A collection in aid of the building fund may then be taken up.*

11. *Then may be sung a suitable hymn.*

12. The Benediction.

Should there be a procession, Psalm lxviii. may appropriately be sung in going to the site of the

New Church, and Psalm xcvi. or the Te Deum in returning from it.

The naming of Churches.—The name of a Church is usually given when the Foundation-stone is laid. It need hardly be said that the affixing of the name of a Saint or Martyr to a church does not mean that the church is dedicated to such Saint or Martyr. This would be sacrilege. A church is dedicated to God only; and if distinguished by the name of a saint, ancient or modern, this is only for a memorial of his or her virtues and services.[1] Our old parish churches usually bore the names either of New Testament saints, or of the early missionaries who planted the Gospel in our land, and who certainly deserve to be kept in grateful remembrance by us. When these names are forgotten, they can sometimes be discovered from the day of the old Parish Fair, which was usually held on the anniversary of the Parish Saint. In many cases, too, an old well in the neighbourhood bore the name of the local saint; but high farming and deep draining have in our day proved fatal to many such fountains, which had been held sacred from the time when their waters had been used to baptize the first converts to the faith. Till

[1] Bingham, book viii. chap. ix. sec. 9.

recently, new churches, such as those built fifty years ago in the new town of Edinburgh, and, still later, the Chapels of Ease in Glasgow, were generally named in the same way. At present there appear to be some sectarian influences at work which are hostile to this ancient Christian usage. It may be admissible to call churches after modern worthies, who deserve to be commemorated, but the saints of former days should have a preference; and after the Apostles, none have such a strong claim upon us as those early missionaries, who were the means of converting our Pagan forefathers to the faith of Christ. It is surely for us, who hold that S. Columba and his followers maintained a form of Christianity, free in a great measure from Romish error, and substantially the same as our own, to honour in this way those Celtic missionaries, who, by their self-denying and zealous labours, in little more than a century, not only diffused the light of the Gospel over the hills and valleys of Scotland, but Christianised Northern and Middle England, and penetrated the recesses of heathenism on the Continent of Europe, where their names are still fresh in the memory of grateful populations who never heard of the "Voluntary Controversy" or the "Ten Years' Conflict," but who will take off their hats to you if you tell them that you are of the race of S. Gall or S. Columbanus.

Dedication or Consecration of a Church.

When a new Church is built, it is the universal custom of Christendom to separate it from common uses, solemnly to set it apart for the Service of God, and to offer special supplications that a blessing may attend the ministration of Word and Sacrament therein. You find forms for such services in several of the Reformed Liturgies; and though there are no directions on the subject in our Church Books, a special service, more or less formal, has, I presume, always been customary in Scotland on such occasions, as is the case at present. One meets with occasional notices of the Consecration of Churches during Episcopal times, as, *e.g.*, that of the Grey Friars, Edinburgh, which was consecrated by Archbishop Spottiswoode in 1619;[1] but such notices are rare, as few churches were erected or renovated till a later period.

It is mentioned as one of the characteristics

---

[1] Johnstone's Hist., MS., Advocates' Lib., quoted in Domestic Annals of Scotland, vol. i. p. 507.

of the sectarian party which arose about 1640, that along with their "scunnering" at the Creed, Lord's Prayer, and Doxology, they began to hold Churches in no more reverence than any other buildings. This was the same leaven which led the Quakers at that time to lift up their testimony against all "steeple houses;" but there is nothing in common between such sectarian conceits and the genuine spirit of the Reformed Church. In an Appendix to the Westminster Directory of Worship, it is stated, and most truly, that no places as such are capable of holiness; and that, on the other hand, the Churches were not so polluted by Romish superstition as to render them unfit for public worship—a fanatical extreme which it was then necessary to guard against. The record of the debates shows that it was not disputed that Churches have a *relative* holiness; and those who do not feel that a House of God is in this sense a more holy place than a Theatre, Music-Hall or Tavern, go against the instincts of mankind, and are wanting both in common-sense and in that reverence which is the root of religion. In 1863 the General Assembly resolved as follows: "The Assembly called for the overture . . . anent the desecration of churches, which was read by the clerk. It was moved and agreed to : That the General Assembly, having taken into consideration the overture anent the practice of using churches for social entertainments and other secular purposes, find that, without claiming for these edifices any inherent sacredness, the said practice is unseemly and incongruous, offensive to the feelings of devout worshippers, and calculated to suggest to the congregation on the Lord's Day recollections which are by no means in harmony with the solemn service for which they are assembled, and enjoin all the ministers and Presbyteries of this Church to take all proper means to discourage the said practice."

Notwithstanding that this injunction is so recent, and that public attention has been frequently called to it, there are ministers who disregard both it and the law of the land; for unquestionably any one who gives the use of his Church for any purpose other than those for which it was built, could be interdicted by the humblest of his parishioners. One is scandalised from time to time by reports in the daily papers of soirees in Churches, at which, as every one knows, one great aim is to produce laughter; of Magic-Lantern Exhibitions, with their comic slides, delighting, no doubt, but in such circumstances demoralising, the young; of Lectures on Wit and Humour, enlivened by the singing of popular songs; and, worst perhaps of all, of Political Meetings, when the candidate mounts the pulpit and addresses an uproarious audience, amid profane allusions to the sacred services to which the building has been dedicated. If the candidate is an Episcopalian, one has the further mortification of knowing that he would not enter it on such an errand were it not that he does not consider it a church at all. Such exhibitions are humiliating and disgraceful, and do much to increase irreverence in the land. Those ministers who have so little regard for the sacred associations of the place where they perform the holiest offices of religion as to allow them, and that, too, in violation of both ecclesiastical and civil law, deserve to be visited with the censures of the Church.

THE SERVICE.

The Dedication or Consecration of a New Church usually takes place on a Week-day, though services of a corresponding character may be appropriately continued on the following Sunday. The service should begin with singing the 24th Psalm at the 7th verse.

The Minister may then give a short exhortation to the following effect: That God has in all ages approved of the acts of His people in erecting sanctuaries for His Worship, and that this House, having been built to the honour of His Name, they are now met to devote it to its intended use. He should then call upon them to join with him in prayer that God would be graciously pleased to pardon their sins, to accept of their persons, and of this, the work of their hands, and to bless all His ordinances administered therein.

Prayer.—After a short invocation appropriate to the occasion, and petitions for pardon and acceptance, he should proceed at once to the Prayer of Dedication, there being a good reason for introducing it as early as possible in the service. He should begin with thanks to God that in His Providence this House has been erected for the worship of His Name, and an acknowledgment that it is of His own His people give unto Him. He should then beseech Him, as they dedicate it to His service, to accept the work of their hands. This should be followed with supplications that God's presence may be in it, and with the assemblies that gather in it for worship; that the ministers who may be ordained or who may officiate in it may be men after His own heart; that His Spirit may be with the preaching of His Word and the administration of His Sacraments; that the prayers and praises and offerings of His people therein may be accepted; that when in seasons of calamity they humble themselves before Him, He may forgive their sins, deliver them out of their troubles, and turn their sorrow into joy; and that He may make the Church a centre of blessing to those who worship in it, and to the community in which they dwell.

Or the prayer may be made more particular, thus: For those who are baptized in it, that they may ever remain in the number of His children; for those who confirm their Baptismal engagements, that they may receive the fulness of His grace, and be faithful to their vows; for those who there show forth the Lord's death, that they may come to His Table with faith, repentance, and charity, and have fellowship and communion with Him; and for those who are there united in Holy Matrimony, that they may keep their vows and remain in perfect love unto their lives' end. The prayer may conclude thus: "Arise, O Lord, into Thy rest, Thou and the Ark of Thy strength.

All Liturgical prayers for such occasions are versions, adapted to Christian times, of Solomon's prayer at the Dedication of the Temple.

The service may then be continued according to the usual order, all the parts of it having some reference to the occasion.

The most suitable Psalms and Lessons to be sung or read are the following: Psalm xxiv., xlviii., lxxxiv., and cxxxii.; 1 Kings viii. 22; Mark xi. 11; 1 Cor. iii.; Heb. ix. 1-15, or Heb. x. 19-26.

Before the Second Prayer—that of Thanksgiving—it is appropriate to introduce the Creed thus: "With Thy Holy Church throughout all the world we profess our faith in Thee," &c., or "I believe," &c. For models of suitable prayers I may refer you to those given in the American (Dutch and German) Reformed Liturgies, from the latter of which the outline I have given is mainly taken.

The 190th Hymn—"Christ is made the sure foundation," or the 191st—"Glorious things of thee are spoken," may follow the prayer of Intercession; and the Service should then close, as usual, with the Benediction.

Concluding Observations.

Having gone over the special subjects on which I purposed addressing you, I shall now conclude with a few general observations.

In Scotland, after the Reformation, other questions than worship mainly absorbed public attention, and the Church, though Liturgical, was less rigidly so than any other, except, perhaps, that of Holland. About the beginning of the seventeenth century both parties in the Church became sensible of defects in the provision made for the devotional services of the sanctuary, and were ready to co-operate in effecting some improvement. But King James's interference with the liberty of the Church, and finally the attempt to supersede the old Liturgy by that of Laud, conspired with other circumstances to bring on a violent reaction against all churchly forms, and for a long period the pendulum swung in that direction. Hence a terrible decline in our worship, a melancholy falling away, not only from the state of things which existed before the adoption of the Westminster Standards, but from the principles and practice of the great Covenanting Divines, toward those sectarian ideas and usages which they deprecated as "the reduction of a minimum which admitted of no reduction whatever," and as "the destruction of the Genevan Reformation, under the pretence of further reforming it." For nearly a century after the Reformation there was daily prayer morning and evening in all the principal churches of the country, Baptism and Marriage were reverently celebrated in God's House, and in towns churches were kept open all day for private devotion. Daily Service was given up after the Directory superseded Knox's Liturgy, and artisans soon began to spend the old accustomed time of prayer in the pothouse instead of in the Church, which was "the occasion of much drinking at that season."[1] At the Restoration in 1660, the Daily Service was restored in many places, and it lingered on in some of the towns for a few years after Presbytery was reintroduced in 1688, but it soon ceased everywhere.

Not only did it disappear, but gradually, in the course of last century, one of the Sunday services was discontinued also in the majority of parishes, first for a few months in winter, and afterwards for the whole year. This was an arrangement which obviously deprived a large part of the

[1] Nicol's Diary.

population of the opportunity of paying their public acts of homage to God once a-week, and at this single service preaching was everything. The Public Worship of God was thus reduced to a minimum never before reached in any Christian country.

Our danger has indeed been from following England—not, however, the Church of England, but those fanatical sects which sprang up during the Commonwealth. When one goes South now and witnesses the extraordinary revival which has taken place within the last few years among all parties, high and low, while humiliated and wellnigh appalled at the contrast between South and North, it is with mingled feelings he calls to mind the protests of our Fathers against the lax practice of the English Church, and recollects that many of the devout and churchly usages of our Southern neighbours were once ours, when they had them not, and that, in short, they have taken our good habits and given us their bad ones.

In a letter which I had a short time ago from a Scottish friend in England, the writer says: " In Scotland religion is made a solemn business on Sundays, and then there is no more worship, or very little, till the next Sunday comes round.

The service at S. N. which we go to is very hearty and bright. Mr —— is very earnest and hardworking; even with three curates, their time and energies are taxed to the utmost. There are two daily services—one at 5.30 P.M. In addition to that, on Wednesday there is a second evening service and sermon at 7.30. On Thursdays, prayers at 11, followed by the Communion, specially intended for elderly people and invalids, and any who prefer avoiding the long 11 o'clock service on Sundays. On Sundays we have a children's service at 9.30; then there is the usual service at 11, evening prayer and sermon at 3, and again evening prayer and sermon at 7. From the 9.30 service all the children belonging to the National Schools . . . go direct to the schools connected with the Parish, presided over by one of the curates. School is again held in the National Schoolroom at 3. On Sunday Evening there is a Bible-class for working men. On Wednesdays, at 12.15, there is a large gathering of children who attend private schools, and who reside at home, held in church. Every Thursday, at 4, there is a Bible-class for female servants in the church; and once a month Mr —— has a class for young communicants. This is only a part of the work done. Our church is crowded:

being free, nearly every available seat is occupied fifteen minutes before the service begins, and many are contented to stand throughout the service, particularly at this season."

This is the sort of work that is going on over a great part of England, and I may add that many churches stand open all day for private devotion, with some such notice as the following affixed to the doors: "Whosoever thou art that entereth this Church, leave it not without one prayer to God for thyself and for those who minister and who worship here." Yet forty or fifty years ago —and there is hope for us in this—Churches in England were only open once or twice during the week, and the service was little better than a duet betwixt the parson and the clerk.

Such an amount of work as is done in many English Parishes would be impossible in Scotland, without a large increase of our clerical staff; and I am only saying what is borne out by the wisdom of ages, when I add that this would be best effected not by the excessive subdivision of parishes, but by the employment of assistants. Experience shows that a population of from five to ten thousand can be much more efficiently worked from one than from several centres, while it is the very genius of Christianity never to divide people into classes when it can by any possibility be avoided. No wonder that Scotsmen going South are amazed at the amount of worship and at the tokens of Church Life which they see on all hands, and that, when they return home, they miss the devotions to which they have become accustomed, and find our services too often dreary and depressing. When one has learned to delight in the Worship of God, no mere intellectual treat from the pulpit will ever be accepted as a substitute for it.

Thanks be to God, there are abundant signs that a revival has begun among us of the kind specially needed,—a revival of worship, and of the reverent observance of Christian ordinances. Evangelical revivals have conferred priceless benefits upon individual souls; but unless supplemented, instead of strengthening the Church, they tend to disintegrate it, and to make every one a church to himself. Nothing keeps Christians in unity save those ordinances which have been appointed for this among other purposes, and nothing is so much needed for their own spiritual wellbeing as an increase of devotion among our people.

The Church herself initiated the change which is now being everywhere felt, by ordering the restoration of the reading of Holy Scripture in Divine Service, by providing a Book of Prayer for her children who are without a ministry in answer to urgent and repeated appeals from her chaplains and missionaries, and by sanctioning the Hymnal, Book of Anthems, and an edition of the Prose Psalms pointed for chanting. The preparation of the Prayer-Book devolved chiefly on the late Professor Crawford of Edinburgh, and its publication marked an important era in the history of Scottish worship. About the same time the late Dr Robert Lee published his Book of Prayer, to which many of the clergy have been greatly indebted; and by his speeches in the Assembly did much to enlighten public opinion, and to help forward the movement. Since 1865 a considerable number of the clergy have combined for the study of the Liturgies, ancient and modern, and for the improvement of the Worship of the Church, in accordance with her old laws and better traditions. Though they met with opposition at first, it is now generally admitted that they have done much to restore devotion to its proper place in God's House, and to increase reverence and heartiness in its services. The movement is an essentially conservative one, and within the domain of religion it is almost the only conservative movement that has much hold of our people. Its promoters, by forming themselves into a Society, have checked the tendency of individuals to introduce inventions of their own, and have kept the Church from drifting into ill-considered changes which rest on no principle, and contribute nothing to hearty and devout worship. Some who sympathised with the movement at first merely on æsthetic grounds, have advanced to a higher platform, and have been led to realise more fully than they did before that reverent, hearty, and orderly worship is a main part of the duty which we owe to Him who is our Lord and King, and who claims His rightful tribute from all the gifts which He bestows upon the children of men.

In conclusion, suffer me to exhort you to pay the greatest attention to this subject. Rightly or wrongly our Church has in this matter "legislated for the heroic virtues." With the few general directions she has supplied, she expects every one of her 1200 clergy to perform all the offices of religion not only in a holy and reverent manner, but with such simplicity and taste as to be edifying and acceptable to all classes of the community. This can only be realised, if at all, by the universal attention of the clergy to the subject, and by their spending much time and thought upon it, which, under other systems, can be devoted to other departments of clerical duty.

Our Church has long had a good reputation for the ability of the sermons preached from her pulpits, and the intelligence of her members. God grant that in the future she may be no less distinguished for the character of her worship and the devotional spirit of her ministers and people.

INDEX.

ABERDEEN, Synod of, 32; Kirk-session of, 139; Town Council of, 165, 166.
Act of Annexation, 232.
Act of Uniformity, 190, 200.
Act Rescissory, 4, 6.
Acts of Parliament as to Worship, 6, 7.
Adamson, Principal, 199.
African Synod, 55.
Alms, 139, 182.
Altare Damascenum, 109, 125.
Anderson of Dumbarton, 5, 101.
Anthems, Book of, 268.
Anwoth, parish of, 198.

Baillie, Principal, 4, 18, 19, 20, 65, 129, 131, 147, 148, 193, 229.
Banns, proclamation of, 143.
Baptism of adults, 79; of infants, 54; private, 57; Romish, 56; repetition of, by Scottish Episcopalians, 56; of children of foreign Protestants, 66; naming of child at, 74; by immersion, 75; sign of Cross in, 77.
Baptismal engagements, 70; forms by Committee on Aids to Devotion, 64, 69, 71, 81.
Baxter, Richard, 99, 194.
Benediction, 44, 95.
Bingham, 12, 40, 44, 83, 200, 211, 253.
Bisset, Rev. Dr, 242.
Bohemian Church, 150.
Books of reference, 52.
Boston, 59, 88, 115, 121, 123, 127, 242.
Bowing in the pulpit, 19.
Boyd, Zachary, 33.

Brichan's Sermons, 133.
Brownists, 42, 61.
Bucer, 55, 99.
Bunsen, 97, 135.
Burial of the dead, 162.
Burnet, Bishop, 5.

Calamy's Autobiography, 201; 'Life of Baxter,' 194.
Calderwood, 28, 34, 61, 109, 125, 127.
Calvin, 11, 15, 24, 56, 92, 95, 99, 105, 124, 243.
Campbell, Principal P. C., 210.
Carlyle's 'Letters of Cromwell,' 196.
Carstairs, Principal, 244.
Catechumens, admission of, 83; service for, 94; Act of Assembly on, 88.
'Catholic Presbyterian,' 150.
Celtic Church, 192.
Censures, Directory for Church, 221.
Ceremonies, the three nocent, 19.
Chambers's 'Domestic Annals of Scotland,' 165, 245.
Chanting, 37.
Chants, 158, 169.
Chrism, 83.
Church architecture, 228.
Church Service Society, 268.
Churches, Reformers did not destroy, 229; internal arrangements and fittings of, 235; naming of, 253; consecration of, 255; service for, 258.
Claim of Right, 186.
Communion, Holy, 98; service, 113; preparatory services, 103; given up during the Commonwealth, 101; vessels, 239; bread, 240;

272 INDEX.

fraction of, 127; the mixed cup, 242; minister receives first, 128; private devotions at, 129; addresses, 130; simultaneous, 128, 131; singing at, 134; English office for, 127; Scottish Episcopal do., 127.
Confirmation, Romish, 84; Episcopal, 85.
Consecration of Communion elements, 117; Romish and Eastern views of, 120.
Coverdale, Bishop, 61.
Cowper, Bishop, works of, 50.
Crawford, Professor, 268.
Creed, the Apostolic, 44, 65, 66, 69, 117, 145; Nicene, 118.
Cromwell, 14, 41, 178, 195.

Daily service, 5, 263.
Deacons, 14, 128, 218, 220.
'Defence of the Lawful Calling of the Ministers of Reformed Churches,' by Bishop P. Forbes, 197.
Degrees in Divinity, 247.
Desecration of churches, resolution of Assembly anent, 256.
Diaconate, the, 188, 218.
Directory, the, turned into a Liturgy, 27, 46.
Discipline, Church, 221.
Dissenting congregations, origin of some, 35.
Donaldson, Mr Andro, 19.
Douglas, Robert, 19, 42.
Dumfries, Synod of, 245.
Dunbar, church of, 233.
Durel's 'Government and Worship of God in the Reformed Churches beyond the Seas,' 34, 35, 101, 191.

Edinburgh, Kirk-session of, 61, 147; Presbytery of, 42.
Edward, minister of Murroes, on the Doxology, 34.
Elders, admission of, 218; formerly elected annually, 219; their office, 220.
England, Church of, 60, 135, 189, 191.
Episcopacy, 189, 190, 201.
Erskine, Dr John, 85, 102, 105.
Eutaxia, 24, 106.
Evelyn's Diary, 101.
Excommunication, order of, 221; the Lesser, 224; the Greater, 225.
Expectants, 217.

Fairley, Bishop of Argyle, 200.
Farel, 105, 243.

Fast days before Communion, 104; private and family fasts, 178; public fasting, 175; fasting in the primitive Church, 175; fasting on Sundays, 176; at opening of the Assembly, 178; at Westminster, 178; at ordinations, 205.
Fencing of tables, 109.
Forbes, Dr John, 197.
Form of process, 8, 221.
Foster, John 202.
Foundation-stone of a church, laying of, 249.
France, Reformed Church of, 35, 91, 244.
Funeral service in the house or church, 170; at the grave, 171; eulogiums, 172.

Geneva, 90, 241.
Gerard, Professor, 31, 80.
Gillespie, George, 18, 27, 82, 121, 125, 198.
Glasgow, Kirk-session of, 147; Presbytery of, 147; Synod of, 102. Assembly of 1638, 58, 199.
Gloria Patri, 19, 33, 34.
God-parents, 61.
Good Friday, 175
Gordon, Bishop, case of, 190.
Gowns, pulpit, 243; Synod of Dumfries on use of, 245.
Greyfriars' Church, Edinburgh, 147; consecration of, 255.
Grindal, Archbishop, 100, 196.

Haddington, Presbytery of, 190.
Hall, Robert, 203.
Harrison on Rubrics, 246.
Harvest festivals, 183.
Hawick, church of, 14.
Henderson, Alexander, 4, 19, 35, 42, 61, 68, 86, 103, 109, 126, 131, 135, 137, 140, 165, 206.
Hill, Principal, 31, 173.
'Historical Vindication of the Church of Scotland,' Baillie's, 230.
Holland, Church of, 75, 80, 191, 262; Churches in, 234.
Hoods, use of, 247.
Hooker, 191.
Hope, Sir Thomas, 147.
Hymns, use of, 8, 33.

Incense at funerals, 166.
Induction of ministers, 214; giving of Bible at, 215.
'Institution of a Christian man,' 189.
'Inverurie and the Earldom of the Garioch,' by Dr Davidson, 242.

INDEX.

Invocation of the Holy Spirit at the Communion, 119.
Irish Episcopal Synod, 124.
Irving, Edward, 123.

Johnstone's 'Hist. MS.,' 255.
'Jus Divinum Ministerii Evangelici,' 193.
Justin Martyr, 11, 93.

Keys of church, custody of, 215.
Kirkcaldy, Presbytery of, 198.
Kneeling at baptism, 81; at prayer, 236.
Knox, John, 25, 28, 61, 164, 177, 187, 194, 229, 230.

Laing, Dr, 42
Lamp of Lothian, 14.
Lasswade, 200.
Law of Church as to worship, 3.
Lawson of Selkirk, 110.
Lee's, Dr Robert, 'Book of Prayer,' 157, 172, 268; 'Reform of the Church of Scotland,' 69.
Lees' Dr, 'Visitation of the Sick,' 162.
Leighton, Archbishop, 5, 27, 30, 66, 86.
Lent, 176, 177.
Lessons, reading of, 26; Act of Assembly on, 82; table of, 29; forms for giving out, 30; comments on, 30.
Lifters and Antilifters, 115.
Liturgies, Scottish, 165; Eastern, 118, 119, 137; study of, 51.
— Liturgy, Ethiopic, 135; of Catholic and Apostolic Church, 25, 118; American German Reformed, 118, 261; American Dutch Reformed, 29, 261; Dutch, 80, 158; Laud's, 4, 262; Savoy, 71, 122; Strasburg, 11.
Livingston, John, 91, 141.
London, 58; Presbytery of, 123; Missionary Society, 242.
Lorimer, Professor P., 25.
Luther, 92.
Lykewakes, 165.

M'Crie, Dr, 42, 248.
M'Gillivray's 'Life of St Chrysostom,' 14.
M'Kerrow's 'History of the Secession,' 36.
'Maitland Club Miscellany,' 147.
Marriage, 143; on Sundays, 147; in church, 146, 148; service, 150; use of ring, 155; sermons, 146, 157.

Melrose Abbey, 229.
Melville, James, 91.
Moncreiff, Sir H., 85.
Morebattle, church of, 233.
Morrison, John, ordination of, 190, 196.

Neal's 'History of the Puritans,' 191.
Nice, Council of, 237.
Nicol's Diary, 101, 263.
'Notes and Queries,' 148, 222.

Oath of purgation, 225.
Order of public worship, 9.
'Order of the General Fast,' 177.
Orders, of the ministry, 188; testimonials of, 193; Anglican, 190.
Ordainers, 186.
Ordinal, English, 190, 204.
Ordination, 184; doctrine of, 186; Act of Assembly on, 187; Scottish Episcopal, 197; by Scottish bishops who conformed to Presbytery, 199; by one bishop, 200; Romish, 193; form of, 204; service, 207; Foster on, 202; laying on of hands at, 196, 204.

Paisley Abbey Church, 233.
Perth Articles. 57, 58; Presbytery of, 19, 215; Communion at, 139.
Postures in worship, 236.
Praise given up by sectaries, 33.
Prayer, morning or evening, 9; service at, 23; private, on entering church, 17.
Prefacing, 21.
Preliminaries to public worship, 17.
Presbyters successors of the Apostles, 187.
Presidents in primitive Church, 189.
Probationers, licensing of, 217.
Protesters, 14, 42, 104.
Psalms and hymns, 36; reading of psalms before lessons, 27.

Quakers, 76, 256.
Questions to sponsors, 65; to catechumens, 95.
Quick's 'Synodicon,' 244.

Ray's account of Worship in Scotland, 13.
Readers, order of, 14.
Readers' service, 14.
Reading of line, 34.
Reading prayers, 5, 19.
'Readings upon the Liturgy,' 11.

INDEX.

Reordination never practised in Scotland, 200.
Resolutioners, 14, 42, 104, 105.
Reynolds, Bishop, of Norwich, 39.
Ring in marriage, 155; in betrothals, 155.
Robes, clerical, 243.
Ross's 'Pastoral Work in Covenanting Times,' 20.
Rutherford, S., 92, 198.

Sacerdotalism, 45, 202.
Sackcloth, 8, 222.
Sacraments, doctrine of Church as to, 64; bodily reference of, 76.
.S. Ambrose, 38.
S. Andrews, 194; Archbishopric of, 192.
S. Augustine, 38, 122.
S. Columba, 254.
S. Columbanus, 255.
S. Gall, 254.
S. Vigeans, church of, 233.
Saravia, Adrian, 191.
Scoon, monastery of, 229.
Scott, Sir Walter, 231.
Scott's 'Continuation of Milner's Church History,' 56.
Scott's 'Fasti,' 102.
Scott's 'History of the Reformers,' 139.
Scottish Episcopal Church, 201.
Scriptural songs, 8.
Scripture, reading of, 30; Act of Assembly on, 32; misquotations of, 50; read by schoolmasters, 14.
Shotts, kirk of, 141.
Sick, visitation of, 161.
Singing, at funerals, 164, 169; responsive, 38.
Socinus, 122; Socinianism, 124.
Somerville, Dr, 148.

Spalding Club, 140.
Spalding's Communion Services, 111, 242.
Sponsors, 62.
Spottiswoode, Archbishop, 163, 197, 198, 255.
Stool of repentance, 41, 222.
Stuart of Pardovan, 70, 140, 144, 212.
Succession, ministerial English, 194; Scottish, 194; old Catholic, 199; Moravian, 199.
Suggestions, 46.
Sunday to be kept from midnight to midnight, 147.
Superintendents, 185, 188, 191.

Tertullian, 12.
Thanksgiving, days of, 180.
Thomson, Dr Andrew, 41.
Toasts at funerals, 167, 168.
Tokens, 139, 140.
Torry, Bishop, 85.
Tranent, minister of, 57.
Treaty of Union, 8.
Trent, Council of, 189.

Webster, Dr A., Memoirs of, 81.
Wemyss, parish of, 198.
Wesleyans, 35, 135, 195.
Whitekirk, Session of, 14.
Whitfield, 51.
Whittingham, Dean of, Durham, 61.
Wightman, Dr, 245.
Wither's Poems, 135.
Wodrow, 163; his 'Analecta,' 40; 'Wodrow Society Miscellany,' 204
'Worship in Spirit and in Truth,' 11.
Worship, revival of, in England, 264; in Scotland, 267.

SELECTED LIST.

St Giles' Lectures—Second Series.

THE FAITHS OF THE WORLD. A CONCISE HISTORY OF THE GREAT RELIGIOUS SYSTEMS OF THE WORLD. By EMINENT CLERGYMEN OF THE CHURCH OF SCOTLAND. Complete in One Volume, crown 8vo, in a handsome binding, price 5s.

Published by Command of Her Majesty.

SERMONS PREACHED BEFORE THE QUEEN AT BALMORAL. By the REV. A. A. CAMPBELL, Minister of Crathie. Crown 8vo, 4s. 6d.

"These sermons are clear in thought, full of a deep pathos, evangelical in sentiment, broad in spirit, and eminently practical.......The volume does honour both to Queen and subject."—*Christian Age.*

"These eight discourses by the minister of Crathie are very attractive....... Clergymen everywhere will read and profit by them."—*Dundee Advertiser.*

THE PASTOR AS PREACHER; OR, PREACHING IN CONNECTION WITH WORK IN THE PARISH AND THE STUDY; being Lectures delivered at the Universities of Edinburgh, Aberdeen, and Glasgow. By HENRY WALLIS SMITH, D.D., Minister of Kirknewton and East Calder; One of the Lecturers on Pastoral Theology appointed by the General Assembly of the Church of Scotland. Crown 8vo, 5s.

A HANDBOOK OF THE CHURCH OF SCOTLAND. By JAMES RANKIN, D.D., Minister of Muthill, Author of 'Character Studies in the Old Testament,' &c. Cheap Edition. Fcap. 8vo, 1s. 6d.

"No loyal son of the Church should be without it. It will enable him to understand the history of his Church, and will put into his hands much useful material for its defence."—*Life and Work.*

THE ORIGIN OF EVIL; AND OTHER SERMONS. Preached in St Peter's, Cranley Gardens. By the REV. A. W. MOMERIE, M.A., D.Sc., Fellow of St John's College, Cambridge; Professor of Logic and Metaphysics in King's College, London. Second Edition, Enlarged. Crown 8vo, 5s.

"There is a cogency, simplicity, and beauty running through each sermon that carries the mind and will of the reader by simple force. We heartily wish that this little volume of sermons could be placed in the hands of every preacher and teacher, whatever their opinions or persuasion."—*Church Union.*

CANONICITY; OR, EARLY TESTIMONIES TO THE EXISTENCE AND USE OF THE BOOKS OF THE NEW TESTAMENT. Based on KIRCHHOFER'S 'QUELLENSAMMLUNG.' Edited by A. H. CHARTERIS, D.D., Professor of Biblical Criticism in the University of Edinburgh. 8vo, 18s.

UNDER THE SHADOW, AND OTHER SERMONS AND LECTURES. By the late WILLIAM M'LEAN, Minister of Penninghame. Edited by ALEXANDER M'LAREN, Minister of Mertoun. Crown 8vo, with Portrait, and other Illustrations, 7s. 6d.

"A volume of unusual excellence."—*Dundee Advertiser.*

THEISM. By ROBERT FLINT, D.D., LL.D., Professor of Divinity in the University of Edinburgh. Being the BAIRD LECTURE for 1876. Second Edition. Crown 8vo, 7s. 6d.

ANTI-THEISTIC THEORIES. By the SAME AUTHOR. Being the BAIRD LECTURE for 1877. Crown 8vo, 10s. 6d.

HOURS OF CHRISTIAN DEVOTION. Translated from the German of A. THOLUCK, D.D., Professor of Theology in the University of Halle. By the late REV. ROBERT MENZIES, D.D. Second Edition. Crown 8vo, 7s. 6d.

SERMONS. By JOHN CAIRD, D.D., Principal of the University of Glasgow. Fourteenth Thousand. Fcap. 8vo, 5s.

THE MYSTERIES OF CHRISTIANITY. By T. J. CRAWFORD, D.D., F R S.E., Professor of Divinity in the University of Edinburgh, &c. Being the BAIRD LECTURE for 1874. Crown 8vo, 7s. 6d.

THE FATHERHOOD OF GOD: Considered in its General and Special Aspects, and particularly in relation to the Atonement; with a Review of Recent Speculations on the subject. By the SAME Third Edition, revised and enlarged, with a Reply to the Strictures of Dr Candlish. 9s.

THE DOCTRINE OF HOLY SCRIPTURE RESPECTING THE ATONEMENT. By the SAME. Third Edition. 8vo, 12s.

SOME FACTS OF RELIGION AND OF LIFE. Sermons preached before Her Majesty the Queen in Scotland, 1866-76. By JOHN TULLOCH, D.D. Second Edition, crown 8vo, 7s. 6d.

THE CHRISTIAN DOCTRINE OF SIN. By the SAME. Being First Series of CROALL LECTURES. Crown 8vo, 6s.

AN HISTORICAL SKETCH OF THE LIFE OF OUR LORD. WITH AN INTRODUCTION AND NOTES. By the REV. W. IRELAND GORDON, M.A., B.D. Cheap Edition. Fcap. 8vo, 2s.]

REST IN JESUS. By the REV. MAXWELL NICHOLSON, D.D., Edinburgh. Sixth Edition. Fcap. 8vo, 4s. 6d.

COMMUNION WITH HEAVEN; AND OTHER SERMONS. By the SAME. Fcap., 5s. 6d.

BOOK OF COMMON ORDER (EUCHOLOGION). Being Forms of Worship issued by THE CHURCH SERVICE SOCIETY. Fourth Edition, Revised. Crown 8vo, 5s.

ORDER FOR THE VISITATION OF THE SICK. For the use of Ministers in Scotland and Others. By the REV. JAMES C. LEES, D.D. Crown 8vo, 4s. 6d.

HOME PRAYERS. By MINISTERS OF THE CHURCH OF SCOTLAND, AND MEMBERS OF THE CHURCH SERVICE SOCIETY. Fcap. 8vo, 3s.

A SELECTION OF HOME PRAYERS. Cloth, 1s. 6d.; sewed, 1s.

SERVICES FOR SUNDAY SCHOOLS. By MINISTERS OF THE CHURCH OF SCOTLAND. Paper, 3d.; cloth, 4d.

THE LIFE AND LABOURS OF THE APOSTLE PAUL. A Continuous Narrative for Schools and Bible Classes. By CHARLES MICHIE, M.A. Third Edition, Revised. Fcap. 8vo, cloth, 1s.

WILLIAM BLACKWOOD & SONS, EDINBURGH AND LONDON.

Catalogue

of

Messrs Blackwood & Sons'

Publications

PHILOSOPHICAL CLASSICS FOR ENGLISH READERS.

EDITED BY WILLIAM KNIGHT, LL.D.,
Professor of Moral Philosophy in the University of St Andrews.

In crown 8vo Volumes, with Portraits, price 3s. 6d.

Contents of the Series.

DESCARTES, by Professor Mahaffy, Dublin.—BUTLER, by Rev. W. Lucas Collins, M.A.—BERKELEY, by Professor Campbell Fraser.—FICHTE, by Professor Adamson, Glasgow.—KANT, by Professor Wallace, Oxford.—HAMILTON, by Professor Veitch, Glasgow.—HEGEL, by the Master of Balliol.—LEIBNIZ, by J. Theodore Merz.—VICO, by Professor Flint, Edinburgh.—HOBBES, by Professor Croom Robertson.—HUME, by the Editor.—SPINOZA, by the Very Rev. Principal Caird, Glasgow.—BACON: Part I. The Life, by Professor Nichol.—BACON: Part II. Philosophy, by the same Author.—LOCKE, by Professor Campbell Fraser.

FOREIGN CLASSICS FOR ENGLISH READERS.

EDITED BY MRS OLIPHANT.

In crown 8vo, 2s. 6d.

Contents of the Series.

DANTE, by the Editor.—VOLTAIRE, by General Sir E. B. Hamley, K.C.B.—PASCAL, by Principal Tulloch.—PETRARCH, by Henry Reeve, C.B.—GOETHE, by A. Hayward, Q.C.—MOLIÈRE, by the Editor and F. Tarver, M.A.—MONTAIGNE, by Rev. W. L. Collins, M.A.—RABELAIS, by Sir Walter Besant.—CALDERON, by E. J. Hasell.—SAINT SIMON, by Clifton W. Collins, M.A.—CERVANTES, by the Editor.—CORNEILLE AND RACINE, by Henry M. Trollope.—MADAME DE SÉVIGNÉ, by Miss Thackeray.—LA FONTAINE, AND OTHER FRENCH FABULISTS, by Rev. W. Lucas Collins, M.A.—SCHILLER, by James Sime, M.A., Author of 'Lessing, his Life and Writings.'—TASSO, by E. J. Hasell.—ROUSSEAU, by Henry Grey Graham.—ALFRED DE MUSSET, by C. F. Oliphant.

ANCIENT CLASSICS FOR ENGLISH READERS.

EDITED BY THE REV. W. LUCAS COLLINS, M.A.

CHEAP RE-ISSUE. In limp cloth, fcap. 8vo, price 1s. each.

Two Volumes will be issued Monthly in the following order:—

HOMER: ILIAD, . . The Editor. HOMER: ODYSSEY, . . The Editor. } *Ready.*	HESIOD AND THEOGNIS, J. Davies. PLAUTUS AND TERENCE, The Editor. } *Sept.*	
HERODOTUS, . . G. C. Swayne. CÆSAR, . . Anthony Trollope. } *March.*	TACITUS, ... W. B. Donne. LUCIAN, ... The Editor. } *Oct.*	
VIRGIL, ... The Editor. HORACE, . Sir Theodore Martin. } *April.*	PLATO, ... C. W. Collins. GREEK ANTHOLOGY, Lord Neaves. } *Nov.*	
ÆSCHYLUS, . Bishop Copleston. XENOPHON, . . Sir Alex. Grant. } *May.*	LIVY, ... The Editor. OVID, . . . Rev. A. Church. } *Dec.*	
CICERO, ... The Editor. SOPHOCLES, . . . C. W. Collins. } *June.*	CATULLUS, TIBULLUS, AND PROPERTIUS, ... J. Davies. DEMOSTHENES, . W. J. Brodribb. } *1898. Jan.*	
PLINY, . Church and Brodribb. EURIPIDES, . . . W. B. Donne. } *July.*	ARISTOTLE, . . Sir Alex. Grant. THUCYDIDES, . . . The Editor. } *Feb.*	
JUVENAL, ... E. Walford. ARISTOPHANES, . . The Editor. } *Aug.*	LUCRETIUS, . . W. H. Mallock. PINDAR, . . Rev. F. D. Morice. } *March.*	

CATALOGUE

OF

MESSRS BLACKWOOD & SONS'
PUBLICATIONS.

ALISON.
History of Europe. By Sir ARCHIBALD ALISON, Bart., D.C.L.
1. From the Commencement of the French Revolution to the Battle of Waterloo.
LIBRARY EDITION, 14 vols., with Portraits. Demy 8vo, £10, 10s.
ANOTHER EDITION, in 20 vols. crown 8vo, £6.
PEOPLE'S EDITION, 13 vols. crown 8vo, £2, 11s.
2. Continuation to the Accession of Louis Napoleon.
LIBRARY EDITION, 8 vols. 8vo, £6, 7s. 6d.
PEOPLE'S EDITION, 8 vols. crown 8vo, 34s.

Epitome of Alison's History of Europe. Thirtieth Thousand, 7s. 6d.

Atlas to Alison's History of Europe. By A. Keith Johnston.
LIBRARY EDITION, demy 4to, £3, 3s.
PEOPLE'S EDITION, 31s. 6d.

Life of John Duke of Marlborough. With some Account of his Contemporaries, and of the War of the Succession. Third Edition. 2 vols. 8vo. Portraits and Maps, 30s.

Essays: Historical, Political, and Miscellaneous. 3 vols. demy 8vo, 45s.

ACROSS FRANCE IN A CARAVAN: BEING SOME ACCOUNT OF A JOURNEY FROM BORDEAUX TO GENOA IN THE "ESCARGOT," taken in the Winter 1889-90. By the Author of 'A Day of my Life at Eton.' With fifty Illustrations by John Wallace, after Sketches by the Author, and a Map. Cheap Edition, demy 8vo, 7s. 6d.

ACTA SANCTORUM HIBERNIÆ; Ex Codice Salmanticensi. Nunc primum integre edita opera CAROLI DE SMEDT et JOSEPHI DE BACKER, e Soc. Jesu, Hagiographorum Bollandianorum; Auctore et Sumptus Largiente JOANNE PATRICIO MARCHIONE BOTHAE. In One handsome 4to Volume, bound in half roxburghe, £2, 2s.; in paper cover, 31s. 6d.

ADOLPHUS. Some Memories of Paris. By F. ADOLPHUS.
Crown 8vo, 6s.

AIKMAN.
Manures and the Principles of Manuring. By C. M. AIKMAN, D.Sc., F.R.S.E., &c., Professor of Chemistry, Glasgow Veterinary College; Examiner in Chemistry, University of Glasgow, &c. Crown 8vo, 6s. 6d.

Farmyard Manure: Its Nature, Composition, and Treatment. Crown 8vo, 1s. 6d.

AIRD. Poetical Works of Thomas Aird. Fifth Edition, with Memoir of the Author by the Rev. JARDINE WALLACE, and Portrait. Crown 8vo, 7s. 6d.

ALLARDYCE.
    The City of Sunshine. By ALEXANDER ALLARDYCE, Author of 'Earlscourt,' &c. New Edition. Crown 8vo, 6s.
    Balmoral: A Romance of the Queen's Country. New Edition. Crown 8vo, 6s.

ALMOND. Sermons by a Lay Head-master. By HELY HUTCHINSON ALMOND, M.A. Oxon., Head-Master of Loretto School. Crown 8vo, 5s.

ANCIENT CLASSICS FOR ENGLISH READERS. Edited by Rev. W. LUCAS COLLINS, M.A. Price 1s. each. *For List of Vols. see p. 2.*

ANDERSON. Daniel in the Critics' Den. A Reply to Dean Farrar's 'Book of Daniel.' By ROBERT ANDERSON, LL.D., Barrister-at-Law, Assistant Commissioner of Police of the Metropolis; Author of 'The Coming Prince,' 'Human Destiny,' &c. Post 8vo, 4s. 6d.

AYTOUN.
    Lays of the Scottish Cavaliers, and other Poems. By W. EDMONDSTOUNE AYTOUN, D.C.L., Professor of Rhetoric and Belles-Lettres in the University of Edinburgh. New Edition. Fcap. 8vo, 3s. 6d.
        ANOTHER EDITION. Fcap. 8vo, 7s. 6d.
        CHEAP EDITION. 1s. Cloth, 1s. 3d.
    An Illustrated Edition of the Lays of the Scottish Cavaliers. From designs by Sir NOEL PATON. Cheaper Edition. Small 4to, 10s. 6d.
    Bothwell: a Poem. Third Edition. Fcap., 7s. 6d.
    Poems and Ballads of Goethe. Translated by Professor AYTOUN and Sir THEODORE MARTIN, K.C.B. Third Edition. Fcap., 6s.
    The Ballads of Scotland. Edited by Professor AYTOUN. Fourth Edition. 2 vols. fcap. 8vo, 12s.
    Memoir of William E. Aytoun, D.C.L. By Sir THEODORE MARTIN, K.C.B. With Portrait. Post 8vo, 12s.

BACH.
    On Musical Education and Vocal Culture. By ALBERT B. BACH. Fourth Edition. 8vo, 7s. 6d.
    The Principles of Singing. A Practical Guide for Vocalists and Teachers. With Course of Vocal Exercises. Second Edition. With Portrait of the Author. Crown 8vo, 6s.
    The Art Ballad: Loewe and Schubert. With Musical Illustrations. With a Portrait of LOEWE. Third Edition. Small 4to, 5s.

BEDFORD & COLLINS. Annals of the Free Foresters, from 1856 to the Present Day. By W. K. R. BEDFORD, W. E. W. COLLINS, and other Contributors. With 55 Portraits and 59 other Illustrations. Demy 8vo, 21s. *net.*

BELLAIRS. Gossips with Girls and Maidens, Betrothed and Free. By LADY BELLAIRS. New Edition. Crown 8vo, 3s. 6d. Cloth, extra gilt edges, 5s.

BELLESHEIM. History of the Catholic Church of Scotland. From the Introduction of Christianity to the Present Day. By ALPHONS BELLESHEIM, D.D., Canon of Aix-la-Chapelle. Translated, with Notes and Additions, by D. OSWALD HUNTER BLAIR, O.S.B., Monk of Fort Augustus. Cheap Edition. Complete in 4 vols. demy 8vo, with Maps. Price 21s. net.

BENTINCK. Racing Life of Lord George Cavendish Bentinck, M.P., and other Reminiscences. By JOHN KENT, Private Trainer to the Goodwood Stable. Edited by the Hon. FRANCIS LAWLEY. With Twenty-three full-page Plates, and Facsimile Letter. Third Edition. Demy 8vo, 25s.

BEVERIDGE.
Culross and Tulliallan; or, Perthshire on Forth. Its History and Antiquities. With Elucidations of Scottish Life and Character from the Burgh and Kirk-Session Records of that District. By DAVID BEVERIDGE. 2 vols. 8vo, with Illustrations, 42s.
Between the Ochils and the Forth; or, From Stirling Bridge to Aberdour. Crown 8vo, 6s.

BICKERDYKE. A Banished Beauty. By JOHN BICKERDYKE, Author of 'Days in Thule, with Rod, Gun, and Camera,' 'The Book of the All-Round Angler,' 'Curiosities of Ale and Beer,' &c. With Illustrations. Crown 8vo, 6s.

BIRCH.
Examples of Stables, Hunting-Boxes, Kennels, Racing Establishments, &c. By JOHN BIRCH, Architect, Author of 'Country Architecture,' &c. With 30 Plates. Royal 8vo, 7s.
Examples of Labourers' Cottages, &c. With Plans for Improving the Dwellings of the Poor in Large Towns. With 34 Plates. Royal 8vo, 7s.
Picturesque Lodges. A Series of Designs for Gate Lodges, Park Entrances, Keepers', Gardeners', Bailiffs', Grooms', Upper and Under Servants' Lodges, and other Rural Residences. With 16 Plates. 4to, 12s. 6d.

BLACK. Heligoland and the Islands of the North Sea. By WILLIAM GEORGE BLACK. Crown 8vo, 4s.

BLACKIE.
Lays and Legends of Ancient Greece. By JOHN STUART BLACKIE, Emeritus Professor of Greek in the University of Edinburgh. Second Edition. Fcap. 8vo, 5s.
The Wisdom of Goethe. Fcap. 8vo. Cloth, extra gilt, 6s.
Scottish Song: Its Wealth, Wisdom, and Social Significance. Crown 8vo. With Music. 7s. 6d.
A Song of Heroes. Crown 8vo, 6s.
John Stuart Blackie: A Biography. By ANNA M. STODDART. With 3 Plates. Third Edition. 2 vols. demy 8vo, 21s.
POPULAR EDITION. With Portrait. Crown 8vo, 6s.

BLACKMORE. The Maid of Sker. By R. D. BLACKMORE, Author of 'Lorna Doone,' &c. New Edition. Crown 8vo, 6s. Cheaper Edition. Crown 8vo, 3s. 6d.

BLACKWOOD.
Annals of a Publishing House. William Blackwood and his Sons; including a History of their Magazine and Friends. By Mrs OLIPHANT. With Four Portraits, demy 8vo. [*Vols. I. and II. in the press.*
Blackwood's Magazine, from Commencement in 1817 to March 1897. Nos. 1 to 977, forming 160 Volumes.
Index to Blackwood's Magazine. Vols. 1 to 50. 8vo, 15s.
Tales from Blackwood. First Series. Price One Shilling each, in Paper Cover. Sold separately at all Railway Bookstalls.
They may also be had bound in 12 vols., cloth, 18s. Half calf, richly gilt, 30s. Or the 12 vols. in 6, roxburghe, 21s. Half red morocco, 28s.
Tales from Blackwood. Second Series. Complete in Twenty-four Shilling Parts. Handsomely bound in 12 vols., cloth, 30s. In leather back, roxburghe style, 37s. 6d. Half calf, gilt, 52s. 6d. Half morocco, 55s.
Tales from Blackwood. Third Series. Complete in Twelve Shilling Parts. Handsomely bound in 6 vols., cloth, 15s.; and in 12 vols., cloth, 18s. The 6 vols. in roxburghe, 21s. Half calf, 25s. Half morocco, 28s.
Travel, Adventure, and Sport. From 'Blackwood's Magazine.' Uniform with 'Tales from Blackwood.' In Twelve Parts, each price 1s. Handsomely bound in 6 vols., cloth, 15s. And in half calf, 25s.

BLACKWOOD.
   New Educational Series. *See separate Catalogue.*
   New Uniform Series of Novels (Copyright).
     Crown 8vo, cloth. Price 3s. 6d. each. Now ready:—

THE MAID OF SKER. By R. D. Blackmore.
WENDERHOLME. By P. G. Hamerton.
THE STORY OF MARGRÉDEL. By D. Storrar Meldrum.
MISS MARJORIBANKS. By Mrs Oliphant.
THE PERPETUAL CURATE, and THE RECTOR. By the Same.
SALEM CHAPEL, and THE DOCTOR'S FAMILY. By the Same.
A SENSITIVE PLANT. By E. D. Gerard.
LADY LEE'S WIDOWHOOD. By General Sir E. B. Hamley.
KATIE STEWART, and other Stories. By Mrs Oliphant.
VALENTINE AND HIS BROTHER. By the Same.
SONS AND DAUGHTERS. By the Same.
MARMORNE. By P. G. Hamerton.

REATA. By E. D. Gerard.
BEGGAR MY NEIGHBOUR. By the Same.
THE WATERS OF HERCULES. By the Same.
FAIR TO SEE. By L. W. M. Lockhart.
MINE IS THINE. By the Same.
DOUBLES AND QUITS. By the Same.
ALTIORA PETO. By Laurence Oliphant.
PICCADILLY. By the Same. With Illustrations.
LADY BABY. By D. Gerard.
THE BLACKSMITH OF VOE. By Paul Cushing.
THE DILEMMA. By the Author of 'The Battle of Dorking.'
MY TRIVIAL LIFE AND MISFORTUNE. By A Plain Woman.
POOR NELLIE. By the Same.

   Standard Novels. Uniform in size and binding. Each complete in one Volume.
     FLORIN SERIES, Illustrated Boards. Bound in Cloth, 2s. 6d.

TOM CRINGLE'S LOG. By Michael Scott.
THE CRUISE OF THE MIDGE. By the Same.
CYRIL THORNTON. By Captain Hamilton.
ANNALS OF THE PARISH. By John Galt.
THE PROVOST, &c. By the Same.
SIR ANDREW WYLIE. By the Same.
THE ENTAIL. By the Same.
MISS MOLLY. By Beatrice May Butt.
REGINALD DALTON. By J. G. Lockhart.

PEN OWEN. By Dean Hook.
ADAM BLAIR. By J. G. Lockhart.
LADY LEE'S WIDOWHOOD. By General Sir E. B. Hamley.
SALEM CHAPEL. By Mrs Oliphant.
THE PERPETUAL CURATE. By the Same.
MISS MARJORIBANKS. By the Same.
JOHN: A Love Story. By the Same.

     SHILLING SERIES, Illustrated Cover. Bound in Cloth, 1s. 6d.

THE RECTOR, and THE DOCTOR'S FAMILY. By Mrs Oliphant.
THE LIFE OF MANSIE WAUCH. By D. M. Moir.
PENINSULAR SCENES AND SKETCHES. By F. Hardman.

SIR FRIZZLE PUMPKIN, NIGHTS AT MESS, &c.
THE SUBALTERN.
LIFE IN THE FAR WEST. By G. F. Ruxton.
VALERIUS: A Roman Story. By J. G. Lockhart.

BON GAULTIER'S BOOK OF BALLADS. Fifteenth Edition. With Illustrations by Doyle, Leech, and Crowquill. Fcap. 8vo, 5s.

BRADDON. Thirty Years of Shikar. By Sir EDWARD BRADDON, K.C.M.G. With Illustrations by G. D. Giles, and Map of Oudh Forest Tracts and Nepal Terai. Demy 8vo, 18s.

BROUGHAM. Memoirs of the Life and Times of Henry Lord Brougham. Written by HIMSELF. 3 vols. 8vo, £2, 8s. The Volumes are sold separately, price 16s. each.

BROWN. The Forester: A Practical Treatise on the Planting and Tending of Forest-trees and the General Management of Woodlands. By JAMES BROWN, LL.D. Sixth Edition, Enlarged. Edited by JOHN NISBET, D.Œc., Author of 'British Forest Trees,' &c. In 2 vols. royal 8vo, with 350 Illustrations, 42s. net.
   Also being issued in 15 Monthly parts, price 2s. 6d. net each.
     [*Parts* 1 *and* 2 *ready*.

BROWN. Stray Sport. By J. MORAY BROWN, Author of 'Shikar Sketches,' 'Powder, Spur, and Spear,' 'The Days when we went Hog-Hunting.' 2 vols. post 8vo, with Fifty Illustrations, 21s.

BROWN. A Manual of Botany, Anatomical and Physiological. For the Use of Students. By ROBERT BROWN, M.A., Ph.D. Crown 8vo, with numerous Illustrations, 12s. 6d.

BRUCE.
In Clover and Heather. Poems by **WALLACE BRUCE.** New and Enlarged Edition. Crown 8vo, 3s. 6d.
A limited number of Copies of the First Edition, on large hand-made paper, 12s. 6d.
Here's a Hand. Addresses and Poems. Crown 8vo, 5s.
Large Paper Edition, limited to 100 copies, price 21s.

BUCHAN. Introductory Text-Book of Meteorology. By **ALEXANDER BUCHAN**, LL.D., F.R.S.E., Secretary of the Scottish Meteorological Society, &c. New Edition. Crown 8vo, with Coloured Charts and Engravings.
[*In preparation.*

BURBIDGE.
Domestic Floriculture, Window Gardening, and Floral Decorations. Being Practical Directions for the Propagation, Culture, and Arrangement of Plants and Flowers as Domestic Ornaments. By F. W. BURBIDGE. Second Edition. Crown 8vo, with numerous Illustrations, 7s. 6d.
Cultivated Plants: Their Propagation and Improvement. Including Natural and Artificial Hybridisation, Raising from Seed, Cuttings, and Layers, Grafting and Budding, as applied to the Families and Genera in Cultivation. Crown 8vo, with numerous Illustrations, 12s. 6d.

BURGESS. The Viking Path: A Tale of the White Christ. By J. J. HALDANE BURGESS, Author of 'Rasmie's Büddie,' 'Shetland Sketches,' &c. Crown 8vo, 6s.

BURKE. The Flowering of the Almond Tree, and other Poems. By CHRISTIAN BURKE. Pott 4to, 5s.

BURROWS.
Commentaries on the History of England, from the Earliest Times to 1865. By MONTAGU BURROWS, Chichele Professor of Modern History in the University of Oxford; Captain R.N.; F.S.A., &c.; "Officier de l'Instruction Publique," France. Crown 8vo, 7s. 6d.
The History of the Foreign Policy of Great Britain. Demy 8vo, 12s.

BURTON.
The History of Scotland: From Agricola's Invasion to the Extinction of the last Jacobite Insurrection. By JOHN HILL BURTON, D.C.L., Historiographer-Royal for Scotland. Cheaper Edition. In 8 monthly vols. Crown 8vo, 3s. 6d. each.
[*Vol. I. ready.*
History of the British Empire during the Reign of Queen Anne. In 3 vols. 8vo. 36s.
The Scot Abroad. Third Edition. Crown 8vo, 10s. 6d.
The Book-Hunter. New Edition. With Portrait. Crown 8vo, 7s. 6d.

BUTCHER. Armenosa of Egypt. A Romance of the Arab Conquest. By the Very Rev. Dean BUTCHER, D.D., F.S.A., Chaplain at Cairo. Crown 8vo, 6s.

BUTE. The Altus of St Columba. With a Prose Paraphrase and Notes. In paper cover, 2s. 6d.

BUTT.
Theatricals: An Interlude. By BEATRICE MAY BUTT. Crown 8vo, 6s.
Miss Molly. Cheap Edition, 2s.
Eugenie. Crown 8vo, 6s. 6d.
Elizabeth, and other Sketches. Crown 8vo, 6s.
Delicia. New Edition. Crown 8vo, 2s. 6d.

CAIRD. Sermons. By **JOHN CAIRD**, D.D., Principal of the University of Glasgow Seventeenth Thousand. Fcap. 8vo, 5s.

CALDWELL. Schopenhauer's System in its Philosophical Significance (the Shaw Fellowship Lectures, 1893). By WILLIAM CALDWELL, M.A., D.Sc., Professor of Moral and Social Philosophy, Northwestern University, U.S.A.; formerly Assistant to the Professor of Logic and Metaphysics, Edin., and Examiner in Philosophy in the University of St Andrews. Demy 8vo, 10s. 6d. net.

CALLWELL. The Effect of Maritime Command on Land Campaigns since Waterloo. By Major C. E. CALLWELL, R.A. With Plans. Post 8vo, 6s. net.

CAMPBELL. Sermons Preached before the Queen at Balmoral. By the Rev. A. A. CAMPBELL, Minister of Crathie. Published by Command of Her Majesty. Crown 8vo, 4s. 6d.

CAMPBELL. Records of Argyll. Legends, Traditions, and Recollections of Argyllshire Highlanders, collected chiefly from the Gaelic. With Notes on the Antiquity of the Dress, Clan Colours, or Tartans of the Highlanders. By Lord ARCHIBALD CAMPBELL. Illustrated with Nineteen full-page Etchings. 4to, printed on hand-made paper, £3, 3s.

CANTON. A Lost Epic, and other Poems. By WILLIAM CANTON. Crown 8vo, 5s.

CARSTAIRS.
Human Nature in Rural India. By R. CARSTAIRS. Crown 8vo, 6s.
British Work in India. Crown 8vo, 6s.

CAUVIN. A Treasury of the English and German Languages. Compiled from the best Authors and Lexicographers in both Languages. By JOSEPH CAUVIN, LL.D. and Ph.D., of the University of Göttingen, &c. Crown 8vo, 7s. 6d.

CHARTERIS. Canonicity; or, Early Testimonies to the Existence and Use of the Books of the New Testament. Based on Kirchhoffer's 'Quellensammlung.' Edited by A. H. CHARTERIS, D.D., Professor of Biblical Criticism in the University of Edinburgh. 8vo, 18s.

CHENNELLS. Recollections of an Egyptian Princess. By her English Governess (MISS E. CHENNELLS). Being a Record of Five Years' Residence at the Court of Ismael Pasha Khédive. Second Edition. With Three Portraits. Post 8vo, 7s. 6d.

CHESNEY. The Dilemma. By General Sir GEORGE CHESNEY, K.C.B., M.P., Author of 'The Battle of Dorking,' &c. New Edition. Crown 8vo, 3s. 6d.

CHRISTISON. Life of Sir Robert Christison, Bart., M.D., D.C.L. Oxon., Professor of Medical Jurisprudence in the University of Edinburgh. Edited by his SONS. In 2 vols. 8vo. Vol. I.—Autobiography. 16s. Vol. II.—Memoirs. 16s.

CHURCH. Chapters in an Adventurous Life. Sir Richard Church in Italy and Greece. By E. M. CHURCH. With Photogravure Portrait. Demy 8vo, 10s. 6d.

CHURCH SERVICE SOCIETY.
A Book of Common Order: being Forms of Worship issued by the Church Service Society. Seventh Edition, carefully revised. In 1 vol. crown 8vo, cloth, 3s. 6d.; French morocco, 5s. Also in 2 vols. crown 8vo, cloth, 4s.; French morocco, 6s. 6d.
Daily Offices for Morning and Evening Prayer throughout the Week. Crown 8vo, 3s. 6d.
Order of Divine Service for Children. Issued by the Church Service Society. With Scottish Hymnal. Cloth, 3d.

CLOUSTON. Popular Tales and Fictions: their Migrations and Transformations. By W. A. CLOUSTON, Editor of 'Arabian Poetry for English Readers,' &c. 2 vols. post 8vo, roxburghe binding, 25s.

COCHRAN. A Handy Text-Book of Military Law. Compiled chiefly to assist Officers preparing for Examination; also for all Officers of the Regular and Auxiliary Forces. Comprising also a Synopsis of part of the Army Act. By Major F. COCHRAN, Hampshire Regiment Garrison Instructor, North British District. Crown 8vo, 7s. 6d.

COLQUHOUN. The Moor and the Loch. Containing Minute Instructions in all Highland Sports, with Wanderings over Crag and Corrie, Flood and Fell. By JOHN COLQUHOUN. Cheap Edition. With Illustrations. Demy 8vo, 10s. 6d.

COLVILE. Round the Black Man's Garden. By Lady Z. COLVILE, F.R.G.S. With 2 Maps and 50 Illustrations from Drawings by the Author and from Photographs. Demy 8vo, 16s.

CONDER. The Bible and the East. By Lieut.-Col. C. R. CONDER, R.E., LL.D., D.C.L., M.R.A.S., Author of 'Tent Work in Palestine,' &c. With Illustrations and a Map. Crown 8vo, 5s.

CONSTITUTION AND LAW OF THE CHURCH OF SCOTLAND. With an Introductory Note by the late Principal Tulloch. New Edition, Revised and Enlarged. Crown 8vo, 3s. 6d.

COTTERILL. Suggested Reforms in Public Schools. By C. C. COTTERILL, M.A. Crown 8vo, 3s. 6d.

COUNTY HISTORIES OF SCOTLAND. In demy 8vo volumes of about 350 pp. each. With 2 Maps. Price 7s. 6d. net.

Fife and Kinross. By ÆNEAS J. G. MACKAY, LL.D., Sheriff of these Counties.

Dumfries and Galloway. By Sir HERBERT MAXWELL, Bart., M.P.

Moray and Nairn. By CHARLES RAMPINI, LL.D., Sheriff-Substitute of these Counties. [Others in preparation.

CRANSTOUN.
The Elegies of Albius Tibullus. Translated into English Verse, with Life of the Poet, and Illustrative Notes. By JAMES CRANSTOUN, LL.D., Author of a Translation of 'Catullus.' Crown 8vo, 6s. 6d.

The Elegies of Sextus Propertius. Translated into English Verse, with Life of the Poet, and Illustrative Notes. Crown 8vo, 7s. 6d.

CRAWFORD. Saracinesca. By F. MARION CRAWFORD, Author of 'Mr Isaacs,' &c., &c. Eighth Edition. Crown 8vo, 6s.

CRAWFORD.
The Doctrine of Holy Scripture respecting the Atonement. By the late THOMAS J. CRAWFORD, D.D., Professor of Divinity in the University of Edinburgh. Fifth Edition. 8vo, 12s.

The Fatherhood of God, Considered in its General and Special Aspects. Third Edition, Revised and Enlarged. 8vo, 9s.

The Preaching of the Cross, and other Sermons. 8vo, 7s. 6d.

The Mysteries of Christianity. Crown 8vo, 7s. 6d.

CROSS. Impressions of Dante, and of the New World; with a Few Words on Bimetallism. By J. W. CROSS, Editor of 'George Eliot's Life, as related in her Letters and Journals.' Post 8vo, 6s.

CUMBERLAND. Sport on the Pamirs and Turkistan Steppes. By Major C. S. CUMBERLAND. With Map and Frontispiece. Demy 8vo, 10s. 6d.

CURSE OF INTELLECT. Third Edition. Fcap. 8vo, 2s. 6d. net.

CUSHING. The Blacksmith of Voe. By PAUL CUSHING, Author of 'The Bull i' th' Thorn,' 'Cut with his own Diamond.' Cheap Edition. Crown 8vo, 3s. 6d.

DAVIES.
Norfolk Broads and Rivers; or, The Waterways, Lagoons, and Decoys of East Anglia. By G. CHRISTOPHER DAVIES. Illustrated with Seven full-page Plates. New and Cheaper Edition. Crown 8vo, 6s.
Our Home in Aveyron. Sketches of Peasant Life in Aveyron and the Lot. By G. CHRISTOPHER DAVIES and Mrs BROUGHALL. Illustrated with full-page Illustrations. 8vo, 15s. Cheap Edition, 7s. 6d.

DE LA WARR. An Eastern Cruise in the 'Edeline.' By the Countess DE LA WARR. In Illustrated Cover. 2s.

DESCARTES. The Method, Meditations, and Principles of Philosophy of Descartes. Translated from the Original French and Latin. With a New Introductory Essay, Historical and Critical, on the Cartesian Philosophy. By Professor VEITCH, LL.D., Glasgow University. Eleventh Edition. 6s. 6d.

DOGS, OUR DOMESTICATED: Their Treatment in reference to Food, Diseases, Habits, Punishment, Accomplishments. By 'MAGENTA.' Crown 8vo, 2s. 6d.

DOUGLAS.
The Ethics of John Stuart Mill. By CHARLES DOUGLAS, M.A., D.Sc., Lecturer in Moral Philosophy, and Assistant to the Professor of Moral Philosophy in the University of Edinburgh. In 1 vol. post 8vo.
[*In the press.*
John Stuart Mill: A Study of his Philosophy. Crown 8vo, 4s. 6d. net.

DOUGLAS. Chinese Stories. By ROBERT K. DOUGLAS. With numerous Illustrations by Parkinson, Forestier, and others. New and Cheaper Edition. Small demy 8vo, 5s.

DOUGLAS. Iras: A Mystery. By THEO. DOUGLAS, Author of 'A Bride Elect.' Crown 8vo, 3s. 6d.

DU CANE. The Odyssey of Homer, Books I.-XII. Translated into English Verse. By Sir CHARLES DU CANE, K.C.M.G. 8vo, 10s. 6d.

DUDGEON. History of the Edinburgh or Queen's Regiment Light Infantry Militia, now 3rd Battalion The Royal Scots; with an Account of the Origin and Progress of the Militia, and a Brief Sketch of the Old Royal Scots. By Major R. C. DUDGEON, Adjutant 3rd Battalion the Royal Scots. Post 8vo, with Illustrations, 10s. 6d.

DUNSMORE. Manual of the Law of Scotland as to the Relations between Agricultural Tenants and the Landlords, Servants, Merchants, and Bowers. By W. DUNSMORE. 8vo, 7s. 6d.

DZIEWICKI. Entombed in Flesh. By M. H. DZIEWICKI. In 1 vol. crown 8vo. [*In the press.*

ELIOT.
George Eliot's Life, Related in Her Letters and Journals. Arranged and Edited by her husband, J. W. CROSS. With Portrait and other Illustrations. Third Edition. 3 vols. post 8vo, 42s.
George Eliot's Life. With Portrait and other Illustrations. New Edition, in one volume. Crown 8vo, 7s. 6d.
Works of George Eliot (Standard Edition). 21 volumes, crown 8vo. In buckram cloth, gilt top, 2s. 6d. per vol.; or in roxburghe binding, 3s. 6d. per vol.
 ADAM BEDE. 2 vols.—THE MILL ON THE FLOSS. 2 vols.—FELIX HOLT, THE RADICAL. 2 vols.—ROMOLA. 2 vols.—SCENES OF CLERICAL LIFE. 2 vols.—MIDDLEMARCH. 3 vols.—DANIEL DERONDA. 3 vols.—SILAS MARNER. 1 vol.—JUBAL. 1 vol.—THE SPANISH GIPSY. 1 vol.—ESSAYS. 1 vol.—THEOPHRASTUS SUCH. 1 vol.
Life and Works of George Eliot (Cabinet Edition). 24 volumes, crown 8vo, price £6. Also to be had handsomely bound in half and full calf. The Volumes are sold separately, bound in cloth, price 5s. each.

ELIOT.
  Novels by George Eliot. Cheap Edition.
    Adam Bede. Illustrated. 3s. 6d., cloth.—The Mill on the Floss. Illustrated. 3s. 6d., cloth.—Scenes of Clerical Life. Illustrated. 3s., cloth.—Silas Marner: the Weaver of Raveloc. Illustrated. 2s. 6d., cloth.—Felix Holt, the Radical. Illustrated. 3s. 6d., cloth.—Romola. With Vignette. 3s. 6d., cloth.
  Middlemarch. Crown 8vo, 7s. 6d.
  Daniel Deronda. Crown 8vo, 7s. 6d.
  Essays. New Edition. Crown 8vo, 5s.
  Impressions of Theophrastus Such. New Edition. Crown 8vo, 5s.
  The Spanish Gypsy. New Edition. Crown 8vo, 5s.
  The Legend of Jubal, and other Poems, Old and New. New Edition. Crown 8vo, 5s.
  Wise, Witty, and Tender Sayings, in Prose and Verse. Selected from the Works of GEORGE ELIOT. New Edition. Fcap. 8vo, 3s. 6d.
  ESSAYS ON SOCIAL SUBJECTS. Originally published in the 'Saturday Review.' New Edition. First and Second Series. 2 vols. crown 8vo, 6s. each.

FAITHS OF THE WORLD, The. A Concise History of the Great Religious Systems of the World. By various Authors. Crown 8vo, 5s.

FALKNER. The Lost Stradivarius. By J. MEADE FALKNER. Second Edition. Crown 8vo, 6s.

FERGUSON. Sir Samuel Ferguson in the Ireland of his Day. By LADY FERGUSON, Author of 'The Irish before the Conquest,' 'Life of William Reeves, D.D., Lord Bishop of Down, Connor, and Druinore,' &c., &c. With Two Portraits. 2 vols. post 8vo, 21s.

FERRIER.
  Philosophical Works of the late James F. Ferrier, B.A. Oxon., Professor of Moral Philosophy and Political Economy, St Andrews. New Edition. Edited by Sir ALEXANDER GRANT, Bart., D.C.L., and Professor LUSHINGTON. 3 vols. crown 8vo, 34s. 6d.
  Institutes of Metaphysic. Third Edition. 10s. 6d.
  Lectures on the Early Greek Philosophy. 4th Edition. 10s. 6d.
  Philosophical Remains, including the Lectures on Early Greek Philosophy. New Edition. 2 vols. 24s.

FLINT.
  Historical Philosophy in France and French Belgium and Switzerland. By ROBERT FLINT, Corresponding Member of the Institute of France, Hon. Member of the Royal Society of Palermo, Professor in the University of Edinburgh, &c. 8vo, 21s.
  Agnosticism. Being the Croall Lecture for 1887-88.
                                                                                       [*In the press.*
  Theism. Being the Baird Lecture for 1876. Ninth Edition, Revised. Crown 8vo, 7s. 6d
  Anti-Theistic Theories. Being the Baird Lecture for 1877. Fifth Edition. Crown 8vo, 10s. 6d.

FOREIGN CLASSICS FOR ENGLISH READERS. Edited by Mrs OLIPHANT. Price 2s. 6d. For List of Volumes, see page 2.

FOSTER. The Fallen City, and other Poems. By WILL FOSTER. Crown 8vo, 6s.

FRANCILLON. Gods and Heroes; or, The Kingdom of Jupiter. By R. E. FRANCILLON. With 8 Illustrations. Crown 8vo, 5s.

FRANCIS. Among the Untrodden Ways. By M. E. FRANCIS (Mrs Francis Blundell), Author of 'In a North Country Village,' 'A Daughter of the Soil,' 'Frieze and Fustian,' &c. Crown 8vo, 3s. 6d.

FRASER.
Philosophy of Theism. Being the Gifford Lectures delivered before the University of Edinburgh in 1894-95. First Series. By ALEXANDER CAMPBELL FRASER, D.C.L. Oxford; Emeritus Professor of Logic and Metaphysics in the University of Edinburgh. Post 8vo, 7s. 6d. net.

Philosophy of Theism. Being the Gifford Lectures delivered before the University of Edinburgh in 1895-96. Second Series. Post 8vo, 7s. 6d. net.

FRASER. St Mary's of Old Montrose: A History of the Parish of Maryton. By the Rev. WILLIAM RUXTON FRASER, M.A., F.S.A. Scot., Emeritus Minister of Maryton; Author of 'History of the Parish and Burgh of Laurencekirk.' Crown 8vo, 3s. 6d.

FULLARTON.
Merlin: A Dramatic Poem. By RALPH MACLEOD FULLARTON. Crown 8vo, 5s.

Tanhäuser. Crown 8vo, 6s.

Lallan Sangs and German Lyrics. Crown 8vo, 5s.

GALT.
Novels by JOHN GALT. With General Introduction and Prefatory Notes by S. R. CROCKETT. The Text Revised and Edited by D. STORRAR MELDRUM, Author of 'The Story of Margrédel.' With Photogravure Illustrations from Drawings by John Wallace. Fcap. 8vo, 3s. net each vol.

ANNALS OF THE PARISH, and THE AYRSHIRE LEGATEES. 2 vols.—SIR ANDREW WYLIE. 2 vols.—THE ENTAIL; or, The Lairds of Grippy. 2 vols.—THE PROVOST, and THE LAST OF THE LAIRDS. 2 vols.

See also STANDARD NOVELS, p. 6.

GENERAL ASSEMBLY OF THE CHURCH OF SCOTLAND.
Scottish Hymnal, With Appendix Incorporated. Published for use in Churches by Authority of the General Assembly. 1. Large type, cloth, red edges, 2s. 6d.; French morocco, 4s. 2. Bourgeois type, limp cloth, 1s.; French morocco, 2s. 3. Nonpareil type, cloth, red edges, 6d.; French morocco, 1s. 4d. 4. Paper covers, 3d. 5. Sunday-School Edition, paper covers, 1d., cloth, 2d. No. 1, bound with the Psalms and Paraphrases, French morocco, 8s. No. 2, bound with the Psalms and Paraphrases, cloth, 2s.; French morocco, 3s.

Prayers for Social and Family Worship. Prepared by a Special Committee of the General Assembly of the Church of Scotland. Entirely New Edition, Revised and Enlarged. Fcap. 8vo, red edges, 2s.

Prayers for Family Worship. A Selection of Four Weeks' Prayers. New Edition. Authorised by the General Assembly of the Church of Scotland. Fcap. 8vo, red edges, 1s. 6d.

One Hundred Prayers. Prepared by the Committee on Aids to Devotion. 16mo, cloth limp, 6d.

Morning and Evening Prayers for Affixing to Bibles. Prepared by the Committee on Aids to Devotion. 1d. for 6, or 1s. per 100.

GERARD.
Reata: What's in a Name. By E. D. GERARD. Cheap Edition. Crown 8vo, 3s. 6d.

Beggar my Neighbour. Cheap Edition. Crown 8vo, 3s. 6d.

The Waters of Hercules. Cheap Edition. Crown 8vo, 3s. 6d.

A Sensitive Plant. Crown 8vo, 3s. 6d.

GERARD.
A Foreigner. An Anglo-German Study. By E. GERARD. Crown 8vo, 6s.

GERARD.
: The Land beyond the Forest. Facts, Figures, and Fancies from Transylvania. With Maps and Illustrations. 2 vols. post 8vo, 25s.
: Bis: Some Tales Retold. Crown 8vo, 6s.
: A Secret Mission. 2 vols. crown 8vo, 17s.
: An Electric Shock, and other Stories. In 1 vol. crown 8vo. [*In the press.*]

GERARD.
: A Spotless Reputation. By DOROTHEA GERARD. Crown 8vo, 6s.
: The Wrong Man. Second Edition. Crown 8vo, 6s.
: Lady Baby. Cheap Edition. Crown 8vo, 3s. 6d.
: Recha. Second Edition. Crown 8vo, 6s.
: The Rich Miss Riddell. Second Edition. Crown 8vo, 6s.

GERARD. Stonyhurst Latin Grammar. By Rev. JOHN GERARD. Second Edition. Fcap. 8vo, 3s.

GILL.
: Free Trade: an Inquiry into the Nature of its Operation. By RICHARD GILL. Crown 8vo, 7s. 6d.
: Free Trade under Protection. Crown 8vo, 7s. 6d.

GORDON CUMMING.
: At Home in Fiji. By C. F. GORDON CUMMING. Fourth Edition, post 8vo. With Illustrations and Map. 7s. 6d.
: A Lady's Cruise in a French Man-of-War. New and Cheaper Edition. 8vo. With Illustrations and Map. 12s. 6d.
: Fire-Fountains. The Kingdom of Hawaii: Its Volcanoes, and the History of its Missions. With Map and Illustrations. 2 vols. 8vo, 25s.
: Wanderings in China. New and Cheaper Edition. 8vo, with Illustrations, 10s.
: Granite Crags: The Yō-semité Region of California. Illustrated with 8 Engravings. New and Cheaper Edition. 8vo, 8s. 6d.

GRAHAM. Manual of the Elections (Scot.) (Corrupt and Illegal Practices) Act, 1890. With Analysis, Relative Act of Sederunt, Appendix containing the Corrupt Practices Acts of 1883 and 1885, and Copious Index. By J. EDWARD GRAHAM, Advocate. 8vo, 4s. 6d.

GRAND.
: A Domestic Experiment. By SARAH GRAND, Author of 'The Heavenly Twins,' 'Ideala: A Study from Life.' Crown 8vo, 6s.
: Singularly Deluded. Crown 8vo, 6s.

GRANT. Bush-Life in Queensland. By A. C. GRANT. New Edition. Crown 8vo, 6s.

GRANT. Life of Sir Hope Grant. With Selections from his Correspondence. Edited by HENRY KNOLLYS, Colonel (H.P.) Royal Artillery, his former A.D.C., Editor of 'Incidents in the Sepoy War;' Author of 'Sketches of Life in Japan,' &c. With Portraits of Sir Hope Grant and other Illustrations. Maps and Plans. 2 vols. demy 8vo, 21s.

GRIER.
: In Furthest Ind. The Narrative of Mr EDWARD CARLYON of Ellswether, in the County of Northampton, and late of the Honourable East India Company's Service, Gentleman. Wrote by his own hand in the year of grace 1697. Edited, with a few Explanatory Notes, by SYDNEY C. GRIER. Post 8vo, 6s.
: His Excellency's English Governess. Crown 8vo, 6s.
: An Uncrowned King: A Romance of High Politics. Crown 8vo, 6s.

GUTHRIE-SMITH. Crispus: A Drama. By H. GUTHRIE-SMITH. Fcap. 4to, 5s.

HAGGARD. Under Crescent and Star. By Lieut.-Col. ANDREW HAGGARD, D.S.O., Author of 'Dodo and I,' 'Tempest Torn,' &c. With a Portrait. Second Edition. Crown 8vo, 6s.

HALDANE. Subtropical Cultivations and Climates. A Handy Book for Planters, Colonists, and Settlers. By R. C. HALDANE. Post 8vo, 9s.

HAMERTON.
Wenderholme: A Story of Lancashire and Yorkshire Life. By P. G. HAMERTON, Author of 'A Painter's Camp.' New Edition. Crown 8vo, 3s. 6d.

Marmorne. New Edition. Crown 8vo, 3s. 6d.

HAMILTON.
Lectures on Metaphysics. By Sir WILLIAM HAMILTON, Bart., Professor of Logic and Metaphysics in the University of Edinburgh. Edited by the Rev. H. L. MANSEL, B.D., LL.D., Dean of St Paul's; and JOHN VEITCH, M.A., LL.D., Professor of Logic and Rhetoric, Glasgow. Seventh Edition. 2 vols. 8vo, 24s.

Lectures on Logic. Edited by the SAME. Third Edition, Revised. 2 vols., 24s.

Discussions on Philosophy and Literature, Education and University Reform. Third Edition. 8vo, 21s.

Memoir of Sir William Hamilton, Bart., Professor of Logic and Metaphysics in the University of Edinburgh. By Professor VEITCH, of the University of Glasgow. 8vo, with Portrait, 18s.

Sir William Hamilton: The Man and his Philosophy. Two Lectures delivered before the Edinburgh Philosophical Institution, January and February 1883. By Professor VEITCH. Crown 8vo, 2s.

HAMLEY.
The Operations of War Explained and Illustrated. By General Sir EDWARD BRUCE HAMLEY, K.C.B., K.C.M.G. Fifth Edition, Revised throughout. 4to, with numerous Illustrations, 30s.

National Defence; Articles and Speeches. Post 8vo, 6s.

Shakespeare's Funeral, and other Papers. Post 8vo, 7s. 6d.

Thomas Carlyle: An Essay. Second Edition. Crown 8vo, 2s. 6d.

On Outposts. Second Edition. 8vo, 2s.

Wellington's Career; A Military and Political Summary. Crown 8vo, 2s.

Lady Lee's Widowhood. New Edition. Crown 8vo, 3s. 6d. Cheaper Edition, 2s. 6d.

Our Poor Relations. A Philozoic Essay. With Illustrations, chiefly by Ernest Griset. Crown 8vo, cloth gilt, 3s. 6d.

The Life of General Sir Edward Bruce Hamley, K.C.B., K.C.M.G. By ALEXANDER INNES SHAND. With two Photogravure Portraits and other Illustrations. Cheaper Edition. With a Statement by Mr EDWARD HAMLEY. 2 vols. demy 8vo, 10s. 6d.

HARE. Down the Village Street: Scenes in a West Country Hamlet. By CHRISTOPHER HARE. Second Edition. Crown 8vo, 6s.

HARRADEN.
In Varying Moods: Short Stories. By BEATRICE HARRADEN, Author of 'Ships that Pass in the Night.' Twelfth Edition. Crown 8vo, 3s. 6d.

Hilda Strafford, and The Remittance Man. Two Californian Stories. Sixth Edition. Crown 8vo, 3s. 6d.

HARRIS.
From Batum to Baghdad, viâ Tiflis, Tabriz, and Persian Kurdistan. By WALTER B. HARRIS, F.R.G.S., Author of 'The Land of an African Sultan; Travels in Morocco,' &c. With numerous Illustrations and 2 Maps. Demy 8vo, 12s.

HARRIS.
Tafilet. The Narrative of a Journey of Exploration to the Atlas Mountains and the Oases of the North-West Sahara. With Illustrations by Maurice Romberg from Sketches and Photographs by the Author, and Two Maps. Demy 8vo, 12s.

A Journey through the Yemen, and some General Remarks upon that Country. With 3 Maps and numerous Illustrations by Forestier and Wallace from Sketches and Photographs taken by the Author. Demy 8vo, 16s.

Danovitch, and other Stories. Crown 8vo, 6s.

HAWKER. The Prose Works of Rev. R. S. HAWKER, Vicar of Morwenstow. Including 'Footprints of Former Men in Far Cornwall.' Re-edited, with Sketches never before published. With a Frontispiece. Crown 8vo, 3s. 6d.

HAY. The Works of the Right Rev. Dr George Hay, Bishop of Edinburgh. Edited under the Supervision of the Right Rev. Bishop STRAIN. With Memoir and Portrait of the Author. 5 vols. crown 8vo, bound in extra cloth, £1, 1s. The following Volumes may be had separately—viz.:
The Devout Christian Instructed in the Law of Christ from the Written Word. 2 vols., 8s.—The Pious Christian Instructed in the Nature and Practice of the Principal Exercises of Piety. 1 vol., 3s.

HEATLEY.
The Horse-Owner's Safeguard. A Handy Medical Guide for every Man who owns a Horse. By G. S. HEATLEY, M.R.C.V.S. Crown 8vo, 5s.

The Stock-Owner's Guide. A Handy Medical Treatise for every Man who owns an Ox or a Cow. Crown 8vo, 4s. 6d.

HEDDERWICK. Lays of Middle Age; and other Poems. By JAMES HEDDERWICK, LL.D., Author of 'Backward Glances.' Price 3s. 6d.

HEMANS.
The Poetical Works of Mrs Hemans. Copyright Editions. Royal 8vo, 5s. The Same with Engravings, cloth, gilt edges, 7s. 6d.

Select Poems of Mrs Hemans. Fcap., cloth, gilt edges, 3s.

HERKLESS. Cardinal Beaton: Priest and Politician. By JOHN HERKLESS, Professor of Church History, St Andrews. With a Portrait. Post 8vo, 7s. 6d.

HEWISON. The Isle of Bute in the Olden Time. With Illustrations, Maps, and Plans. By JAMES KING HEWISON, M.A., F.S.A. (Scot.), Minister of Rothesay. Vol. I., Celtic Saints and Heroes. Crown 4to, 15s. net. Vol. II., The Royal Stewards and the Brandanes. Crown 4to, 15s. net.

HIBBEN. Inductive Logic. By JOHN GRIER HIBBEN, Ph.D., Assistant Professor of Logic in Princeton University, U.S.A. Crown 8vo, 3s. 6d. net.

HILDEBRAND. The Early Relations between Britain and Scandinavia. Being the Rhind Lectures in Archæology for 1896. By Dr HANS HILDEBRAND, Royal Antiquary of Sweden. With Illustrations. In 1 vol. post 8vo. [In the press.

HOME PRAYERS. By Ministers of the Church of Scotland and Members of the Church Service Society. Second Edition. Fcap. 8vo, 3s.

HORNBY. Admiral of the Fleet Sir Geoffrey Phipps Hornby, G.C.B. A Biography. By Mrs FRED. EGERTON. With Three Portraits. Demy 8vo, 16s.

HUTCHINSON. Hints on the Game of Golf. By HORACE G. HUTCHINSON. Ninth Edition, Enlarged. Fcap. 8vo, cloth, 1s.

HYSLOP. The Elements of Ethics. By JAMES H. HYSLOP, Ph.D., Instructor in Ethics, Columbia College, New York, Author of 'The Elements of Logic.' Post 8vo, 7s. 6d. net.

IDDESLEIGH. Life, Letters, and Diaries of Sir Stafford Northcote, First Earl of Iddesleigh. By ANDREW LANG. With Three Portraits and a View of Pynes. Third Edition. 2 vols. post 8vo, 31s. 6d.
POPULAR EDITION. With Portrait and View of Pynes. Post 8vo, 7s. 6d.

INDEX GEOGRAPHICUS: Being a List, alphabetically arranged, of the Principal Places on the Globe, with the Countries and Subdivisions of the Countries in which they are situated, and their Latitudes and Longitudes. Imperial 8vo, pp. 676, 21s.

JEAN JAMBON. Our Trip to Blunderland; or, Grand Excursion to Blundertown and Back. By JEAN JAMBON. With Sixty Illustrations designed by CHARLES DOYLE, engraved by DALZIEL. Fourth Thousand. Cloth, gilt edges, 6s. 6d. Cheap Edition, cloth, 3s. 6d. Boards, 2s. 6d.

JEBB. A Strange Career. The Life and Adventures of JOHN GLADWYN JEBB. By his Widow. With an Introduction by H. RIDER HAGGARD, and an Electrogravure Portrait of Mr Jebb. Third Edition. Demy 8vo, 10s. 6d. CHEAP EDITION. With Illustrations by John Wallace. Crown 8vo, 3s. 6d.

Some Unconventional People. By Mrs GLADWYN JEBB, Author of 'Life and Adventures of J. G. Jebb.' With Illustrations. Crown 8vo, 3s. 6d.

JENNINGS. Mr Gladstone: A Study. By LOUIS J. JENNINGS, M.P., Author of 'Republican Government in the United States,' 'The Croker Memoirs,' &c. Popular Edition. Crown 8vo, 1s.

JERNINGHAM.
Reminiscences of an Attaché. By HUBERT E. H. JERNINGHAM. Second Edition. Crown 8vo, 5s.

Diane de Breteuille. A Love Story. Crown 8vo, 2s. 6d.

JOHNSTON.
The Chemistry of Common Life. By Professor J. F. W. JOHNSTON. New Edition, Revised. By ARTHUR HERBERT CHURCH, M.A. Oxon.; Author of 'Food: its Sources, Constituents, and Uses,' &c. With Maps and 102 Engravings. Crown 8vo, 7s. 6d.

Elements of Agricultural Chemistry. An entirely New Edition from the Edition by Sir CHARLES A. CAMERON, M.D., F.R.C.S.I., &c. Revised and brought down to date by C. M. AIKMAN, M.A., B.Sc., F.R.S.E., Professor of Chemistry, Glasgow Veterinary College. 17th Edition. Crown 8vo, 6s. 6d.

Catechism of Agricultural Chemistry. An entirely New Edition from the Edition by Sir CHARLES A. CAMERON. Revised and Enlarged by C. M. AIKMAN, M.A., &c. 95th Thousand. With numerous Illustrations. Crown 8vo, 1s.

JOHNSTON. Agricultural Holdings (Scotland) Acts, 1883 and 1889; and the Ground Game Act, 1880. With Notes, and Summary of Procedure, &c. By CHRISTOPHER N. JOHNSTON, M.A., Advocate. Demy 8vo, 5s.

JOKAI. Timar's Two Worlds. By MAURUS JOKAI. Authorised Translation by Mrs HEGAN KENNARD. Cheap Edition. Crown 8vo, 6s.

KEBBEL. The Old and the New: English Country Life. By T. E. KEBBEL, M.A., Author of 'The Agricultural Labourers,' 'Essays in History and Politics,' 'Life of Lord Beaconsfield.' Crown 8vo, 5s.

KERR. St Andrews in 1645-46. By D. R. KERR. Crown 8vo, 2s. 6d.

KINGLAKE.
History of the Invasion of the Crimea. By A. W. KINGLAKE. Cabinet Edition, Revised. With an Index to the Complete Work. Illustrated with Maps and Plans. Complete in 9 vols., crown 8vo, at 6s. each.

—— Abridged Edition for Military Students. Revised by Lieut.-Col. Sir GEORGE SYDENHAM CLARKE, K.C.M.G., R.E. In 1 vol, demy 8vo.
[In the press.

History of the Invasion of the Crimea. Demy 8vo. Vol. VI. Winter Troubles. With a Map, 16s. Vols. VII. and VIII. From the Morrow of Inkerman to the Death of Lord Raglan With an Index to the Whole Work. With Maps and Plans. 28s.

KINGLAKE.
　　Eothen. A New Edition, uniform with the Cabinet Edition of the 'History of the Invasion of the Crimea.' 6s.
　　　　CHEAPER EDITION. With Portrait and Biographical Sketch of the Author. Crown 8vo, 3s. 6d.
KIRBY. In Haunts of Wild Game: A Hunter-Naturalist's Wanderings from Kahlamba to Libombo. By FREDERICK VAUGHAN KIRBY, F.Z.S. (Maqaqamba). With numerous Illustrations by Charles Whymper, and a Map. Large demy 8vo, 25s.
KLEIN. Among the Gods. Scenes of India, with Legends by the Way. By AUGUSTA KLEIN. With 22 Full-page Illustrations. Demy 8vo, 15s.
KNEIPP. My Water-Cure. As Tested through more than Thirty Years, and Described for the Healing of Diseases and the Preservation of Health. By SEBASTIAN KNEIPP, Parish Priest of Wörishofen (Bavaria). With a Portrait and other Illustrations. Authorised English Translation from the Thirtieth German Edition, by A. de F. Cheap Edition. With an Appendix, containing the Latest Developments of Pfarrer Kneipp's System, and a Preface by E. Gerard. Crown 8vo, 3s. 6d.
KNOLLYS. The Elements of Field-Artillery. Designed for the Use of Infantry and Cavalry Officers. By HENRY KNOLLYS, Colonel Royal Artillery; Author of 'From Sedan to Saarbrück,' Editor of 'Incidents in the Sepoy War,' &c. With Engravings. Crown 8vo, 7s. 6d.

LANG. Life, Letters, and Diaries of Sir Stafford Northcote, First Earl of Iddesleigh. By ANDREW LANG. With Three Portraits and a View of Pynes. Third Edition. 2 vols. post 8vo, 31s. 6d.
　　　　POPULAR EDITION. With Portrait and View of Pynes. Post 8vo, 7s. 6d.
LEES. A Handbook of the Sheriff and Justice of Peace Small Debt Courts. With Notes, References, and Forms. By J. M. LEES, Advocate, Sheriff of Stirling, Dumbarton, and Clackmannan. 8vo, 7s. 6d.
LINDSAY.
　　Recent Advances in Theistic Philosophy of Religion. By Rev. JAMES LINDSAY, M.A., B.D., B.Sc., F.R.S.E., F.G.S., Minister of the Parish of St Andrew's, Kilmarnock. Demy 8vo, 12s. 6d. net.
　　The Significance of the Old Testament for Modern Theology. Crown 8vo, 1s. net.
　　The Progressiveness of Modern Christian Thought. Crown 8vo, 6s.
　　Essays, Literary and Philosophical. Crown 8vo, 3s. 6d.
LOCKHART.
　　Doubles and Quits. By LAURENCE W. M. LOCKHART. New Edition. Crown 8vo, 3s. 6d.
　　Fair to See. New Edition. Crown 8vo, 3s. 6d.
　　Mine is Thine. New Edition. Crown 8vo, 3s. 6d.
LOCKHART.
　　The Church of Scotland in the Thirteenth Century. The Life and Times of David de Bernham of St Andrews (Bishop), A.D. 1239 to 1253. With List of Churches dedicated by him, and Dates. By WILLIAM LOCKHART, A.M., D.D., F.S.A. Scot., Minister of Colinton Parish. 2d Edition. 8vo, 6s.
　　Dies Tristes: Sermons for Seasons of Sorrow. Crown 8vo, 6s.
LORIMER.
　　The Institutes of Law: A Treatise of the Principles of Jurisprudence as determined by Nature. By the late JAMES LORIMER, Professor of Public Law and of the Law of Nature and Nations in the University of Edinburgh. New Edition, Revised and much Enlarged. 8vo, 18s.
　　The Institutes of the Law of Nations. A Treatise of the Jural Relation of Separate Political Communities. In 2 vols. 8vo. Volume I., price 16s. Volume II., price 20s.

LUGARD. The Rise of our East African Empire : Early Efforts in Uganda and Nyasaland. By F. D. LUGARD, Captain Norfolk Regiment. With 130 Illustrations from Drawings and Photographs under the personal superintendence of the Author, and 14 specially prepared Maps. In 2 vols. large demy 8vo, 42s.

M'CHESNEY.
Miriam Cromwell, Royalist : A Romance of the Great Rebellion. By DORA GREENWELL M'CHESNEY. Crown 8vo, 6s.
Kathleen Clare : Her Book, 1637-41. With Frontispiece, and five full-page Illustrations by James A. Shearman. Crown 8vo, 6s.

M'COMBIE. Cattle and Cattle-Breeders. By WILLIAM M'COMBIE, Tillyfour. New Edition, Enlarged, with Memoir of the Author by JAMES MACDONALD, F.R.S.E., Secretary Highland and Agricultural Society of Scotland. Crown 8vo, 3s. 6d.

M'CRIE.
Works of the Rev. Thomas M'Crie, D.D. Uniform Edition. 4 vols. crown 8vo, 24s.
Life of John Knox. Crown 8vo, 6s. Another Edition, 3s. 6d.
Life of Andrew Melville. Crown 8vo, 6s.
History of the Progress and Suppression of the Reformation in Italy in the Sixteenth Century. Crown 8vo, 4s.
History of the Progress and Suppression of the Reformation in Spain in the Sixteenth Century. Crown 8vo, 3s. 6d.

M'CRIE. The Public Worship of Presbyterian Scotland. Historically treated. With copious Notes, Appendices, and Index. The Fourteenth Series of the Cunningham Lectures. By the Rev. CHARLES G. M'CRIE, D.D. Demy 8vo, 10s. 6d.

MACDONALD. A Manual of the Criminal Law (Scotland) Procedure Act, 1887. By NORMAN DORAN MACDONALD. Revised by the LORD JUSTICE-CLERK. 8vo, 10s. 6d.

MACDONALD AND SINCLAIR. History of Polled Aberdeen and Angus Cattle. Giving an Account of the Origin, Improvement, and Characteristics of the Breed. By JAMES MACDONALD and JAMES SINCLAIR. Illustrated with numerous Animal Portraits. Post 8vo, 12s. 6d.

MACDOUGALL AND DODDS. A Manual of the Local Government (Scotland) Act, 1894. With Introduction, Explanatory Notes, and Copious Index. By J. PATTEN MACDOUGALL, Legal Secretary to the Lord Advocate, and J. M. DODDS. Tenth Thousand, Revised. Crown 8vo, 2s. 6d. net.

MACINTYRE. Hindu - Koh : Wanderings and Wild Sports on and beyond the Himalayas. By Major-General DONALD MACINTYRE, V.C., late Prince of Wales' Own Goorkhas, F.R.G.S. Dedicated to H.R.H. *The Prince of Wales.* New and Cheaper Edition, Revised, with numerous Illustrations. Post 8vo, 3s. 6d.

MACKAY.
A Manual of Modern Geography ; Mathematical, Physical, and Political. By the Rev. ALEXANDER MACKAY, LL.D., F.R.G.S. 11th Thousand, Revised to the present time. Crown 8vo, pp. 688, 7s. 6d.
Elements of Modern Geography. 55th Thousand, Revised to the present time. Crown 8vo, pp. 300, 3s.
The Intermediate Geography. Intended as an Intermediate Book between the Author's 'Outlines of Geography' and 'Elements of Geography.' Eighteenth Edition, Revised. Fcap. 8vo, pp. 238, 2s.
Outlines of Modern Geography. 191st Thousand, Revised to the present time. Fcap. 8vo, pp. 128, 1s.
Elements of Physiography. New Edition. Rewritten and Enlarged. With numerous Illustrations. Crown 8vo. [*In the press.*

MACKENZIE. Studies in Roman Law. With Comparative Views of the Laws of France, England, and Scotland. By Lord MACKENZIE, one of the Judges of the Court of Session in Scotland. Sixth Edition, Edited by JOHN KIRKPATRICK, M.A., LL.B., Advocate, Professor of History in the University of Edinburgh. 8vo, 12s.

MACPHERSON. Glimpses of Church and Social Life in the Highlands in Olden Times. By ALEXANDER MACPHERSON, F.S.A. Scot. With 6 Photogravure Portraits and other full-page Illustrations. Small 4to, 25s.

M'PHERSON. Golf and Golfers. Past and Present. By J. GORDON M'PHERSON, Ph.D., F.R.S.E. With an Introduction by the Right Hon. A. J. BALFOUR, and a Portrait of the Author. Fcap. 8vo, 1s. 6d.

MACRAE. A Handbook of Deer-Stalking. By ALEXANDER MACRAE, late Forester to Lord Henry Bentinck. With Introduction by Horatio Ross, Esq. Fcap. 8vo, with 2 Photographs from Life. 3s. 6d.

MAIN. Three Hundred English Sonnets. Chosen and Edited by DAVID M. MAIN. New Edition. Fcap. 8vo, 3s. 6d.

MAIR. A Digest of Laws and Decisions, Ecclesiastical and Civil, relating to the Constitution, Practice, and Affairs of the Church of Scotland. With Notes and Forms of Procedure. By the Rev. WILLIAM MAIR, D.D., Minister of the Parish of Earlston. New Edition, Revised. Crown 8vo, 9s. net.

MARCHMONT AND THE HUMES OF POLWARTH. By One of their Descendants. With numerous Portraits and other Illustrations. Crown 4to, 21s. net.

MARSHMAN. History of India. From the Earliest Period to the present time. By JOHN CLARK MARSHMAN, C.S.I. Third and Cheaper Edition. Post 8vo, with Map, 6s.

MARTIN.
The Æneid of Virgil. Books I.-VI. Translated by Sir THEODORE MARTIN, K.C.B. Post 8vo, 7s. 6d.
Goethe's Faust. Part I. Translated into English Verse. Second Edition, crown 8vo, 6s. Ninth Edition, fcap. 8vo, 3s. 6d.
Goethe's Faust. Part II. Translated into English Verse. Second Edition, Revised. Fcap. 8vo, 6s.
The Works of Horace. Translated into English Verse, with Life and Notes. 2 vols. New Edition. Crown 8vo, 21s.
Poems and Ballads of Heinrich Heine. Done into English Verse. Third Edition. Small crown 8vo, 5s.
The Song of the Bell, and other Translations from Schiller, Goethe, Uhland, and Others. Crown 8vo, 7s. 6d.
Madonna Pia: A Tragedy; and Three Other Dramas. Crown 8vo, 7s. 6d.
Catullus. With Life and Notes. Second Edition, Revised and Corrected. Post 8vo, 7s. 6d.
The 'Vita Nuova' of Dante. Translated, with an Introduction and Notes. Third Edition. Small crown 8vo, 5s.
Aladdin: A Dramatic Poem. By ADAM OEHLENSCHLAEGER. Fcap. 8vo, 5s.
Correggio: A Tragedy. By OEHLENSCHLAEGER. With Notes. Fcap. 8vo, 3s.

MARTIN. On some of Shakespeare's Female Characters. By HELENA FAUCIT, Lady MARTIN. Dedicated by permission to Her Most Gracious Majesty the Queen. Fifth Edition. With a Portrait by Lehmann. Demy 8vo, 7s. 6d.

MARWICK. Observations on the Law and Practice in regard to Municipal Elections and the Conduct of the Business of Town Councils and Commissioners of Police in Scotland. By Sir JAMES D. MARWICK, LL.D., Town-Clerk of Glasgow. Royal 8vo, 30s.

MATHESON.
Can the Old Faith Live with the New? or, The Problem of Evolution and Revelation. By the Rev. GEORGE MATHESON, D.D. Third Edition. Crown 8vo, 7s. 6d.
The Psalmist and the Scientist; or, Modern Value of the Religious Sentiment. Third Edition. Crown 8vo, 5s.
Spiritual Development of St Paul. Third Edition. Cr. 8vo, 5s.
The Distinctive Messages of the Old Religions. Second Edition. Crown 8vo, 5s.
Sacred Songs. New and Cheaper Edition. Crown 8vo, 2s. 6d.

MATHIESON. The Supremacy and Sufficiency of Jesus Christ our Lord, as set forth in the Epistle to the Hebrews. By J. E. MATHIESON, Superintendent of Mildmay Conference Hall, 1880 to 1890. Second Edition. Crown 8vo, 3s. 6d.

MAURICE. The Balance of Military Power in Europe. An Examination of the War Resources of Great Britain and the Continental States. By Colonel MAURICE, R.A., Professor of Military Art and History at the Royal Staff College. Crown 8vo, with a Map, 6s.

MAXWELL.
A Duke of Britain. A Romance of the Fourth Century. By Sir HERBERT MAXWELL, Bart., M.P., F.S.A., &c., Author of 'Passages in the Life of Sir Lucian Elphin.' Fourth Edition. Crown 8vo, 6s.
Life and Times of the Rt. Hon. William Henry Smith, M.P. With Portraits and numerous Illustrations by Herbert Railton, G. L. Seymour, and Others. 2 vols. demy 8vo, 25s.
POPULAR EDITION. With a Portrait and other Illustrations. Crown 8vo, 3s. 6d.
Scottish Land-Names: Their Origin and Meaning. Being the Rhind Lectures in Archæology for 1893. Post 8vo, 6s.
Meridiana: Noontide Essays. Post 8vo, 7s. 6d.
Post Meridiana: Afternoon Essays. Post 8vo, 6s.
Dumfries and Galloway. Being one of the Volumes of the County Histories of Scotland. With Four Maps. Demy 8vo, 7s. 6d. net.

MELDRUM.
The Story of Margrédel: Being a Fireside History of a Fifeshire Family. By D. STORRAR MELDRUM. Cheap Edition. Crown 8vo, 3s. 6d.
Grey Mantle and Gold Fringe. Crown 8vo, 6s.

MERZ. A History of European Thought in the Nineteenth Century. By JOHN THEODORE MERZ. Vol. I., post 8vo, 10s. 6d. net.

MICHIE.
The Larch: Being a Practical Treatise on its Culture and General Management. By CHRISTOPHER Y. MICHIE, Forester, Cullen House. Crown 8vo, with Illustrations. New and Cheaper Edition, Enlarged, 5s.
The Practice of Forestry. Crown 8vo, with Illustrations. 6s.

MIDDLETON. The Story of Alastair Bhan Comyn; or, The Tragedy of Dunphail. A Tale of Tradition and Romance. By the Lady MIDDLETON. Square 8vo, 10s. Cheaper Edition, 5s.

MIDDLETON. Latin Verse Unseens. By G. MIDDLETON, M.A., Lecturer in Latin, Aberdeen University; late Scholar of Emmanuel College, Cambridge; Joint-Editor of 'Student's Companion to Latin Authors.' In 1 vol. crown 8vo. [In the press.

MILLER. The Dream of Mr H——, the Herbalist. By HUGH MILLER, F.R.S.E., late H.M. Geological Survey, Author of 'Landscape Geology.' With a Photogravure Frontispiece. Crown 8vo, 2s. 6d.

MILLS. Greek Verse Unseens. By T. R. MILLS, M.A., late Lecturer in Greek, Aberdeen University; formerly Scholar of Wadham College, Oxford; Joint-Editor of 'Student's Companion to Latin Authors.' In 1 vol. crown 8vo. [In the press.

MINTO.
A Manual of English Prose Literature, Biographical and Critical: designed mainly to show Characteristics of Style. By W. MINTO, M.A., Hon. LL.D. of St Andrews; Professor of Logic in the University of Aberdeen. Third Edition, Revised. Crown 8vo, 7s. 6d.
Characteristics of English Poets, from Chaucer to Shirley. New Edition, Revised. Crown 8vo, 7s. 6d.
Plain Principles of Prose Composition. Crown 8vo, 1s. 6d.
The Literature of the Georgian Era. Edited, with a Biographical Introduction, by Professor KNIGHT, St Andrews. Post 8vo, 6s.

MOIR. **Life of Mansie Wauch, Tailor in Dalkeith.** By D. M. MOIR. With CRUIKSHANK'S Illustrations. Cheaper Edition. Crown 8vo, 2s. 6d. Another Edition, without Illustrations, fcap. 8vo, 1s. 6d.

MOLE. **For the Sake of a Slandered Woman.** By MARION MOLE. Fcap. 8vo, 2s. 6d. net.

MOMERIE.
Defects of Modern Christianity, and other Sermons. By Rev. ALFRED WILLIAMS MOMERIE, M.A., D.Sc., LL.D. Fifth Edition. Crown 8vo, 5s.
The Basis of Religion. Being an Examination of Natural Religion. Third Edition. Crown 8vo, 2s. 6d.
The Origin of Evil, and other Sermons. Eighth Edition, Enlarged. Crown 8vo, 5s.
Personality. The Beginning and End of Metaphysics, and a Necessary Assumption in all Positive Philosophy. Fifth Edition, Revised. Crown 8vo, 3s.
Agnosticism. Fourth Edition, Revised. Crown 8vo, 5s.
Preaching and Hearing; and other Sermons. Fourth Edition, Enlarged. Crown 8vo, 5s.
Belief in God. Third Edition. Crown 8vo, 3s.
Inspiration; and other Sermons. Second Edition, Enlarged. Crown 8vo, 5s.
Church and Creed. Third Edition. Crown 8vo, 4s. 6d.
The Future of Religion, and other Essays. Second Edition. Crown 8vo, 3s. 6d.
The English Church and the Romish Schism. Second Edition. Crown 8vo, 2s. 6d.

MONCREIFF.
The Provost-Marshal. A Romance of the Middle Shires. By the Hon. FREDERICK MONCREIFF. Crown 8vo, 6s.
The X Jewel. A Romance of the Days of James VI. Crown 8vo, 6s.

MONTAGUE. **Military Topography.** Illustrated by Practical Examples of a Practical Subject. By Major-General W. E. MONTAGUE, C.B., P.S.C., late Garrison Instructor Intelligence Department, Author of 'Campaigning in South Africa.' With Forty-one Diagrams. Crown 8vo, 5s.

MONTALEMBERT. **Memoir of Count de Montalembert.** A Chapter of Recent French History. By Mrs OLIPHANT, Author of the 'Life of Edward Irving,' &c. 2 vols. crown 8vo, £1, 4s.

MORISON.
Doorside Ditties. By JEANIE MORISON. With a Frontispiece. Crown 8vo, 3s. 6d.
Æolus. A Romance in Lyrics. Crown 8vo, 3s.
There as Here. Crown 8vo, 3s.
⁎ *A limited impression on hand-made paper, bound in vellum, 7s. 6d.*
Selections from Poems. Crown 8vo, 4s. 6d.
Sordello. An Outline Analysis of Mr Browning's Poem. Crown 8vo, 3s.

MORISON.
 Of "Fifine at the Fair," "Christmas Eve and Easter Day," and other of Mr Browning's Poems. Crown 8vo, 3s.
 The Purpose of the Ages. Crown 8vo, 9s.
 Gordon : An Our-day Idyll. Crown 8vo, 3s.
 Saint Isadora, and other Poems. Crown 8vo, 1s. 6d.
 Snatches of Song. Paper, 1s. 6d. ; cloth, 3s.
 Pontius Pilate. Paper, 1s. 6d. ; cloth, 3s.
 Mill o' Forres. Crown 8vo, 1s.
 Ane Booke of Ballades. Fcap. 4to, 1s.

MUNRO. The Lost Pibroch, and other Sheiling Stories. By NEIL MUNRO. Crown 8vo, 6s.

MUNRO.
 Rambles and Studies in Bosnia-Herzegovina and Dalmatia. With an Account of the Proceedings of the Congress of Archæologists and Anthropologists held at Sarajevo in 1894. By ROBERT MUNRO, M.A., M.D., F.R.S.E., Author of 'The Lake-Dwellings of Europe,' &c. With numerous Illustrations. Demy 8vo, 12s. 6d. net.
 Prehistoric Problems. With numerous Illustrations. In 1 vol. demy 8vo. [In the press.

MUNRO. On Valuation of Property. By WILLIAM MUNRO, M.A., Her Majesty's Assessor of Railways and Canals for Scotland. Second Edition, Revised and Enlarged. 8vo, 3s. 6d.

MURDOCH. Manual of the Law of Insolvency and Bankruptcy: Comprehending a Summary of the Law of Insolvency, Notour Bankruptcy, Composition - Contracts, Trust - Deeds, Cessios, and Sequestrations; and the Winding-up of Joint-Stock Companies in Scotland; with Annotations on the various Insolvency and Bankruptcy Statutes; and with Forms of Procedure applicable to these Subjects. By JAMES MURDOCH, Member of the Faculty of Procurators in Glasgow. Fifth Edition, Revised and Enlarged. 8vo, 12s. net.

MURRAY. A Popular Manual of Finance. By SYDNEY J. MURRAY. In 1 vol. crown 8vo. [In the press.

MY TRIVIAL LIFE AND MISFORTUNE : A Gossip with no Plot in Particular. By A PLAIN WOMAN. Cheap Edition. Crown 8vo, 3s. 6d.
 By the SAME AUTHOR.
 POOR NELLIE. Cheap Edition. Crown 8vo, 3s. 6d.

MY WEATHER - WISE COMPANION. Presented by B. T. Fcap. 8vo, 1s. net.

NAPIER. The Construction of the Wonderful Canon of Logarithms. By JOHN NAPIER of Merchiston. Translated, with Notes, and a Catalogue of Napier's Works, by WILLIAM RAE MACDONALD. Small 4to, 15s. *A few large-paper copies on Whatman paper*, 30s.

NEAVES. Songs and Verses, Social and Scientific. By An Old Contributor to 'Maga.' By the Hon. Lord NEAVES. Fifth Edition. Fcap. 8vo, 4s.

NICHOLSON.
 A Manual of Zoology, for the Use of Students. With a General Introduction on the Principles of Zoology. By HENRY ALLEYNE NICHOLSON, M.D., D.Sc., F.L.S., F.G.S., Regius Professor of Natural History in the University of Aberdeen. Seventh Edition, Rewritten and Enlarged. Post 8vo, pp. 956, with 555 Engravings on Wood, 18s.
 Text-Book of Zoology, for Junior Students. Fifth Edition, Rewritten and Enlarged. Crown 8vo, with 358 Engravings on Wood, 10s. 6d.
 Introductory Text-Book of Zoology, for the Use of Junior Classes. New Edition, Revised and Enlarged. [In the press.

NICHOLSON.
Outlines of Natural History, for Beginners: being Descriptions of a Progressive Series of Zoological Types. Third Edition, with Engravings, 1s. 6d.
A Manual of Palæontology, for the Use of Students. With a General Introduction on the Principles of Palæontology. By Professor H. ALLEYNE NICHOLSON and RICHARD LYDEKKER, B.A. Third Edition, entirely Rewritten and greatly Enlarged. 2 vols. 8vo, £3, 3s.
The Ancient Life-History of the Earth. An Outline of the Principles and Leading Facts of Palæontological Science. Crown 8vo, with 276 Engravings, 10s. 6d.
On the "Tabulate Corals" of the Palæozoic Period, with Critical Descriptions of Illustrative Species. Illustrated with 15 Lithographed Plates and numerous Engravings. Super-royal 8vo, 21s.
Synopsis of the Classification of the Animal Kingdom. 8vo, with 106 Illustrations, 6s.
On the Structure and Affinities of the Genus Monticulipora and its Sub-Genera, with Critical Descriptions of Illustrative Species. Illustrated with numerous Engravings on Wood and Lithographed Plates. Super-royal 8vo, 18s.

NICHOLSON.
Thoth. A Romance. By JOSEPH SHIELD NICHOLSON, M.A., D.Sc., Professor of Commercial and Political Economy and Mercantile Law in the University of Edinburgh. Third Edition. Crown 8vo, 4s. 6d.
A Dreamer of Dreams. A Modern Romance. Second Edition. Crown 8vo, 6s.

NICOLSON AND MURE. A Handbook to the Local Government (Scotland) Act, 1889. With Introduction, Explanatory Notes, and Index. By J. BADENACH NICOLSON, Advocate, Counsel to the Scotch Education Department, and W. J. MURE, Advocate, Legal Secretary to the Lord Advocate for Scotland. Ninth Reprint. 8vo, 5s.

OLIPHANT.
Masollam: A Problem of the Period. A Novel. By LAURENCE OLIPHANT. 3 vols. post 8vo, 25s. 6d.
Scientific Religion; or, Higher Possibilities of Life and Practice through the Operation of Natural Forces. Second Edition. 8vo, 16s.
Altiora Peto. Cheap Edition. Crown 8vo, boards, 2s. 6d.; cloth, 3s. 6d. Illustrated Edition. Crown 8vo, cloth, 6s.
Piccadilly. With Illustrations by Richard Doyle. New Edition, 3s. 6d. Cheap Edition, boards, 2s. 6d.
Traits and Travesties; Social and Political. Post 8vo, 10s. 6d.
Episodes in a Life of Adventure; or, Moss from a Rolling Stone. Cheaper Edition. Post 8vo, 3s. 6d.
Haifa: Life in Modern Palestine. Second Edition. 8vo, 7s. 6d.
The Land of Gilead. With Excursions in the Lebanon. With Illustrations and Maps. Demy 8vo, 21s.
Memoir of the Life of Laurence Oliphant, and of Alice Oliphant, his Wife. By Mrs M. O. W. OLIPHANT. Seventh Edition. 2 vols. post 8vo, with Portraits. 21s.
POPULAR EDITION. With a New Preface. Post 8vo, with Portraits. 7s. 6d.

OLIPHANT.
Annals of a Publishing House. William Blackwood and his Sons; including a History of their Magazine and Friends. With Four Portraits. Demy 8vo. [Vols. I. and II. in the press.
Who was Lost and is Found. By Mrs OLIPHANT. Second Edition. Crown 8vo, 6s.
Miss Marjoribanks. New Edition. Crown 8vo, 3s. 6d.

OLIPHANT.
  The Perpetual Curate, and The Rector. New Edition. Crown 8vo, 3s. 6d.
  Salem Chapel, and The Doctor's Family. New Edition. Crown 8vo, 3s. 6d.
  Katie Stewart, and other Stories. New Edition. Crown 8vo, cloth, 3s. 6d.
  Katie Stewart. Illustrated boards, 2s. 6d.
  Valentine and his Brother. New Edition. Crown 8vo, 3s. 6d.
  Sons and Daughters. Crown 8vo, 3s. 6d.
  Two Stories of the Seen and the Unseen. The Open Door —Old Lady Mary. Paper covers, 1s.

OLIPHANT. Notes of a Pilgrimage to Jerusalem and the Holy Land. By F. R. OLIPHANT. Crown 8vo, 3s. 6d.

OSWALD. By Fell and Fjord; or, Scenes and Studies in Iceland. By E. J. OSWALD. Post 8vo, with Illustrations. 7s. 6d.

PAGE.
  Introductory Text-Book of Geology. By DAVID PAGE, LL.D., Professor of Geology in the Durham University of Physical Science, Newcastle. With Engravings and Glossarial Index. New Edition. Revised by Professor LAPWORTH of Mason Science College, Birmingham. [In preparation.
  Advanced Text-Book of Geology, Descriptive and Industrial. With Engravings, and Glossary of Scientific Terms. New Edition. Revised by Professor LAPWORTH. [In preparation.
  Introductory Text-Book of Physical Geography. With Sketch-Maps and Illustrations. Edited by Professor LAPWORTH, LL.D., F.G.S., &c., Mason Science College, Birmingham. Thirteenth Edition, Revised and Enlarged. 2s. 6d.
  Advanced Text-Book of Physical Geography. Third Edition. Revised and Enlarged by Professor LAPWORTH. With Engravings. 5s.

PATON.
  Spindrift. By Sir J. NOEL PATON. Fcap., cloth, 5s.
  Poems by a Painter. Fcap., cloth, 5s.

PATON. Body and Soul. A Romance in Transcendental Pathology. By FREDERICK NOEL PATON. Third Edition. Crown 8vo, 1s.

PATRICK. The Apology of Origen in Reply to Celsus. A Chapter in the History of Apologetics. By the Rev. J. PATRICK, D.D. Post 8vo, 7s. 6d.

PAUL. History of the Royal Company of Archers, the Queen's Body-Guard for Scotland. By JAMES BALFOUR PAUL, Advocate of the Scottish Bar. Crown 4to, with Portraits and other Illustrations. £2, 2s.

PEILE. Lawn Tennis as a Game of Skill. By Lieut.-Col. S. C. F. PEILE, B.S.C. Revised Edition, with new Scoring Rules. Fcap. 8vo, cloth, 1s.

PETTIGREW. The Handy Book of Bees, and their Profitable Management. By A. PETTIGREW. Fifth Edition, Enlarged, with Engravings. Crown 8vo, 3s. 6d.

PFLEIDERER. Philosophy and Development of Religion. Being the Edinburgh Gifford Lectures for 1894. By OTTO PFLEIDERER, D.D. Professor of Theology at Berlin University. In 2 vols. post 8vo, 15s. net.

PHILLIPS. The Knight's Tale. By F. EMILY PHILLIPS, Author of 'The Education of Antonia.' Crown 8vo, 3s. 6d.

PHILOSOPHICAL CLASSICS FOR ENGLISH READERS. Edited by WILLIAM KNIGHT, LL.D., Professor of Moral Philosophy, University of St Andrews. In crown 8vo volumes, with Portraits, price 3s. 6d.
  [For List of Volumes, see page 2.

POLLARD. A Study in Municipal Government: The Corporation of Berlin. By JAMES POLLARD, C.A., Chairman of the Edinburgh Public Health Committee, and Secretary of the Edinburgh Chamber of Commerce. Second Edition, Revised. Crown 8vo, 3s. 6d.

POLLOK. The Course of Time: A Poem. By ROBERT POLLOK, A.M. Cottage Edition, 32mo, 8d. The Same, cloth, gilt edges, 1s. 6d. Another Edition, with Illustrations by Birket Foster and others, fcap., cloth, 3s. 6d., or with edges gilt, 4s.

PORT ROYAL LOGIC. Translated from the French; with Introduction, Notes, and Appendix. By THOMAS SPENCER BAYNES, LL.D., Professor in the University of St Andrews. Tenth Edition, 12mo, 4s.

POTTS AND DARNELL.

Aditus Faciliores: An Easy Latin Construing Book, with Complete Vocabulary By A. W. POTTS, M.A., LL.D., and the Rev. C. DARNELL, M.A., Head-Master of Cargilfield Preparatory School Edinburgh. Tenth Edition, fcap. 8vo, 3s. 6d.

Aditus Faciliores Graeci. An Easy Greek Construing Book, with Complete Vocabulary. Fifth Edition, Revised. Fcap. 8vo, 3s.

POTTS. School Sermons. By the late ALEXANDER WM. POTTS LL.D., First Head-Master of Fettes College. With a Memoir and Portrait. Crown 8vo, 7s. 6d.

PRINGLE. The Live Stock of the Farm. By ROBERT O. PRINGLE. Third Edition. Revised and Edited by JAMES MACDONALD. Crown 8vo, 7s. 6d.

PRYDE. Pleasant Memories of a Busy Life. By DAVID PRYDE, M.A., LL.D., Author of 'Highways of Literature,' 'Great Men in European History,' 'Biographical Outlines of English Literature,' &c. With a Mezzotint Portrait. Post 8vo, 6s.

PUBLIC GENERAL STATUTES AFFECTING SCOTLAND from 1707 to 1847, with Chronological Table and Index. 3 vols. large 8vo, £3, 3s.

PUBLIC GENERAL STATUTES AFFECTING SCOTLAND, COLLECTION OF. Published Annually, with General Index.

RAE. The Syrian Church in India. By GEORGE MILNE RAE, M.A., D.D., Fellow of the University of Madras; late Professor in the Madras Christian College. With 6 full-page Illustrations. Post 8vo, 10s. 6d.

RAMSAY. Scotland and Scotsmen in the Eighteenth Century. Edited from the MSS. of JOHN RAMSAY, Esq. of Ochtertyre, by ALEXANDER ALLARDYCE, Author of 'Memoir of Admiral Lord Keith, K.B.,' &c. 2 vols. 8vo, 31s. 6d.

RANKIN.

A Handbook of the Church of Scotland. By JAMES RANKIN, D.D., Minister of Muthill; Author of 'Character Studies in the Old Testament, &c. An entirely New and much Enlarged Edition. Crown 8vo, with 2 Maps, 7s. 6d.

The First Saints. Post 8vo, 7s. 6d.

The Creed in Scotland. An Exposition of the Apostles Creed. With Extracts from Archbishop Hamilton's Catechism of 1552, John Calvin's Catechism of 1556, and a Catena of Ancient Latin and other Hymns. Post 8vo, 7s. 6d.

The Worthy Communicant. A Guide to the Devout Observance of the Lord's Supper. Limp cloth, 1s. 3d.

The Young Churchman. Lessons on the Creed, the Commandments, the Means of Grace, and the Church. Limp cloth, 1s. 3d.

First Communion Lessons. 25th Edition. Paper Cover, 2d.

RANKINE. A Hero of the Dark Continent. Memoir of Rev. Wm. Affleck Scott, M.A., M.B., C.M., Church of Scotland Missionary at Blantyre, British Central Africa. By W. HENRY RANKINE, B.D., Minister at St Boswells. With a Portrait and other Illustrations. Crown 8vo, 5s.

RECORDS OF THE TERCENTENARY FESTIVAL OF THE UNIVERSITY OF EDINBURGH. Celebrated in April 1884. Published under the Sanction of the Senatus Academicus. Large 4to, £2, 12s. 6d.

ROBERTSON. The Early Religion of Israel. As set forth by Biblical Writers and Modern Critical Historians. Being the Baird Lecture for 1888-89. By JAMES ROBERTSON, D.D., Professor of Oriental Languages in the University of Glasgow. Fourth Edition. Crown 8vo, 10s. 6d.

ROBERTSON.
Orellana, and other Poems. By J. LOGIE ROBERTSON, M.A. Fcap. 8vo. Printed on hand-made paper. 6s.
A History of English Literature. For Secondary Schools. With an Introduction by Professor MASSON, Edinburgh University. Cr. 8vo, 3s.
English Verse for Junior Classes. In Two Parts. Part I.—Chaucer to Coleridge. Part II.—Nineteenth Century Poets. Crown 8vo, each 1s. 6d. net.

ROBERTSON. Our Holiday among the Hills. By JAMES and JANET LOGIE ROBERTSON. Fcap. 8vo, 3s. 6d.

ROBERTSON. Essays and Sermons. By the late W. ROBERTSON, B.D., Minister of the Parish of Sprouston. With a Memoir and Portrait. Crown 8vo, 5s. 6d.

ROBINSON. Wild Traits in Tame Animals. Being some Familiar Studies in Evolution. By LOUIS ROBINSON, M.D. With Illustrations by STEPHEN J. DADD. In 1 vol. crown 8vo. [*In the press.*

RODGER. Aberdeen Doctors at Home and Abroad. The Story of a Medical School. By ELLA HILL BURTON RODGER. Demy 8vo, 10s. 6d.

ROSCOE. Rambles with a Fishing-Rod. By E. S. ROSCOE. Crown 8vo, 4s. 6d.

ROSS AND SOMERVILLE. Beggars on Horseback : A Riding Tour in North Wales. By MARTIN ROSS and E. Œ. SOMERVILLE. With Illustrations by E. Œ. SOMERVILLE. Crown 8vo, 3s. 6d.

RUTLAND.
Notes of an Irish Tour in 1846. By the DUKE OF RUTLAND, G.C.B. (Lord JOHN MANNERS). New Edition. Crown 8vo, 2s. 6d.
Correspondence between the Right Honble. William Pitt and Charles Duke of Rutland, Lord-Lieutenant of Ireland, 1781-1787. With Introductory Note by JOHN DUKE OF RUTLAND. 8vo, 7s. 6d.

RUTLAND.
Gems of German Poetry. Translated by the DUCHESS OF RUTLAND (Lady JOHN MANNERS). [*New Edition in preparation.*
Impressions of Bad-Homburg. Comprising a Short Account of the Women's Associations of Germany under the Red Cross. Crown 8vo, 1s. 6d.
Some Personal Recollections of the Later Years of the Earl of Beaconsfield, K.G. Sixth Edition. 6d.
Employment of Women in the Public Service. 6d.
Some of the Advantages of Easily Accessible Reading and Recreation Rooms and Free Libraries. With Remarks on Starting and Maintaining them. Second Edition. Crown 8vo, 1s.
A Sequel to Rich Men's Dwellings, and other Occasional Papers. Crown 8vo, 2s. 6d.
Encouraging Experiences of Reading and Recreation Rooms, Aims of Guilds, Nottingham Social Guide, Existing Institutions, &c., &c. Crown 8vo, 1s.

SAINTSBURY. The Flourishing of Romance and the Rise of Allegory (12th and 13th Centuries). By GEORGE SAINTSBURY, M.A., Professor of Rhetoric and English Literature in Edinburgh University. Being the first volume issued of "PERIODS OF EUROPEAN LITERATURE." Edited by Professor SAINTSBURY. Crown 8vo, 5s. net.

SALMON. Songs of a Heart's Surrender, and other Verse.
By ARTHUR L. SALMON. Fcap. 8vo, 2s.
SCHEFFEL. The Trumpeter. A Romance of the Rhine. By
JOSEPH VICTOR VON SCHEFFEL. Translated from the Two Hundredth German
Edition by JESSIE BECK and LOUISA LORIMER. With an Introduction by Sir
THEODORE MARTIN, K.C.B. Long 8vo, 3s. 6d.
SCHILLER. Wallenstein. A Dramatic Poem. By FRIEDRICH
VON SCHILLER. Translated by C. G. N. LOCKHART. Fcap. 8vo, 7s. 6d.
SCOTT. Tom Cringle's Log. By MICHAEL SCOTT. New Edition.
With 19 Full-page Illustrations. Crown 8vo, 3s. 6d.
SCOUGAL. Prisons and their Inmates; or, Scenes from a
Silent World. By FRANCIS SCOUGAL. Crown 8vo, boards, 2s.
SELKIRK. Poems. By J. B. SELKIRK, Author of 'Ethics and
Æsthetics of Modern Poetry,' 'Bible Truths with Shakespearian Parallels,' &c.
New and Enlarged Edition. Crown 8vo, printed on antique paper, 6s.
SELLAR'S Manual of the Acts relating to Education in Scotland. By J. EDWARD GRAHAM, B.A. Oxon., Advocate. Ninth Edition. Demy 8vo, 12s. 6d.
SETH.
Scottish Philosophy. A Comparison of the Scottish and
German Answers to Hume. Balfour Philosophical Lectures, University of
Edinburgh. By ANDREW SETH, LL.D., Professor of Logic and Metaphysics in
Edinburgh University. Second Edition. Crown 8vo, 5s.
Hegelianism and Personality. Balfour Philosophical Lectures.
Second Series. Second Edition. Crown 8vo, 5s.
Man's Place in the Cosmos, and other Essays. In 1 vol. post
8vo. [In the press.
SETH. A Study of Ethical Principles. By JAMES SETH, M.A.,
Professor of Philosophy in Cornell University, U.S.A. Second Edition, Revised.
Post 8vo, 10s. 6d. net.
SHADWELL. The Life of Colin Campbell, Lord Clyde. Illustrated by Extracts from his Diary and Correspondence. By Lieutenant-General
SHADWELL, C.B. With Portrait, Maps, and Plans. 2 vols. 8vo, 36s.
SHAND.
The Life of General Sir Edward Bruce Hamley, K.C.B.,
K.C.M.G. By ALEX. INNES SHAND, Author of 'Kilcarra,' 'Against Time,' &c.
With two Photogravure Portraits and other Illustrations. Cheaper Edition, with
a Statement by Mr Edward Hamley. 2 vols. demy 8vo, 10s. 6d.
Half a Century; or, Changes in Men and Manners. Second
Edition. 8vo, 12s. 6d.
Letters from the West of Ireland. Reprinted from the
'Times.' Crown 8vo, 5s.
SHARPE. Letters from and to Charles Kirkpatrick Sharpe.
Edited by ALEXANDER ALLARDYCE, Author of 'Memoir of Admiral Lord Keith,
K.B.,' &c. With a Memoir by the Rev. W. K. R. BEDFORD. In 2 vols. 8vo.
Illustrated with Etchings and other Engravings. £2, 12s. 6d.
SIM. Margaret Sim's Cookery. With an Introduction by L. B.
WALFORD, Author of 'Mr Smith: A Part of his Life,' &c. Crown 8vo, 5s.
SIMPSON. The Wild Rabbit in a New Aspect; or, Rabbit-
Warrens that Pay. A book for Landowners, Sportsmen, Land Agents, Farmers,
Gamekeepers, and Allotment Holders. A Record of Recent Experiments conducted on the Estate of the Right Hon. the Earl of Wharncliffe at Wortley Hall.
By J. SIMPSON. Second Edition, Enlarged. Small crown 8vo, 5s.
SINCLAIR. Audrey Craven. By MAY SINCLAIR. Crown
8vo, 6s.
SKELTON.
The Table-Talk of Shirley. By JOHN SKELTON, Advocate,
C.B., LL.D., Author of 'The Essays of Shirley.' With a Frontispiece. Sixth
Edition, Revised and Enlarged. Post 8vo, 7s. 6d.

SKELTON.
    The Table-Talk of Shirley. Second Series. Summers and Winters at Balmawhapple. With Illustrations. Two Volumes. Second Edition. Post 8vo, 10s. net.
    Maitland of Lethington; and the Scotland of Mary Stuart. A History. Limited Edition, with Portraits. Demy 8vo, 2 vols., 28s. net.
    The Handbook of Public Health. A Complete Edition of the Public Health and other Sanitary Acts relating to Scotland. Annotated, and with the Rules, Instructions, and Decisions of the Board of Supervision brought up to date with relative forms. Second Edition. With Introduction, containing the Administration of the Public Health Act in Counties. 8vo, 8s. 6d.
    The Local Government (Scotland) Act in Relation to Public Health. A Handy Guide for County and District Councillors, Medical Officers, Sanitary Inspectors, and Members of Parochial Boards. Second Edition. With a new Preface on appointment of Sanitary Officers. Crown 8vo, 2s.

SKRINE. Columba: A Drama. By JOHN HUNTLEY SKRINE, Warden of Glenalmond; Author of 'A Memory of Edward Thring.' Fcap. 4to, 6s.

SMITH.
    Thorndale; or, The Conflict of Opinions. By WILLIAM SMITH, Author of 'A Discourse on Ethics,' &c. New Edition. Crown 8vo, 10s. 6d.
    Gravenhurst; or, Thoughts on Good and Evil. Second Edition. With Memoir and Portrait of the Author. Crown 8vo, 8s.
    The Story of William and Lucy Smith. Edited by GEORGE MERRIAM. Large post 8vo, 12s. 6d.

SMITH. Memoir of the Families of M'Combie and Thoms, originally M'Intosh and M'Thomas. Compiled from History and Tradition. By WILLIAM M'COMBIE SMITH. With Illustrations. 8vo, 7s. 6d.

SMITH. Greek Testament Lessons for Colleges, Schools, and Private Students, consisting chiefly of the Sermon on the Mount and the Parables of our Lord. With Notes and Essays. By the Rev. J. HUNTER SMITH, M.A., King Edward's School, Birmingham. Crown 8vo, 6s.

SMITH. The Secretary for Scotland. Being a Statement of the Powers and Duties of the new Scottish Office. With a Short Historical Introduction, and numerous references to important Administrative Documents. By W. C. SMITH, LL.B., Advocate. 8vo, 6s.

"SON OF THE MARSHES, A."
    From Spring to Fall; or, When Life Stirs. By "A SON OF THE MARSHES." Cheap Uniform Edition. Crown 8vo, 3s. 6d.
    Within an Hour of London Town: Among Wild Birds and their Haunts. Edited by J. A. OWEN. Cheap Uniform Edition. Crown 8vo, 3s. 6d.
    With the Woodlanders and by the Tide. Cheap Uniform Edition. Crown 8vo, 3s. 6d.
    On Surrey Hills. Cheap Uniform Edition. Crown 8vo, 3s. 6d.
    Annals of a Fishing Village. Cheap Uniform Edition. Crown 8vo, 3s. 6d.

SORLEY. The Ethics of Naturalism. Being the Shaw Fellowship Lectures, 1884. By W. R. SORLEY, M.A., Fellow of Trinity College, Cambridge, Professor of Moral Philosophy in the University of Aberdeen. Crown 8vo, 6s.

SPROTT. The Worship and Offices of the Church of Scotland. By GEORGE W. SPROTT, D.D., Minister of North Berwick. Crown 8vo, 6s.

STATISTICAL ACCOUNT OF SCOTLAND. Complete, with Index. 15 vols. 8vo, £16, 16s.

STEEVENS. The Land of the Dollar. By G. W. STEEVENS, Author of 'Naval Policy,' &c. Crown 8vo, 6s.

STEPHENS.
The Book of the Farm; detailing the Labours of the Farmer,
Farm-Steward, Ploughman, Shepherd, Hedger, Farm-Labourer, Field-Worker,
and Cattle-man. Illustrated with numerous Portraits of Animals and Engravings
of Implements, and Plans of Farm Buildings. Fourth Edition. Revised, and
in great part Re-written, by JAMES MACDONALD, F.R.S.E., Secretary Highland
and Agricultural Society of Scotland. Complete in Six Divisional Volumes,
bound in cloth, each 10s. 6d., or handsomely bound, in 3 volumes, with leather
back and gilt top, £3, 3s.
Catechism of Practical Agriculture. 22d Thousand. Revised
by JAMES MACDONALD, F.R.S.E. With numerous Illustrations. Crown 8vo, 1s.
The Book of Farm Implements and Machines. By J. SLIGHT
and R. SCOTT BURN, Engineers. Edited by HENRY STEPHENS. Large 8vo, £2, 2s.

STEVENSON. British Fungi. (Hymenomycetes.) By Rev.
JOHN STEVENSON, Author of 'Mycologia Scotica,' Hon. Sec. Cryptogamic Society
of Scotland. Vols. I. and II., post 8vo, with Illustrations, price 12s. 6d. net each.

STEWART. Advice to Purchasers of Horses. By JOHN
STEWART, V.S. New Edition. 2s. 6d.

STEWART. Boethius: An Essay. By HUGH FRASER STEWART,
M.A., Trinity College, Cambridge. Crown 8vo, 7s. 6d.

STODDART. Angling Songs. By THOMAS TOD STODDART.
New Edition, with a Memoir by ANNA M. STODDART. Crown 8vo, 7s. 6d.

STODDART.
John Stuart Blackie: A Biography. By ANNA M. STODDART.
With 3 Plates. Third Edition. 2 vols. demy 8vo, 21s.
POPULAR EDITION, with Portrait. Crown 8vo, 6s.
Sir Philip Sidney: Servant of God. Illustrated by MARGARET
L. HUGGINS. With a New Portrait of Sir Philip Sidney. Small 4to, with a
specially designed Cover. 5s.

STORMONTH.
Dictionary of the English Language, Pronouncing, Etymological, and Explanatory. By the Rev. JAMES STORMONTH. Revised by the
Rev. P. H. PHELP. Library Edition. New and Cheaper Edition, with Supplement. Imperial 8vo, handsomely bound in half morocco, 18s. net.
Etymological and Pronouncing Dictionary of the English
Language. Including a very Copious Selection of Scientific Terms. For use in
Schools and Colleges, and as a Book of General Reference. The Pronunciation
carefully revised by the Rev. P. H. PHELP, M.A. Cantab. Thirteenth Edition,
with Supplement. Crown 8vo, pp. 800. 7s. 6d.
The School Etymological Dictionary and Word-Book. New
Edition, Revised. [In preparation.

STORY. The Apostolic Ministry in the Scottish Church (The
Baird Lecture for 1897). By ROBERT HERBERT STORY, D.D. (Edin.), F.S.A.
Scot., Professor of Ecclesiastical History in the University of Glasgow; Principal
Clerk of the General Assembly; and Chaplain to the Queen. Crown 8vo, 7s. 6d.

STORY.
Nero; A Historical Play. By W. W. STORY, Author of
'Roba di Roma.' Fcap. 8vo, 6s.
Vallombrosa. Post 8vo, 5s.
Poems. 2 vols., 7s. 6d.
Fiammetta. A Summer Idyl. Crown 8vo, 7s. 6d.
Conversations in a Studio. 2 vols. crown 8vo, 12s. 6d.
Excursions in Art and Letters. Crown 8vo, 7s. 6d.
A Poet's Portfolio: Later Readings. 18mo, 3s. 6d.

STRACHEY. Talk at a Country House. Fact and Fiction.
By Sir EDWARD STRACHEY, Bart. With a Portrait of the Author. Crown 8vo,
4s. 6d. net.

STURGIS. Little Comedies, Old and New. By JULIAN STURGIS. Crown 8vo, 7s. 6d.

SUTHERLAND. Handbook of Hardy Herbaceous and Alpine Flowers, for General Garden Decoration. Containing Descriptions of upwards of 1000 Species of Ornamental Hardy Perennial and Alpine Plants; along with Concise and Plain Instructions for their Propagation and Culture. By WILLIAM SUTHERLAND, Landscape Gardener; formerly Manager of the Herbaceous Department at Kew. Crown 8vo, 7s. 6d.

TAYLOR. The Story of my Life. By the late Colonel MEADOWS TAYLOR, Author of 'The Confessions of a Thug,' &c., &c. Edited by his Daughter. New and Cheaper Edition, being the Fourth. Crown 8vo, 6s.

THOMAS. The Woodland Life. By P. E. THOMAS. With a Frontispiece. In 1 vol. square 8vo. [*In the press.*

THOMSON.
The Diversions of a Prime Minister. By Basil Thomson. With a Map, numerous Illustrations by J. W. Cawston and others, and Reproductions of Rare Plates from Early Voyages of Sixteenth and Seventeenth Centuries. Small demy 8vo, 15s.

South Sea Yarns. With 10 Full-page Illustrations. Cheaper Edition. Crown 8vo, 3s. 6d.

THOMSON.
Handy Book of the Flower-Garden: Being Practical Directions for the Propagation, Culture, and Arrangement of Plants in Flower-Gardens all the year round. With Engraved Plans. By DAVID THOMSON, Gardener to his Grace the Duke of Buccleuch, K.T., at Drumlanrig. Fourth and Cheaper Edition. Crown 8vo, 5s.

The Handy Book of Fruit-Culture under Glass: Being a series of Elaborate Practical Treatises on the Cultivation and Forcing of Pines, Vines, Peaches, Figs, Melons, Strawberries, and Cucumbers. With Engravings of Hothouses, &c. Second Edition, Revised and Enlarged. Crown 8vo, 7s. 6d.

THOMSON. A Practical Treatise on the Cultivation of the Grape Vine. By WILLIAM THOMSON, Tweed Vineyards. Tenth Edition. 8vo, 5s.

THOMSON. Cookery for the Sick and Convalescent. With Directions for the Preparation of Poultices, Fomentations, &c. By BARBARA THOMSON. Fcap. 8vo, 1s. 6d.

THORBURN. Asiatic Neighbours. By S. S. THORBURN, Bengal Civil Service, Author of 'Bannú; or, Our Afghan Frontier,' 'David Leslie: A Story of the Afghan Frontier,' 'Musalmans and Money-Lenders in the Panjab.' With Two Maps. Demy 8vo, 10s. 6d. net.

THORNTON. Opposites. A Series of Essays on the Unpopular Sides of Popular Questions. By LEWIS THORNTON. 8vo, 12s. 6d.

TRANSACTIONS OF THE HIGHLAND AND AGRICULTURAL SOCIETY OF SCOTLAND. Published annually, price 5s.

TRAVERS.
Mona Maclean, Medical Student. A Novel. By GRAHAM TRAVERS. Twelfth Edition. Crown 8vo, 6s.

Fellow Travellers. Third Edition. Crown 8vo, 6s.

TRYON. Life of Vice-Admiral Sir George Tryon, K.C.B. By Rear-Admiral C. C. PENROSE FITZGERALD. With Two Portraits and numerous Illustrations. Second Edition. Demy 8vo, 21s.

TULLOCH.
Rational Theology and Christian Philosophy in England in the Seventeenth Century. By JOHN TULLOCH, D.D., Principal of St Mary's College in the University of St Andrews, and one of her Majesty's Chaplains in Ordinary in Scotland. Second Edition. 2 vols. 8vo, 16s.

Modern Theories in Philosophy and Religion. 8vo, 15s.

TULLOCH.
Luther, and other Leaders of the Reformation. Third Edition, Enlarged. Crown 8vo, 3s. 6d.
Memoir of Principal Tulloch, D.D., LL.D. By Mrs OLIPHANT, Author of 'Life of Edward Irving.' Third and Cheaper Edition. 8vo, with Portrait, 7s. 6d.

TWEEDIE. The Arabian Horse: His Country and People. By Major-General W. TWEEDIE, C.S.I., Bengal Staff Corps; for many years H.B.M.'s Consul-General, Baghdad, and Political Resident for the Government of India in Turkish Arabia. In one vol. royal 4to, with Seven Coloured Plates and other Illustrations, and a Map of the Country. Price £3, 3s. net.

TYLER. The Whence and the Whither of Man. A Brief History of his Origin and Development through Conformity to Environment. The Morse Lectures of 1895. By JOHN M. TYLER, Professor of Biology, Amherst College, U.S.A. Post 8vo, 6s. net.

VEITCH.
Memoir of John Veitch, LL.D., Professor of Logic and Rhetoric, University of Glasgow. By MARY R. L. BRYCE. With Portrait and 3 Photogravure Plates. Demy 8vo, 7s. 6d.
Border Essays. By JOHN VEITCH, LL.D., Professor of Logic and Rhetoric, University of Glasgow. Crown 8vo, 4s. 6d. *net.*
The History and Poetry of the Scottish Border: their Main Features and Relations. New and Enlarged Edition. 2 vols. demy 8vo, 16s.
Institutes of Logic. Post 8vo, 12s. 6d.
The Feeling for Nature in Scottish Poetry. From the Earliest Times to the Present Day. 2 vols. fcap. 8vo, in roxburghe binding, 15s.
Merlin and other Poems. Fcap. 8vo, 4s. 6d.
Knowing and Being. Essays in Philosophy. First Series. Crown 8vo, 5s.
Dualism and Monism; and other Essays. Essays in Philosophy. Second Series. With an Introduction by R. M. Wenley. Crown 8vo, 4s. 6d. net.

VIRGIL. The Æneid of Virgil. Translated in English Blank Verse by G. K. RICKARDS, M.A., and Lord RAVENSWORTH. 2 vols. fcap. 8vo, 10s.

WACE. Christianity and Agnosticism. Reviews of some Recent Attacks on the Christian Faith. By HENRY WACE, D.D., Principal of King's College, London; Preacher of Lincoln's Inn; Chaplain to the Queen. Second Edition. Post 8vo, 10s. 6d. net.

WADDELL. An Old Kirk Chronicle: Being a History of Auldhame, Tyninghame, and Whitekirk, in East Lothian. From Session Records, 1615 to 1850. By Rev. P. HATELY WADDELL, B.D., Minister of the United Parish. Small Paper Edition, 200 Copies. Price £1. Large Paper Edition, 50 Copies. Price £1, 10s.

WALDO. The Ban of the Gubbe. By CEDRIC DANE WALDO. Crown 8vo, 2s. 6d.

WALFORD. Four Biographies from 'Blackwood': Jane Taylor, Hannah More, Elizabeth Fry, Mary Somerville. By L. B. WALFORD. Crown 8vo, 5s.

WARREN'S (SAMUEL) WORKS:—
Diary of a Late Physician. Cloth, 2s. 6d.; boards, 2s.
Ten Thousand A-Year. Cloth, 3s. 6d.; boards, 2s. 6d.
Now and Then. The Lily and the Bee. Intellectual and Moral Development of the Present Age. 4s. 6d.
Essays: Critical, Imaginative, and Juridical. 5s.

WENLEY.
 Socrates and Christ: A Study in the Philosophy of Religion. By R. M. WENLEY, M.A., D.Sc., D.Phil., Professor of Philosophy in the University of Michigan, U.S.A. Crown 8vo, 6s.
 Aspects of Pessimism. Crown 8vo, 6s.

WHITE.
 The Eighteen Christian Centuries. By the Rev. JAMES WHITE. Seventh Edition. Post 8vo, with Index, 6s.
 History of France, from the Earliest Times. Sixth Thousand. Post 8vo, with Index, 6s.

WHITE.
 Archæological Sketches in Scotland—Kintyre and Knapdale. By Colonel T. P. WHITE, R.E., of the Ordnance Survey. With numerous Illustrations. 2 vols. folio, £4, 4s. Vol. I., Kintyre, sold separately, £2, 2s.
 The Ordnance Survey of the United Kingdom. A Popular Account. Crown 8vo, 5s.

WILLIAMSON. The Horticultural Handbook and Exhibitor's Guide. A Treatise on Cultivating, Exhibiting, and Judging Plants, Flowers, Fruits, and Vegetables. By W. WILLIAMSON, Gardener. Revised by MALCOLM DUNN, Gardener to his Grace the Duke of Buccleuch and Queensberry, Dalkeith Park. New and Cheaper Edition, enlarged. Crown 8vo, paper cover, 2s.; cloth, 2s. 6d.

WILLIAMSON. Poems of Nature and Life. By DAVID R. WILLIAMSON, Minister of Kirkmaiden. Fcap. 8vo, 3s.

WILLS. Behind an Eastern Veil. A Plain Tale of Events occurring in the Experience of a Lady who had a unique opportunity of observing the Inner Life of Ladies of the Upper Class in Persia. By C. J. WILLS, Author of 'In the Land of the Lion and Sun,' 'Persia as it is,' &c., &c. Cheaper Edition. Demy 8vo, 5s.

WILSON.
 Works of Professor Wilson. Edited by his Son-in-Law, Professor FERRIER. 12 vols. crown 8vo, £2, 8s.
 Christopher in his Sporting-Jacket. 2 vols., 8s.
 Isle of Palms, City of the Plague, and other Poems. 4s.
 Lights and Shadows of Scottish Life, and other Tales. 4s.
 Essays, Critical and Imaginative. 4 vols., 16s.
 The Noctes Ambrosianæ. 4 vols., 16s.
 Homer and his Translators, and the Greek Drama. Crown 8vo, 4s.

WORSLEY.
 Poems and Translations. By PHILIP STANHOPE WORSLEY, M.A. Edited by EDWARD WORSLEY. Second Edition, Enlarged. Fcap. 8vo, 6s.
 Homer's Odyssey. Translated into English Verse in the Spenserian Stanza. By P. S. Worsley. New and Cheaper Edition. Post 8vo, 7s. 6d. net.
 Homer's Iliad. Translated by P. S. Worsley and Prof. Conington. 2 vols. crown 8vo, 21s.

YATE. England and Russia Face to Face in Asia. A Record of Travel with the Afghan Boundary Commission. By Captain A. C. YATE, Bombay Staff Corps. 8vo, with Maps and Illustrations, 21s.

YATE. Northern Afghanistan; or, Letters from the Afghan Boundary Commission. By Major C. E. YATE, C.S.I., C.M.G., Bombay Staff Corps, F.R.G.S. 8vo, with Maps, 18s.

YULE. Fortification: For the use of Officers in the Army, and Readers of Military History. By Colonel YULE, Bengal Engineers. 8vo, with Numerous Illustrations, 10s.

3/97.

www.ingramcontent.com/pod-product-compliance
Lightning Source LLC
Chambersburg PA
CBHW022019240426
43667CB00042B/986